Dependent Development

Dependent Development

THE ALLIANCE OF MULTINATIONAL, STATE, AND LOCAL CAPITAL IN BRAZIL

by Peter Evans

PRINCETON UNIVERSITY PRESS
PRINCETON, NEW JERSEY

All Rights Reserved
Library of Congress Cataloging in Publication Data will be
found on the last printed page of this book

Publication of this book has been aided by a grant from
The Andrew W. Mellon Foundation

This book has been composed in V.I.P. Caledonia
Clothbound editions of Princeton University Press books
are printed on acid-free paper, and binding materials are
chosen for strength and durability.

Printed in the United States of America by Princeton
University Press, Princeton, New Jersey

*Aos Brasileiros que recusaram
largar a visão de uma sociedade justa,
livre, e igualitária*

Contents

Foreword

ONE who agrees to write a foreword often ends up with the same feeling of frustration as a young man who finds an attractive dancing partner just as the music is ending. What is there to say after everything has been said? Strictly speaking, if the writer of a foreword answers this question in all modesty, he is left with nothing to say. The author and the book speak for themselves. That is what has happened in this case.

I read the manuscript during the first half of 1977 before the preparation of the final version. I had met the author the year before at a lecture I gave in New York. We were able to develop our relations further thanks to a visit on his part to Yale and an opportunity on my part to give a talk at Brown University. From the beginning, he seemed to me an unlikely character, as if he had come out of one of those old Gary Cooper films, one of those individuals who embodies the "basic (or archetypal) North American." Only rarely can a person of this type be found in the day-to-day life of the United States of "mass society" and the megalopolis. On reading his manuscript I discovered that he belonged to the tradition of critical thinking which has Veblen and C. Wright Mills among its exponents but is little cultivated in North American universities. So, it is not hard to see that I liked both the author and the book—and that I consider this foreword superfluous.

I am not going to dwell on the obvious. First, the vast bibliography which the author uses as a point of departure in the formulation of his theoretical syntheses. Second, the rich documentation which he puts forward and uses, as a rule, honestly and meticulously. Without indulging in mindless and unnecessary quantification, he demonstrates quantitatively certain characteristics and tendencies basic to the incorporation of Brazil into the system of monopoly capitalism. Third, the extent to which he moves forward along a creative and original path within political economy, and the extent to which he enriches the theoretical contribution of Paul Baran, his principal interlocutor (visible or invisible). Fourth, his love of clarity and thorough exposition, which creates, here and there, a few excesses (the author does not allow himself overly selective quotations, incomplete descriptions, or partial explanations, and this creates a false impression of prolixity). In the end, the scholar is always a scholar: conservative, liberal, or radical, he loves learning and works in its service. The prevalence of the spirit of erudition is not a defect: it is well counterbalanced by a severely critical attitude that is exemplary, and a sense of militancy in relation to the world.

In my opinion, what makes this book stand out, making it a striking contribution to modern sociological research, is the way in which it returns to the theory of imperialism, its method of considering the Brazilian case, and its interpretative approach. These three things enable one to place the book both in terms of the theoretical advance it has achieved and in terms of its significance for social scientists, for the socialist movement, and for understanding the current epoch.

One may feel that certain authors were neglected, especially Bukharin (whose *Economic Theory of the Period of the Transition* seems to me to be the most important sourcebook for scholars of dependency) and Luxemburg (whose interpretation of the dynamics of the economies of the center in relation to the transformation, exploitation, and shaping of peripheral capitalist economies is still far from having been adequately reevaluated). Nevertheless, the effort made to give precedence to the theory of imperialism is constructive and useful in an academic environment that has shown itself so timid up to now in making use of analyses of capitalism that depart from a conservative orbit. It is particularly important to reject decisively what has been done to the so-called "theory of dependency" in the United States. It has been vulgarized, sanitized, and sterilized. Evans corrects this

error and moves in the right direction by associating the analysis
of dependency with the general theory of imperialism. I do have
a small point of disagreement since I do not think that there is
such a thing as the *theory of dependency*; what exists is a theory
of imperialism of which the body of hypothesis and explanations
relating to the effects of imperialist domination on the periphery
of the capitalist world form one part. But this does not prevent
me from being enthusiastic about his approach, which locates
imperialism at the center of the theory and focuses on relations of
dependency as seen in the light of the dynamics of expansion of
large corporations, the modern capitalist state, and the model for
control of the periphery formed by the two of them in an era
when the "division of the world" has been redefined by internationalization and worldwide counterrevolution.

The Brazilian case has been grasped, as Marx would say, with a
view toward understanding the "unity in diversity." It is for this
reason that Evans gives so much attention to the investigations,
analyses, and discoveries of his Brazilian and Latin American colleagues (as well as other authors who have been concerned with
the analysis of capitalism emphasizing the center-periphery
dialectic). Unlike those "Brazilianists" who neglect the ideas of
Brazilians and other Latin Americans, Evans not only begins
with them, but critiques and elaborates them. He also tries to en-
rich them, bringing forward possibilities of theoretical syntheses
and supplementary interpretation based on investigations of
capitalism in the hegemonic countries of the center (in particular,
the U.S.A. and the complex of power relations engendered by
the final confrontation with socialism). Consequently, his approach is extremely rich and conveys the multiplicity of relationships that connect his empirical data to the reality of which they
are a part. It is not just that it goes beyond the false dichotomy of
center-periphery (something which had already been achieved
by Brazilian and Latin American scholars); in superseding this
dichotomy it provides a global context for the apprehension and
refinement of the theory, the context of the totality of the con-

temporary capitalist system and the importance of the periphery
within this system and *for* it. This leaves, of course, room for a
theoretical understanding of what dependent capitalist development, "national" or "local" bourgeoisies of the periphery itself,
and their openly dictatorial states all mean to the equilibrium of
the world capitalist system and the coexistence of capitalism and
socialism (in this difficult and tormented phase of human history).
What can be seen is not only the "imperialization of Brazil," "dependent modernization" as an historical reality, or the dead end
of the delayed bourgeois revolution. What can be seen is what
Brazil signifies for the empirical, theoretical, and critical understanding, not only of dependent capitalism and associated peripheral development, but also, and principally, for the revolution which the periphery imposes on the capitalist nations of the
center and on the world capitalist system of power. In short, the
history of capitalism, in our times, reveals itself more clearly in
the *periphery* than in the *center*. Brazil's present not only illumi-
nates the future of other nations of the periphery, it reflects what
capitalism and imperialism are doing to "modern Western civili-
zation" and to humanity. "Bourgeois democracy" is rapidly becoming obsolete and its evolution, which is most obvious in extreme cases like the Brazilian one, constitutes the real movement
of history in the whole capitalist world (in spite of some rhetoric
with regard to "human rights").

The question of the interpretive orientation implicit in the
foregoing discussion is too complex to be discussed in a foreword.
I would suggest, however, that we should return to the classics of
revolutionary socialism, which were not afraid to rely on diverse
sources of knowledge. In fact, they "squeezed dry" their sources,
worrying more about eliminating the ideological infusions con-
tained in political economy, for example, than in excluding positive contributions that were partially or essentially valid. The
prejudice which subsequently became implanted in the "socialist
academic environment" severely impoverished those "engaged"
or "radical" analyses which avoided the pitfalls and limitations of

the practitioners of supposed "ethical neutrality." Thus, in the name of an orthodoxy poorly understood and poorly practiced socialists turned to writing catechisms or constructing sterile dogmatism, banishing the creative imagination from the orbit of socialist social science. Evans escapes this deformed intellectual leftism, which is truly an infantile beginner's disorder. One may regret the lack of emphasis on the direct analysis of class relations and class conflict, or on the fundamental contradictions of contemporary monopoly capitalism (which include the pressures created by the growth of the socialist sphere on central and peripheral capitalist countries and on the world capitalist system of power). But, this is an almost inevitable flaw. One cannot do everything, and even Evans's Latin American colleagues have had to operate to varying degrees within such limitations. What matters is the general significance of the interpretative orientation. It is an orientation that indicates there is a movement underway in the United States from an abstract radicalism to a new type of Marxism. This transition is very important for those who complain about the political isolation of the American university and the lack of more direct influence from the working class movement on the pattern of intellectual work among North American social scientists.

The value of a book does not guarantee that it will have an effect. By the same token, the significance of an author's position does not insure he will be accepted or that his importance will be recognized. We operate in the sphere of potentiality. Nonetheless, the potential justifies some optimism and certain hopes. We can hope that the author and his book will enjoy a balanced and constructive reception, and that both lay readers and specialists will benefit from the insights into the complex world historical situation of the final quarter of the twentieth century that the book has to offer.

FLORESTAN FERNANDES
São Paulo, January 6, 1978

Acknowledgments

BOOKS are never written by individuals. The work and thinking of an extraordinarily large number of people have gone into producing the chapters that follow. A few are acknowledged briefly in the footnotes, but most are not. In some ways, it would be fairer to leave them unacknowledged since they had no say in the final shape of the product. But, without trying to shift any of the responsibility for the outcome, which is mine alone, some of the contributors need mentioning.

Among the most important contributors, but least responsible for the book itself, are the business executives of various nationalities. Without their generosity in sharing their time this study would not have been possible. I doubt they will be happy with the result, but I hope that it bears enough resemblance to reality to provoke them to think about why they see things differently.

Since the research on which this book is based began almost ten years ago, I have also accumulated a number of debts to various funding agencies. My initial fieldwork in Brazil as a graduate student would not have been possible without the support of the National Institutes of Mental Health and the Ford Foundation. Support from the Carnegie Foundation through the Harvard Center for International Affairs gave me some valuable rethinking time after the completion of my dissertation. Funds from the Ford Foundation enabled me to return to Brazil, and a grant from the Brazil office of the Ford Foundation was essential to the completion of that period of fieldwork. The writing itself could not have been accomplished in the absence of a fellowship from the Howard Foundation.

During the time I spent in Brazil the sympathy and support

of Brazilian friends, colleagues, and students made fieldwork a pleasure and, more important from the point of view of the book, contributed immeasurably to my understanding of what was going on in Brazil. If my work has escaped some of the naive views common to North Americans, there are a large number of Brazilians who deserve the credit. While I cannot cite all of them individually, Maurício Vinhas de Queiroz must be mentioned. Our many discussions of the history of large firms, local and multinational, in Brazil were a very important part of my education and Chapter 3 is largely the product of a research project in which we collaborated. At a much later stage, conversations with Florestan Fernandes were important in stimulating me to rethink my theoretical approach to Brazilian politics. For this, for his generous foreword, and most of all for having provided an exemplar of steadfastness to principle for so many years, I would like to thank him.

That I ended up working on a study of Brazil at all is due to some intriguing lectures by David Maybury-Lewis. Likewise, the fascination with organizational structures which Harrison White manages to convey is responsible for the organizational side of my approach to multinational corporations. A number of people read parts of the manuscript and provided valuable comments. Barbara Rosen, Jake Oser, and Bob Hill were helpful critics of the earlier versions of the first two chapters. Warren Dean not only took the time to go through the whole manuscript but also suggested some necessary changes in the second chapter. Some ideas from Ken Mericle and Harry Broadman have improved Chapter 5. Ken Erickson, Lou Goodman, Ted Moran, Bob Packenham, and Tom Weisskopf all read the entire manuscript and provided some new directions for its revision.

The "Working Group on Multinational Corporations in Latin America in the Context of the World System," organized by the Social Science Research Council under the leadership of Al Stepan and Lou Goodman and supported by funds from the Ford and Tinker Foundations, has been one of the most important intellectual influences on my work. The members of this group not only listened to my ideas and helped to reshape them, but also provided me with constant stimulation and new ideas by presenting their own work. Their contribution went far beyond what is evident from my footnotes.

There were a number of other kinds of support, both generalized and practical, without which the manuscript would never have been completed. My parents taught me to examine conventionally accepted explanations for social behavior critically long before I understood the words "social" or "behavior," and they have supported my efforts in this direction ever since. Elaine Haste and Norma MacDonald both typed multiple drafts of different chapters with an efficiency that was embarrassingly superior to that of the work that proceeded theirs. Kate Dunnigan not only typed but also provided crucial general aid in the production of the final draft. Sandy Thatcher's enthusiasm, good advice, and effectiveness more than lived up to his widespread reputation as an editor of exceptional caliber. Dietrich Rueschemeyer was an ideal colleague throughout the period I worked on the manuscript, always quick to respond to my ideas, always interested in what I was doing, and always understanding when another deadline passed unmet. Louise Lamphere was not only supportive, but also provided me with a model of intellectual honesty and clear thinking; to the extent that either of these qualities is embodied in the manuscript she deserves the major credit.

A number of individuals had to put up with living in the same house with me during the writing of this book. They tolerated lapses in the performance of my domestic responsibilities and created an environment that often made me wonder how authors who lack such a community survive. I can only hope that Ed Benson, Sue Benson, Kate Dunnigan, Louise Lamphere, Barbara Melosh, Ruth Milkman, Tina Simmons, and Bruce Tucker feel that they have gotten something close to the support for their own work that I feel I have gotten for mine.

Finally, I would like to thank my two sons, Benjamin and Alexander, for talking about superheroes with me, playing football with me, and valuing my companionship for reasons that had nothing whatsoever to do with whether I ever finished this work.

Dependent Development

Introduction

THE day the workers stopped the buses will be remembered for a long time in Brasília. The local bus company probably expected complaints and grumbling when it redesignated most of the buses that took the working population of the city to their homes in the "satellite towns" as "special" and "express" buses, and doubled or tripled the fares. The workers first watched the few remaining "regular" vehicles pass by with no room, followed by "express" and "special" buses going by almost empty. Realizing that they could not pay the new fares and survive, the people exploded. They smashed the windows of the buses, dragged trees onto the roads in front of them, or set fire to them. It was even said later that when the police arrived, they were told to go home. For those living in Brasília, the explosion of violence against the buses revealed the extent of pent-up grievances even more starkly than the overwhelming electoral defeat of the government party that took place in the same year, 1974.

Unexpectedly, the protests were successful. The company was persuaded to lower its fares again. However minor the victory, it showed that even in a well-institutionalized, efficient, and generally ruthless repressive state such as Brazil, people could be pushed only so far. The smashing of the buses brought back memories of the strikes at Contagem and Osasco in 1968 and the massive student demonstrations of that time. It was another reminder that the Brazilian people would continue to struggle to keep the elite from monopolizing the fruits of the country's economic growth, that they would continue to play a role in making Brazil's history, regardless of the desire of those on top to exclude them.

For me, the smashing of the buses was another indication that the fundamental conflict in Brazil is between the 1, or perhaps 5, percent of the population that comprises the elite and the 80 percent that has been left out of the "Brazilian model" of development. Unfortunately, this insight provides no automatic guidance as to the proper method of analyzing that development. Class struggle may be the essence of history, but how should it be studied? Ideally, one should examine the contending classes and the relations between them. But, for students without the brilliance and endurance of Marx, this choice usually leads to a superficial and generally disappointing presentation. If the aim is to begin with a detailed, empirical analysis, as faithful as possible to the complexities of the specific historical situation, before an attempt is made to derive more general theoretical implications, then a more restricted scope is necessary. One way of limiting the focus would be to concentrate on the conditions of the mass of the population, their political successes and failures, the circumstances that divide them from each other, and the possible strategies for overcoming these divisions. While I would consider such a focus useful and necessary, I chose another.

The "other side" is the object of my analysis. I have concentrated on the internal structure of the Brazilian elite to produce a study of collaboration and competition among its different segments. I examine the bases for conflict and cooperation among representatives of international capital, owners of local capital, and the top echelons of the state apparatus. One important reason for studying the internal dynamics of the elite is the conviction, shared, of course, by most Brazilian social scientists, that both development and class conflict must be seen as international phenomena, that one cannot understand the development of Brazil without understanding the development of the international economy and the development of the advanced capitalist countries. The links between Brazil and the rest of the capitalist world are most evident when the examination focuses on the elite, which makes a work of this kind particularly appropriate for a North American interested in Brazil.

Choosing to examine the internal structure of Brazilian elite and its relation to the prevailing international system could have led me to highlight a number of different issues. Questions of the maintenance of the elite's monopoly on violence and the role of external forces in preserving this monopoly are of central importance. Equally fascinating are questions concerning international finance (public and private), and the machinations involved in preserving Brazil's financial equilibrium. In my opinion, however, the study of the accumulation of industrial capital is most fundamental. Questions of ideology, politics, repression, and of course finance must enter, but the core of my discussion revolves around the interrelationship of foreign capital, local capital, and the state in building an industrialized economy.

Multinational corporations emerge naturally as main characters in this story. Given a focus on industrialization, there is no way of avoiding them. Examining multinational corporations has the additional benefit of making it easier to demonstrate that the struggle between elite and mass in Brazil cannot be separated from the conflict of classes in the United States. Also, analyzing the role of the multinationals provides an opportunity to use the sociological literature on complex organizations, a literature whose potential contribution to the study of development is still very underexploited.

Multinationals are approached here from what I consider to be a sociological perspective: not sociological in the sense that it relies primarily on literature from the discipline of sociology, but rather in the sense that it looks at corporate strategies as being determined to an important degree by "nonmarket" considerations. Decisions depend on who makes them. They are made in the context of industries that are complex structures of firms, not just simple sets of buyers and sellers. Decisions are always based on guesses about the future, and differences between guesses depend on perceptions of the broader social context, not on costs and prices in the narrow sense. This "sociological" approach is, of course, an orientation applicable to the other segments of the elite—local capitalists and servants of the state—just as it applies to the multinationals.

Throughout the analysis I have tried to consider industrialization not only sociologically but also concretely. Specific configurations of companies and specific strategic choices are always the starting point. I have concentrated on the evolution of only a small number of industries and the behavior of only a small number of firms, and spent considerable time on "technical" questions, such as how the research and development efforts of foreign firms in the pharmaceutical industry compare with those of local firms. For those who see the outcome of the class struggle as the only problem of development, such issues may appear trivial. I cannot agree. To be sure, many of those who analyze business behavior give the impression that finding solutions to technical problems, increasing the efficiency of production, and raising profit levels are synonymous with "development." But this does not obviate the fact that real comprehension of the broader issues that divide elite and mass must be built on a solid understanding of how business firms and the men who manage them behave under specific circumstances.

The method of my investigation is a consequence of the way I defined the subject matter. In order to understand the decision making that goes on within firms, one must talk to the men who run them. A major part of the primary empirical evidence on which my analysis is based comes from interviews with executives, conducted in both the United States and Brazil over a period of five years. While they number less than 150 in total and were never intended to be a "sample," they provided extremely useful insights as to how the contemporary Brazilian industrial system is perceived by men in different positions. In addition, of course, interviews yielded a large amount of "objective" information on the operations of different industries.

Material gathered in interviews was combined with company reports and other information produced by the companies themselves. Business publications primarily aimed at the business elite were also a source of valuable information, albeit information that came in fragments which needed piecing together. Another very different sort of data are the myriad descriptive statistics compiled by Brazilian and U.S. government bodies and by researchers, Brazilian and foreign.

Statistical sources were especially important in looking at the historical course of industrialization. In examining patterns of investment and business behavior during earlier phases of Brazil's industrialization, statistical patterns could not be checked against the perceptions of living decision-makers and the statistics had to carry heavier weight. In compensation, of course, the scholarly literature on Brazilian industrialization includes the excellent work of people like Warren Dean, John Wirth, and Richard Graham. I have relied heavily on this literature in my attempt to provide a historical context for the contemporary pattern of industrialization.

Throughout the research and writing of this book, I have been made uncomfortable by the discrepancies between the messy and eclectic style of my work and the neat and well-disciplined models that I remembered from textbooks on methodology. It is only a moderate exaggeration to say that the following description of the methods of Dashiell Hammett's Continental Op comes closer to my experience:

What he soon discovers is that the "reality" that anyone involved will swear to is in fact itself a construction, a fabrication, a fiction, a faked and alternate reality—and that it has been gotten together long before he arrived on the scene. And the

Op's work therefore is to deconstruct, decompose, deplot and
defictionalize that "reality" and to construct or reconstruct out
of it a true fiction, i.e., an account of what "really" happened.
. . . What one both begins and ends with, then is a story, a
narrative, a coherent yet questionable account of the world.[1]

I hope that I have ended up with a coherent account. I also
hope that I have been sufficiently careful in my use of evidence so
that it is a convincing account. But, I have no doubt that for many
readers it will be a questionable account. Among those who study
international business and Brazilian development there will be
many who will disagree vehemently with my version of the story.
Even those I see as my theoretical mentors may well disagree
with my emphases and certain of my conclusions. As long as
there are also those who find it contributes to their thinking on
imperialism and dependency, provokes them to look at the evidence differently, or suggests new ways of proceeding in their
own investigations, then it is a useful account.

For readers familiar with the imperialism/dependency tradition, the outlines of my argument will hardly appear novel. I
have drawn freely on the work of others to provide the theoretical context for my investigation. My general conceptions of "development" have been shaped by a gamut of social scientists including economic historians such as David Landes and Alexander
Gerschenkron, sociologists such as Barrington Moore Jr. and
Immanuel Wallerstein, anthropologists such as Eric Wolf and
Karl Polanyi, and economists such as Albert Hirschman. More
specifically, my view of Brazilian industrialization has been
shaped by my attempts to come to terms with the literature on
imperialism and dependency theory. This literature, which

[1] The quote is from Steven Marcus's introduction to Dashiell Hammett's *The
Continental Op* (New York: Random House, 1974, xx, xxii). I am grateful to Fred
Gross for bringing it to my attention.

began in Europe with Lenin and Hobson, was developed in the United States by Marxists such as Baran and Frank, and has undergone its most creative recent extensions in the hands of Latin Americans such as Celso Furtado, Fernando Henrique Cardoso, Florestan Fernandes, and Oswaldo Sunkel, seems to me to be the most valid interlocutor for anyone studying industrialization in Latin America. It is an eclectic body of work and even individual authors within the tradition are not always consistent in their arguments. Those who would use it are forced first to make clear how they have interpreted it. I have devoted my first chapter to this task.

I have also used the first chapter to foreshadow the outlines of the argument itself. The development of a capitalist world economy in which multinational corporations are the major organizational actors has made it impossible to look at all third world countries as simply "the periphery." A number of the larger and richer ones no longer stand at the edge of the international division of labor, exporting primary products to the center and receiving manufactured goods in return. They belong instead to a distinct category, which Wallerstein has called the "semiperiphery." These third world countries have now within their borders an increasingly diversified industrial capacity. At the same time, the penetration of international capital into their social and economic life is increasingly thorough. International capital is an integral part of the domestic Brazilian economy, and the representatives of international capital are an integral part of the Brazilian political and social order.

Foreign capital is no longer an external force whose interests are represented internally by compradores and agrarian exporters. Instead, foreign capital, now operating locally, shares with local capital, both private and state-controlled, an interest in the further development of local industry. This is not to deny that there is differentiation of local and foreign capital within the industrial structure; it is only to say that conflicts of interest are now more subtle. Over the issue of industrialization in general there is no split.

Capital accumulation took place in the periphery even under conditions of "classic dependence," that is, the export of primary products in exchange for manufactured goods. The process of accumulation as it is currently occurring in countries such as Brazil is, however, of a different order. It is different because it includes a substantial degree of industrialization, and also the more complex internal division of labor and increased productivity that this implies. I have labeled the current process "dependent development." This label risks our confusing the contemporary Brazilian situation with other forms of dependence, but it should help make clear that I do not feel that the kind of accumulation now going on in Brazil eliminates dependence.

When I argue that Brazil has been incorporated into the capitalist world economy in a new way, I have tried to avoid giving the impression that dependent development has been produced by some cataclysmic break with the past. No one would deny that the external sector has had a central influence on the shape of the domestic economy and social structure from the beginning, even when Brazil was a simple colony with a role in the international division of labor that placed it unequivocally on the periphery. As I have tried to show in my second chapter, foreign capital played a part in the development of local manufacturing even during the period of classic dependence, when its primary function was maintaining "export-oriented growth." Substantial involvement of foreign capital in local manufacturing dates from the beginning of the century, even though, as I have tried to show in Chapters 2 and 3, it is unlikely that foreign capital would have sponsored industrialization on its own without continual stimulation and pressure from the local elite. Finally, dependent development is not a break with the past in that many of the contradictions of classic dependence remain, especially those created by the exclusion of the mass population from participation in development.

Some chroniclers of the growth of the multinationals leave the impression that geographic boundaries and the governments organized around them are becoming anachronisms. I have tried in the fifth chapter to make it clear that my own view is quite the reverse. The direct role of the Brazilian state in the process of industrialization has increased dramatically. The internalization of imperialism has given the state a new position of power from which to bargain with the multinationals. If classic dependence was associated with weak states, dependent development is associated with the strengthening of strong states in the "semiperiphery." The consolidation of state power may even be considered a prerequisite of dependent development.

Another misconstruction of the notion of dependent development is that the internalization of imperialism implies the final demise of the "national industrial bourgeoisie." I have tried to show in Chapter 3 that the "national industrial bourgeoisie" is alive and well. Certain of its members now operate increasingly in collaboration with international capital. This collaboration, like that between the state and the multinationals, is one that leaves substantial ability to bargain in the hands of local capital. At the same time, the gap separating the local capitalists who are able to play a role in shaping the process of accumulation from those who are not in a position to do so grows larger.

The end result of the incorporation of the periphery into the international capitalist system, as far as the elite is concerned, is to create a complex alliance between elite local capital, international capital, and state capital, which I have called here "the triple alliance." The result is not a monolith. Each of the partners comes at industrialization with different strengths, and their interests vary accordingly. As in any economy, there are differences among sectors of industry. In addition, goals vary among the branches of the state apparatus. Over and above the differences, however, is the consensus that all members of the alliance will benefit from the accumulation of industrial capital within Brazil.

Consensus between local and foreign capital around the issue of accumulation is a fundamental part of the explanation of the successes of Brazilian industrialization. To understand the distortions and failures of that industrialization requires a return to the older theories of imperialism and a closer consideration of the logic of the multinational corporation. I contend that, while circumstances have pushed the multinational into becoming an important instrument for the industrialization of certain areas of the periphery, there remain contradictions between the logic of growth as seen from the perspective of the multinational and the development of the periphery as seen from a broader perspective—contradictions more severe than those which separate corporations and society in the countries of the center.

In Chapter 4, I have attempted to lay out what I consider to be the centripetal logic of strategies for growth coming out of multinational headquarters. The consequence of industrializing on the basis of this logic is the exclusion of most of the population from the potential benefits of industrialization. The state, as I have tried to show in Chapter 5, has been a powerful force for modifying the logic of the multinational when the issue is where the accumulation of capital will take place (in Brazil or in the center). But, even as it wins this battle, the state is constrained by the necessity of fostering the enthusiastic participation of both the multinationals and local capitalists, constrained in a way that makes it extremely difficult to adopt a developmental strategy that would spread the benefits of industrialization more widely. Even if there is substantial support within the state apparatus for more welfare-oriented policies, adopting such policies would threaten the whole elite consensus on which industrialization itself is based.

In the end we are back to questions of elite and mass. One of the implications of my analysis is that the industrializing elite alliance that currently holds sway in Brazil is inherently incapable of serving the needs of the mass of the population. Furthermore, the argument has been developed in terms that suggest that the characteristics of Brazil's dependent development are not peculiar to Brazil or even to military regimes. Many countries of the periphery may not have sufficient resources or markets to attract the cooperation of multinationals and undertake dependent development; but those which do are likely to experience a form of industrialization that follows the pattern described here. In the final chapter I discuss the extent to which problems of Brazil's people are shared, at least potentially, by the people of most of the larger, more dynamic countries of the periphery. I also examine the implications of dependent development for the people of the center.

Most of Brazil's population are absent from this analysis because they are absent from the decision making that is being described. Yet the pressure of their unsatisfied needs remains the constant backdrop for the elite's strategies of industrialization. As long as the current alliance is successful in its own terms, an ever increasing surplus will provide the possibility of some satisfaction of mass demands. In addition, as long as the elite is united, the rest of the population will have a hard time pressing its grievances beyond sporadic protests. Should the alliance falter, a confrontation will come sooner, but even if it does not, the redistribution of economic rewards and political power can only be postponed for a certain period. The workers who burned the buses will not remain indefinitely a passive audience at the political drama that accompanies dependent development.

1.

Imperialism, Dependency, and Dependent Development*

IMPERIALISM worried John Hobson. He was skeptical of its "civilizing" impact on the people of Asia, Africa, and Latin America and fearful of its consequences for Britain. While most of his contemporaries saw England's imperial might as a solution to its internal problems, Hobson talked of "the gigantic peril of a Western parasitism, a group of advanced industrial nations whose upper classes draw vast tribute from Asia and Africa with which they support tame masses of retainers no longer engaged in the staple industries of agriculture and manufacture but kept in the performance of personal or minor industrial services under the control of a new financial aristocracy" (quoted in Lenin, 1966:248). Over the long run, he argued, the export of capital could result in the development of industry on the periphery, thereby undermining the economic supremacy of the center. Speaking of China, he speculated about a "third stage" of imperialism in which "fully equipped for future internal development in all necessary productive powers, such a nation may turn upon her civilizer, untrammelled by need for further industrial aid, undersell him in his own market, take away his other foreign markets and secure for herself what further development work

* My article "Industrialization and Imperialism: Growth and Stagnation on the Periphery," published by the *Berkeley Journal of Sociology* in 1975 (20:113-145), represents my first attempt to write this chapter. While I have been forced to rework a number of my ideas, I am grateful to the editors of the *Berkeley Journal* for providing me with some valuable early feedback.

remains to be done in other underdeveloped parts of the earth" (Hobson, 1938:308).

The inversion of imperialism has not come to pass. No self-interested member of the British working class would trade places with a worker in Asia, Africa, or Latin America. For all the television sets it may import from Taiwan, the United States remains firmly in the center of the international system and Taiwan remains on the periphery. Still, as the United States, plagued by unemployment and inflation, exports lumber to Asia in order to import clothing, steel, and television sets, Hobson seems more prescient than his contemporaries.

Industrialization on the periphery has not proved as threatening to the interests of center country capital as Hobson expected. The development of the multinational corporation has enabled international capital to retain greater control over third world factories than Hobson could have imagined possible. Nonetheless, the international division of labor, measured in terms of the kinds of goods produced in different locations, has changed substantially in the direction that Hobson predicted. Manchester no longer makes cloth for Indians or Brazilians. The larger countries of the periphery manufacture their own consumer goods and some capital goods. A few are substantial exporters of manufactured goods.

As certain third world countries have been allowed to industrialize, the gap between those few and the rest of the periphery has grown. Industrialization on the periphery has involved the creation of internally differentiated economies, the emergence of more sophisticated state apparatuses, and the formation of new kinds of links among locally dominant elites, international capital, and center country states. Even favored third world countries are still fundamentally dependent, but they are as different from the stereotype of the simple agrarian exporting society as the United States is from its own agrarian past.

Accompanying the changes in the international division of labor and relations between center and periphery there has been a complex and continuous elaboration of theoretical perspectives on third world countries and their relation to the capitalist center. Most important has been the development of more sophisticated analyses of the character of peripheral societies. A rich body of literature on dependency and peripheral social formations, focusing on the internal dynamics of less developed countries, now complements the literature on the dynamics of imperialism in advanced capitalist countries. These new characterizations of the periphery must be set in the context of the theoretical tradition that produced them. They have emerged in response to changes in the world economy, but they are based on critical analysis and refinement of previous theoretical formulations. In the words of one of the most impressive of the new theoreticians, Samir Amin (1977b:25), "The starting point, as always, is imperialism."

Imperialism

From Hobson onwards, imperialism has been defined as a combination of economic expansion and political domination. Simply put, imperialism is a system of capital accumulation based on the export of capital from advanced countries to less developed regions (or more precisely, center capital's acquisition of control over the means of the production in those regions) accompanied by the utilization of political and military resources to protect and maintain the means of production over which control has been acquired.

Political empires do not qualify as imperialism in the post-Hobson sense unless they are designed to foster the accumulation of capital. Extraction of the surplus product of a less developed country by a more developed country is not imperialism unless the dominant country has acquired control over the means of production in the poorer country. The theory of imperialism assumes that the system works primarily to the benefit of capital controlled by citizens of the dominant country, but not necessarily to the benefit of the dominant country taken as a whole.

Hobson stressed this last point most of all. He was convinced that England maintained its colonial empire for the sake of the trusts and combines that looked abroad to solve problems created by the "mal-distribution of consuming power which prevents the absorption of commodities and capital within the country." The political and military costs of maintaining the empire were being borne by the country as a whole in order to protect the profits of a few. He was enraged by "the illicit nature of this use of public resources of the nation to safeguard and improve private investments" (Hobson, 1938:85, 358) and concluded that no nation which kept good books and had the interests of the majority at heart would practice imperialism. Social reform was the answer. Social reform would create the necessary domestic market and make imperialism unnecessary even from the point of view of the trusts and combines.

Lenin had no illusions that investors would see income redistribution as an acceptable alternative to imperialism and assumed that investors would continue to use the political and military power of the nation to further their own interests. But he did find merit in Hobson's model and agreed with him that imperialism should stimulate the development of the periphery: "The export of capital greatly accelerates the development of capitalism in those countries to which it is exported. While, therefore, the export of capital may tend to a certain extent to arrest the development of capitalism in the countries exporting capital it can do so only by expanding and deepening the further development of capitalism throughout the world" (Lenin, 1966:217). He argued that capital would be exported to "backward countries" because low wages, low rents, and cheap raw materials make investments profitable. In 1916, Lenin was already willing to argue that on the periphery the "elementary conditions for industrial development have been created."

Why should not the expanding and deepening of capitalism on the periphery upset England's privileged economic position as Hobson predicted? For Lenin, the answer to this question was that the center economies that produced imperialism were based on monopoly, resulting in finance capitalism and not the competitive variety. He followed Hilferding in believing that "finance capital does not want liberty, it wants domination." Regular market competition was a "thing of the past." Monopolists aimed at control of markets and raw materials, and the political structure of colonialism was a reflection of their economic needs. According to Lenin, "Colonial possession alone gives complete guarantee of success to the monopolies against all risks of the struggle with competitors. . . ." Since monopoly control characterized the whole system, there was no real prospect of the center being "undersold" by competitors on the periphery (Lenin, 1966:232-234).

In this model, competition had to be political. Since political hegemony was the mechanism by which markets were controlled, the struggle over the "redivision" of markets would also be political. Such redivision would become necessary whenever the productive capacity of a particular nation's monopolies got out of line with the amount of territory over which it held sway. Lenin asked rhetorically, ". . . is there *under capitalism* any means of remedying the disparity between the development of the productive forces and the accumulation of capital on the one side and the division of colonies and 'spheres of influence' by finance capital on the other side—other than by resorting to war?" (1966:245). Political control of the periphery was inextricably part of the expansion of capitalism, and struggle among the metropolitan powers was the most likely source of instability.

Neither Hobson nor Lenin was in a position to analyze the

consequences of imperialism for the countries of the periphery. A model of imperialism that attempted to lay out the internal logic of capitalist development within underdeveloped countries did not emerge until later. When it did emerge, it offered a very different perspective on industrialization in the periphery. Writing in the fifties, Paul Baran (1968:197), argued that instead of "expanding and deepening the further development of capitalism" throughout the world, the "main task" of imperialism was to "slow down and to control the economic development of underdeveloped countries."

Baran had little disagreement with Lenin's image of imperialism as the penetration of monopoly capitalism into the third world. But, while Lenin emphasized the tendency of monopoly to produce stagnation in the metropole, Baran saw it as having this effect even more strongly on the periphery. In Baran's view, the main interest of foreign investors lay in freezing the international division of labor so that the less developed countries continued to be producers of raw materials. He treated the destruction of the Indian textile industry, which Hobson had considered to represent only the "first stage" of imperialism, as typical of the attitude of metropolitan corporations toward industry in the third world. He also agreed with Hans Singer (1950) and other non-Marxists who believed that the interests of companies exporting raw materials to the markets of the metropole did not lie in the general economic development of the host country. "For whichever aspect of economic development we may consider," he wrote, "it is manifestly detrimental to the prosperity of the raw materials producing corporations" (Baran, 1968:197).

Like Lenin and Hobson, Baran saw imperialism as a political phenomenon as well as an economic one. His political analysis focused on the class structure of the countries of the periphery. Lenin spoke of the "solid bonds" created between foreign capital and the bourgeoisie in less developed countries (1966:235). Baran tried to spell out the nature of these bonds and their consequences for industrialization. Foreign capital, because it is not interested in fostering industrialization, allies itself with those elements of the local elite who also oppose it. The merchants who handle the manufactured goods imported from the metropole become a compradore class. Agriculture remains essentially feudal. With the possibility of "self-sustaining" growth in the manufacturing sector wiped out early by free-trade agreements with the metropole, the local industrialists that remain are entrenched monopolists. Local industry moves from handicrafts to monopoly capitalism without ever experiencing the dynamic stage of competitive accumulation: "Having lived through all the pains and frustrations of childhood it never experienced the vigor and exuberance of youth, and began displaying at an early age all the grievous features of senility and decadence." The extension of capitalism from the center to the periphery, far from resulting in a class structure dominated by a dynamic industrial bourgeoisie, makes such a social structure impossible. "What results is a political and social coalition of wealthy compradores, powerful monopolists and large landowners dedicated to the defense of the existing social order" (Baran, 1968:177, 195).

Baran provided a convincing model of how the penetration of international capitalism might lead toward stagnation. But his investors did not appear to follow the normal rules of capitalist behavior. Lenin and Hobson assumed that investors would put their factories wherever they could make the highest profits. Baran argued that profits were higher on the periphery (1968:229), but that capitalists would send most of these profits back to the center countries where profit rates were lower.

On the surface, Baran's investors look irrational. The irrationality disappears once the context in which they would have operated is taken into account. Reinvesting in the periphery would have meant diversifying into manufacturing and this would have introduced a new set of uncertainties. The fact that extractive and commercial ventures made high profits was no guarantee that more diversified investments would produce the same profits. Manufacturing operations, as Baran recognized, are much more integrated into the local economy. The problems of organization and control that they present are complex and difficult. Unless the operation can be effectively controlled, there is no way to profit from the advantages, such as cheap labor, that a foreign location might offer.

Because profits depended on the decisions of other investors, the risk of a peripheral location was even harder to judge. Complementary investments in manufacturing in a given location might produce a boom and good profits for all. But if one investor decided to go in and no one else followed, he would find himself facing a stagnant market. Extractive investors who exported their output back to the metropole did not have to worry about the development of the local market. The manufacturer, on the other hand, would have to make predictions about local sales which meant making predictions about future local development. It is hardly surprising that foreign investors chose to take their risks at home.

Foreign investors might have been forced to undertake more risky investments in the periphery if they had been under enough competitive pressure. But as long as the periphery represented a comfortable monopoly situation, there was no compulsion to take risks. Economically, the local industrial bourgeoisie was not in a position to challenge the foreign investor. Insofar as the foreign investor came from a monopoly capitalist home economy, he was likely to have already reached agreements that would keep corporations from his home base from engaging in "cutthroat competition."

More important than the lack of pressure from other firms was the political side of the environment. Lenin's statement about the "complete guarantees" provided by colonial possession is apt. As long as the investor could count on the political protection of his home state he was unthreatened by either competition from the corporations of other nationalities or politically motivated coercion on the part of the local elite. If colonial possession was not possible, then a well-defined sphere of influence situation might suffice to produce the same security.

As long as these political and economic conditions held, imperialism could show its monopolistic face. Stagnation was a consistent result. Looking mainly at factors internal to the peripheral nations, Baran saw little reason to believe that much change was possible within a framework of capitalist development. (He did admit, nonetheless, the possibility of "new deal type regimes" that might put foreign investors under some pressure.) Writing during the heyday of American hegemony, he also seemed to discount the possibility of changes in the political and economic situation of the metropolitan powers as a potential source of instability.

The elegance of Baran's argument connecting imperialism and stagnation made it seem that the social structures he described should endure indefinitely. Of course they did not. Both the international structure of imperialism and its consequences for peripheral social formations had begun to change even before Baran began his work. The post-World War II period saw the tension between imperialism as a monopolistic system of control and as a dynamic mode of accumulation begin to work itself out in new ways. By the beginning of the seventies, the growth of peripheral industrial production and manufactured exports led some observers to argue that the association of imperialism with stagnation was simply a temporary aberration. Bill Warren (1973:42) expressed this view well: "It can now be seen that the elements inhibiting capitalist industrialization, which operated in the period of political control, were comparatively short-lived and that the post-war period is witnessing the full re-emergence of those elements of imperialism conducive to capitalist industrialization."

The roots of the gradual transformation of imperialism were

diverse. They included new conditions of competition among the center countries, consequent changes in the bargaining position of third world states, and even changes within multinational corporations themselves. Perhaps most fundamental was the simple fact that the center countries could not sustain a stable monopolistic division of the periphery. Containing the tremendous expansion of the productive capacity of the center countries within a fixed system of colonial empires or spheres of influence was not possible. Redivision of the world market by violence was unacceptable. After two world wars had produced horrendous destruction and the loss to the capitalist system of the Soviet Union and China, it became clear that the center nations could not afford violent competition among themselves.

The hegemony of the United States after World War II gave an appearance of stability to the system, but did not provide quite the same sort of comfortable monopoly position that colonial empires or well-defined spheres of influence did. As a general caretaker for the center nations the United States was not in a position to exclude the capital of other center countries from the periphery. To do so would have raised again the specter of violent redivision, and the dangers of this had become even more unacceptable with the emergence of the Soviet Union as a potential participant in such a redivision. While corporations based in the United States enjoyed substantial advantage, the consequences of the partial nature of U.S. control over the periphery became evident as soon as German, Japanese, and firms from other center countries were ready, economically and organizationally, to compete. In short, a reluctance to risk a violent redivision increased the possibility of economic competition among center-based corporations within the third world.

In the sixties doubts began to arise about the use of force by the center power to maintain its interests in the periphery. The costly and frustrating fight against socialist- and communist-led movements of national liberation, culminating in the debacle of

Indochina, made some decentralization of the means of violence appear advantageous even from the point of view of the United States. It began to seem easier to train and equip local police and armed forces than to try to maintain order by sending in the marines.

Support for the decentralization of the means of violence can be seen even among those closest to the multinationals. Raymond Vernon (1971), for example, has argued that the multinationals should try to improve their political position locally by formally rejecting the protection of the metropole. Once the origins of international capital in a peripheral country become diverse, there is another reason to turn for protection to a forceful local regime rather than to the center. Relying on the center means relying on a particular country which might favor its own investors over others. Whatever its disadvantages, local administration of the means of violence is more likely to be neutral among different investors than administration by a competing center country.

Greater dependence on local elites to control the means of violence meant increasing local bargaining power vis-à-vis the international firms in their territories. But decentralization of the means of violence was simply a new element in a process already underway. Attempts by third world governments to improve their economic bargaining position had been going on for some time. The great depression had shaken the faith of third world politicians that their nations had a secure economic future as producers of primary products. They wanted industry established within their own territories and began to push foreign investors in that direction.

Conveniently, foreign investors themselves were evolving in ways that enabled them to respond to the demands. The increased organizational sophistication achieved by American corporations during the first decades of the twentieth century is well documented. Improved means of information processing and transformations of organizational structures made it possible to control corporate empires of enormous scale and diversity (Chandler, 1962). These techniques, developed for coping with the domestic market, became important for overseas expansion (Fouraker and Stopford, 1968; Stopford and Wells, 1972). Once the organizational barriers were overcome, direct investment in third world manufacturing operations became potentially more profitable. At the same time, increased international competition and pressure from third world governments made it a competitive necessity.

The changed situation was reflected in a dramatic rise in direct investment during the fifties and sixties. United States direct investment in manufacturing in Latin America rose from $400 million just after World War II to $9 billion by 1976. In the sixties, German and Japanese investment grew even more rapidly. The growth and diversification of foreign investment was self-reinforcing. Multinationals operating in the third world could no longer afford simply to consider the environment too risky; they were forced to confront the possibility that if they did not make a given investment someone else might. This in turn increased the bargaining position of third world states still further.

By the sixties it was necessary to recognize that imperialism might be consistent with a certain kind of development in the periphery, development that would include the growth of a local manufacturing sector. It was also clear that the course of this dependent development would be shaped, not only by events in the center of the system but also by the internal evolution of peripheral societies themselves. "Dependency theory," largely a third world product itself, attempted to deal with these concerns.

Imperialism and Dependence

The founders of dependency theory included critical Latin American sociologists and historians such as Caio Prado, Jr., Sergio Bagu, and Florestan Fernandes (see Cardoso, 1977; Kahl, 1976), the work of Baran as applied to the Latin American context by André Gundar Frank (1967), and the structuralist revisions of development economics that had been worked out by Raul Prebisch, Celso Furtado, and others (see Girvan, 1973). Drawing on this body of work, dependency theorists then aimed at discovering "those characteristics of national societies which express external relations" (Cardoso and Faletto, 1973:28).

More recently, the Latin American originators of dependency theory have been joined by others, such as Samir Amin, who work more directly with the theory of imperialism but who share dependency theory's focus on the consequences of imperialism for the internal evolution of peripheral countries.

The starting point is still relations with the external world. A dependent country is one whose development is "conditioned by the development and expansion of another economy" (Dos Santos, 1970:236). Dependent countries are classically those whose histories of involvement with the international market have led them to specialize in the export of a few primary products. While the income from these few products is absolutely central to the process of accumulation in the dependent country, for the center each product represents only a tiny fraction of total imports, and can usually be obtained from several different sources. The development of the dependent country, however, requires the continued acceptance of its products in the center. Therefore, economic fluctuations in the center may have severe negative consequences for the periphery, whereas an economic crisis in the periphery offers no real threat to accumulation in the center.

Complementing and often underlying dependence based on trade relations, is dependence based on foreign ownership of the productive apparatus of the dependent country. When the principal aspect of dependence is that key sectors of the local productive apparatus are integral parts of capital that is controlled elsewhere, then accumulation in the dependent country is externally conditioned more by the "development and expansion of center-based capital" rather than by the "development and expansion of another country." The asymmetry is there nonetheless.

Dependence is then defined most simply as a situation in which the rate and direction of accumulation are externally conditioned. Curiously, however, while external relations are the starting point for the analysis of dependence, most of the emphasis of dependency theorists is on the internal class relations of dependent countries. As Cardoso and Faletto (1973:140) say, ". . . there is no such thing as a metaphysical relation of dependency between one nation and another, one state and another. Such relations are made concrete possibilities through the existence of a network of interests and interactions which link certain social groups to other social groups, certain social classes to other classes."

Dependence includes a wide range of disparate situations. OPEC and the oil crisis provided a powerful reminder that exporting primary products does not universally entail having a weak position in international trade. Even more important, saying that a country is "dependent" does not indicate that its relation to the international economic system is immutably fixed. It means rather that the historic process of accumulation in that country exhibits certain distinctive features that are shared by other countries of the periphery and set it apart from the nations of the center.

Contemporary dependency theorists see the international division of labor as shifting substantially on the surface while continuing to have the same fundamental effect. Curiously, the most carefully elaborated theoretical underpinning for this view comes not from within the dependency tradition itself but rather from the latest version of the theory of comparative advantage, known as the "product life cycle model" (Vernon, 1966; Johnson, 1968; Wells, 1972). According to the product life cycle model, new products are likely to be first produced and sold in the center, later produced in the center and exported to the periphery, and finally produced in the periphery. Over time, more and more products will be manufactured in the periphery, but these products will continue to share certain characteristics.

Production moves to the periphery only after the technology involved has become routinized. At this point uncertainties are small and savings from cheap labor make a difference. Thus, the Schumpeterian "windfall profits" associated with new products always remain the prerogative of the center. In addition, the periphery is forced to rely on the low cost of its labor for its comparative advantage in the international market, making low living standards the basis of dependent development.[1]

The introduction of manufacturing on the periphery also lacks the traditional "multiplier effect" associated with manufacturing investments in the center. Peripheral economies are "disarticulated," that is, firms on the periphery are not connected to each other in the same way as firms in an autocentric economy. Firms in dependent countries buy their equipment and other capital goods from outside, so that the "multiplier effect" of new investments is transferred back to the center. Increases in the output of export sectors, dramatic as they may be, do not feed back into the peripheral economy in the same way that they would feed back into an autocentric economy. As Amin (1976:239) puts it: "When the iron ore of Lorraine is eventually worked out this may create a difficult reconversion problem for the region, but it will be able to overcome these difficulties, for an infrastructure has been formed on the basis of the mineral, which could be imported

[1] One stream of thinking which speaks to this point and has been left unexplored here is Arrighi Emmanuel's (1972) "theory of unequal exchange." In the absence of concrete work on Latin America which links the theory of unequal exchange to the dependency theory tradition, I decided to neglect Emmanuel's contribution, despite its important place in the development of the theory of imperialism. For a brief exposition of the theory of unequal exchange, see Amin (1976:138-154).

from elsewhere. But when the iron ore of Mauritania is worked out, that country will go back to the desert."

Disarticulation between technology and social structure reinforces the economy's lack of integration. Celso Furtado (1969:15) speaks of the importation of technology as contributing to a "structural deformation" of the peripheral economy. Productive technologies imported from the center are not designed to absorb the huge reserves of underemployed agricultural labor. Products developed in the center and assimilated by the periphery are luxury products in the context of the periphery. Their production uses scarce resources and results in a "distortion in the allocation of resources in favor of those products and to the detriment of mass consumption goods" (Amin, 1977b:9).

For the elite, disarticulation is an obstacle to self-sustained, autocentric accumulation, but for the mass its consequence is exclusion. Because accumulation depends primarily either on exports or on goods beyond their means, the mass of the population can be excluded as consumers. Capital intensive technologies in the modern sector make it possible to marginalize them as producers. Because they are effectively barred from economic participation, to allow them political participation would be disruptive. Social and cultural exclusion follow from political and economic exclusion.

Exclusion, like disarticulation, is a constant feature of dependency. The gross gap between elite and mass that characterized classic dependence was expected to diminish once a domestic manufacturing sector was established. But the record of the sixties shows increasing inequality (cf. Adelman and Morris, 1973; Chase-Dunn, 1975; Evans and Timberlake, 1977). On the political level, populism has not proved an enduring strategy. As O'Donnell's (1973) pessimistic but convincing comparative analysis of Latin American countries shows, the ruling groups in the more advanced peripheral societies have discovered that the kind of economic development they need to sustain their own lifestyles requires the increasing political exclusion of the mass of the population.

The internal disarticulation of the peripheral society is complemented and exacerbated by the integration of elites internationally. Contemporary elites do not send their shirts to Europe to be laundered as the traditional colonial rulers of Latin America supposedly did, but they are part of what Sunkel calls "the transnational kernel," that is, "a complex of activities, social groups and regions in different countries . . . which are closely linked transnationally through many concrete interests as well as by similar styles, ways and levels of living and cultural affinities" (1973:146).

Arguing that certain features of dependent social structures will persist despite industrialization has been one main task of dependency theory, but mapping change and variation has been equally central. From the beginning, dependency theory has recognized that hand in hand with changes in the shape of imperialism have gone changes in peripheral social formations. In Latin America, where classic dependency occurred in the context of formal political independence, the great depression is usually seen as the "moment of the transition." The period of classic dependency in which primary products provided the basis of "externally oriented expansion" ran until the beginning of the thirties (Cardoso and Faletto, 1973:39-51). The crisis of the depression made survival on the old basis impossible and forced the transition to a focus on the dependent's internal market.

The "consolidation of the internal market," which is to say the growth of "easy" import-substituting industrialization, is followed in turn by the "internationalization" of the domestic market (Cardoso and Faletto, 1973:114-138) during which the penetration of the multinationals becomes more intense as import substitution moves from consumer nondurables to consumer durables, intermediary goods, and some capital goods. O'Donnell (1973:60-61) speaks of this as the transition from "horizontal" to "vertical" industrialization, and agrees with Cardoso and

Faletto that its internal character, political as well as economic, is distinct from the earlier phase of import substitution.[2]

In Asia and Africa, the political crisis of World War II marked the beginning of the transition. In most of these countries consolidation of the internal market is still going on and "vertical industrialization" is a project for the future. Nonetheless, the relations between local industrial bourgeoisies and international capital have changed in ways that are quite similar to the evolution of the more advanced countries of Latin America.

Amin (1977a:35) talks of the local bourgeoisies as having "won victories that led to independence, agrarian reforms and industrial achievements" and suggests that their victories "led to the integration of these bourgeoisies into the imperialist alliance." Amin's description of the class alliances of the "second phase" of imperialism echoes themes common to Latin American descriptions of the recent history of dependency. Once the "internationalization of the domestic market" has occurred then the stage is set for an "internationalized bourgeoisie" (Cardoso and Faletto, 1973:134) or, in Sunkel's language, the dominance of the "transnational kernel." Alliance of local and international capital is the common element in all these descriptions.

Cardoso's model of "associated-dependent development" pushes the idea of alliance the furthest. Associated-dependent development involves, he says, "the simultaneous and differentiated expansion of three sectors of the economy: the private national, the foreign and the public" (Cardoso, 1974:57). Politically, associated-dependent development requires the "structuring of a system of relations among the social groups which control these economic sectors" (Cardoso and Faletto, 1973:130).

Dependency theory and the contributions of theorists like

[2] A number of parallel periodizations exist. Sunkel (1973), for example, emphasizes the rise of the multinational as a retreat from the rule of laissez-faire and so characterizes the contemporary period as the "age of neo-mercantilism." Pereira (1970) emphasizes the internal side of the transformation and speaks of "peripheral industrialization." Dos Santos (1970) simply uses the term "new dependence" for the post-World War II period.

Amin lead away from the construction of models of stagnation and toward an analysis of dependent development. If we join Cardoso in defining development as "the accumulation of capital and its effect on the differentiation of the productive system" (1974:57), then dependent development implies both the accumulation of capital and some degree of industrialization on the periphery. Dependent development is a special instance of dependency, characterized by the association or alliance of international and local capital. The state also joins the alliance as an active partner, and the resulting triple alliance is a fundamental factor in the emergence of dependent development.

Dependent development was taking place even during the period of classic dependence and "export-oriented growth," at least in those countries which were later able to make the transition to the "consolidation of the internal market." If capital accumulation and some degree of industrialization had not been occurring in these countries, the transition to a more industrially oriented growth would have been impossible. But dependent development was the emerging antithesis rather than the main theme of classic dependency. Under classic dependence, the accumulation of industrial capital took place in spite of the interests of the dominant elite.

In countries characterized by the internationalization of the internal market (the "second phase" of imperialism, or "vertical industrialization"), however, dependent development is the dominant aspect of dependence. It is these instances of dependence to which the label "dependent development" applies in an unambiguous way. Throughout this study, "dependent development" will be used to refer to cases where capital accumulation and diversified industrialization of a more than superficial sort are not only occurring in a peripheral country, but are dominating the transformation of its economy and social structure.

Dependent development is *not*, it should be stressed, the negation of dependence. It is rather dependence combined with development. Amin (1976:287) even goes so far as to argue that "none of the features that define the structure of the periphery is weakened as economic growth proceeds: on the contrary these features are accentuated." Nor does dependent development eradicate contradictions between center and periphery. As Cardoso writes, "when one examines the relations between economies of 'dependent-associated development' and the central economies, it is not hard to perceive that the international division of labor persists, based on very unequal degrees of wealth, on unequal forms of appropriation of the international surplus and on monopolization of the dynamic capitalist sectors by the central countries" (1977:20).

Dependent development is not a phase that all peripheral countries will be able to reach. Only a few are chosen. International stratification is accentuated rather than leveled as those countries in which the local bourgeoisie and international capital can arrive at an alliance become increasingly differentiated from the majority of the third world. Wallerstein (1974b, 1974c) claims that the more advanced exemplars of dependent development occupy their own distinct position within the international system. They form the "semi-periphery."[3]

Those which "make it" into the semi-periphery have an ambiguous relation to those left behind. All are still disadvantaged vis-à-vis the center, but the semi-periphery is advantaged vis à vis its neighbors. The political and military resources of the semi-periphery may not be sufficient to generate "subimperialism" (cf. Marini, 1972), but it remains plausible that they "could advance faster on the path of the new dependence if they

[3] Wallerstein is not a *dependentista*. His focus on the world system rather than on the internal social structures of peripheral nations gives his work a quite different theoretical orientation. He is included here both because of the obvious relevance of his concept of the "semi-periphery" to any discussion of dependent development and because, like Amin, he is a contributor to the theory of imperialism who has definitely drawn on and been influenced by dependency theory.

also had markets in the less developed countries and if they could have direct and cheap access to their supplies of raw materials and food" (Amin, 1977b:14-15).

The distinctive position of semi-periphery in the international economy makes the course of dependent development in these countries critical to the future of imperialism. The commitment of center country capital to the semi-periphery is sufficient for a crisis in these economies to have significant consequences not only for firms involved in raw materials production but for a broad range of multinationals. The poorest countries of the periphery can stagnate without their plight being reflected in any serious disturbances in the center, but crisis in the semi-periphery would rob the multinationals in several industries of an important alternate arena for accumulation. Should crisis in the semi-periphery result in the political disaffection of these states, the political stability of the overall system would be threatened as well. In Wallerstein's (1974c:3) view at least, "the creation of 'middle' sectors which tend to think of themselves as better off than the lower sector rather than as worse off than the upper sector" has been a major means of averting the political polarization of the international system.

The most recent phase of dependency entails a restructuring of external relations, but changes in this area depend upon the nature of capital accumulation within the countries of the semi-periphery; and this in turn is based on the triple alliance of the multinationals, the state, and the local bourgeoisie. The three partners and their interrelationships are the starting point for any analysis of the institutional basis of dependent development.

The Multinationals[4]

Multinational corporations are the organizational embodiment of international capital. Their decisions reflect the dictates of

---

[4] The term "multinationals" is obviously a misnomer in the fundamental sense that most multinationals are controlled by capital from a single center country.

imperialism. At the same time, these decisions are more than reflections of external exigencies; the organizational form itself has consequences. Just as imperialism is not simply capitalism, multinational corporations are not simply profit-making capitalist firms. Corporations remove control over production from those engaged in production; multinationals extend the alienation across political boundaries. Strategic decisions are made in the center. Even if a strategy is first conceived locally it must be validated in the center. Operational decisions may be made locally. Personnel who work in the periphery may influence strategy. The fact remains that long-term plans and the "larger picture" are put together in the center. For those who live in the periphery this realization is frustrating, perhaps even more for elites than for the mass of the population.

Many who analyze imperialism discount the question of who makes the decisions and where. Arrighi Emmanuel (1974:75) presents the case clearly:

> I must confess that I have never understood what Canadian workers or the Canadian people would gain if the decision making centers of their industry were shifted from offices located in the skyscrapers of New York or Chicago to others located in the tower blocks of Montreal or Toronto and still less have I ever understood what the Indian masses, with their per capita income of $100 per annum, would stand to lose if the day came when capitalists with Indian passports handed over to capitalists with North American or Japanese ones.

Unfortunately, the behavior of capitalists is not as simple as Emmanuel suggests. To be sure, the structure of imperialism as a whole creates a common environment to which any firm, local or

---

The newer term "transnational" is more accurate. I have continued to use "multinational" mainly because I feel that the language used in the analysis of dependent development contains more than its share of departures from common usage and that most readers have a reasonably clear idea of the empirical universe of corporations to which the term multinational refers.

international must respond. But the logic of accumulation for individual firms depends on their specific relation to that environment.

Multinationals have opportunities that local firms do not have. They will maximize their profits in terms of a global strategy, not a local one. In addition, the logic of profit is always ambiguous. What a corporation does depends on what opportunities it can see. Corporations, no matter how sophisticated, make decisions on the basis of incomplete, uncertain information (cf. Goodman, 1975). Choices about what products to produce, where to produce them, and how to produce them must be based on educated guesses and the direction of the guess depends on the environment in which it is made. Organization theorists describe the problem as "bounded rationality" (Simon, 1965; March and Simon, 1958; Cyert and March, 1963). By this they mean that a decision is rational only within the cognitive boundaries created by the information available to the decision maker. What information is available depends on who makes the decision and where it is made. A rational profit maximizer who grew up in Kansas City and works in Chicago brings different information to a decision from one who grew up in São Paulo and works there.

Bounded rationality helps explain why foreign investors did not spontaneously start manufacturing operations in the periphery during the earlier phase of imperialism. From where they were sitting it did not look worth the risk. Sometimes they may have been right not to invest. The point is that if and when they were wrong, they were likely to be wrong in the direction of overestimating the riskiness of investment on the periphery. The classic entrepreneur is just the opposite. When he is wrong, it is likely to be because he underestimates risk. Bounded rationality makes the foreign investor a poor candidate for the entrepreneurial role, just as Baran argued.

The organizational logic of the multinational tends to slow down the implantation of industry on the periphery. It also helps to impose the kind of international division of labor implied by the product life cycle model and to reinforce the disarticulation of technology and social structure. Imperialism as a system of accumulation ensures that any profit-making firm will tend to gravitate toward technology designed for center country social conditions and focus on low return, routine kinds of production in peripheral locations, but the interests of multinationals powerfully increase these tendencies.

The ability to produce new products which other firms cannot replicate is one of the most important sources of multinationals' profits. Knowledge is hard to monopolize—harder if its production is not highly centralized. Multinationals have then every motivation to keep the innovative side of their businesses as close to home as possible. As long as they are free to make that choice, the industrialization of the periphery will remain partial. Facilities for the production of new knowledge will not be located there. New technology will continue to be generated by the center countries and later assimilated by the periphery.

A multinational also has every reason to try to persuade consumers on the periphery to imitate customers in the center. The further it can spread the products and ideas over which it has control the more profits it can make. The added cost of using technology in a new market is negligible compared to the cost of developing the technology in the first place. This applies, of course, to methods of production as well as to new products. The proprietary interests of the multinational lie in making the peripheral economy as permeable as possible to center technology. Reluctant to invest in innovative activities that might produce a more locally appropriate technology, the multinational is anxious to market existing ideas regardless of appropriateness.

New products will be sold in the third world as soon as the multinational can create a market for them, but unless political considerations intervene, their production will be moved there only after it becomes routine. As Barnet and Müller illustrate nicely in the case of television (1974:129-133), following the logic of the product cycle enables a multinational to prolong its returns on a given product over the longest possible period.

Finally, the products offered by the multinationals will, because of their rich country origins, find their market primarily among third world elites. Thus, multinationals have both an interest in keeping wages low so that they can make a profit on routine manufacturing operations and an interest in income concentration so that they will have a market for the kinds of products they are trying to sell. If they look after their own corporate interests, multinationals will exacerbate both the exclusionary tendencies of dependent development and the disarticulation of technology and social conditions.

The interests of the multinationals as firms contribute to other kinds of disarticulation as well. They provide natural channels for pulling their local managers and their other local allies into the "transnational kernel." They have connections with center country suppliers and servicing organizations, relationships that reinforce the tendency toward disconnection between the multinationals and other local firms. The efficiency of the ties that bind the corporate core of the multinational to its far-flung parts multiplies the "missing links" in the periphery (Amin, 1976:212). The phone circuits that connect downtown São Paulo with downtown New York are rapidly improved while those linking São Paulo to its own rural hinterland remain primitive and undependable.

Multinationals are more than the representatives of the international economic order. They are organizations whose internal structures both reflect and shape the international economy. The contradictions between the interests of the multinationals and development on the periphery were not just figments of Baran's imagination or transitional aberrations. They persist even after multinationals have begun to engage in manufacturing on the periphery, even in the context of the "internationalization of the internal market," "associated-dependent development," and the emergence of new partnerships with the national bourgeoisie.

Local Capital

The "national industrial bourgeoisie" is the stepchild of imperialism, never completely abandoned but never given a full opportunity to develop. The industrial bourgeoisie, insofar as it develops at all on the periphery, enters the scene under conditions severely disadvantageous to its own interests. Center country bourgeoisies have already "preempted" the world historic role of the "conquering bourgeoisie" (see Fernandes, 1975:295). Furthermore, imperialism, as Baran pointed out, stimulates the growth of its more favored children—the export-oriented agrarian capitalists and a mercantile compradore class.

Even with the transformation of imperialism and the advent of industrialization in certain third world countries, hegemony was not the lot of the "national industrial bourgeoisie." One of the contributions of dependency theory has been to point out that industrialization was a project built on compromise and not on bourgeois domination. As Cardoso and Faletto (1973:93) put it, "This industrialization represented more a policy of accords, between diverse groups from agrarian to popular-urban, than the imposition of interests or will to power of a 'conquering bourgeoisie.' " Traditional agrarian and export interests lost some ground but remained powerful, while the industrial bourgeoisie acquired new competitors.

Along with industrialization came the "presence of the masses" (Cardoso and Faletto, 1973:92), urban working class groups who, if organized in the context of a relatively open political system, could represent a substantial political force. At the same time the "new dependency," in the form of foreign investment in manufacturing, brought a new kind of competitive pressure on local industrialists. Dependent industrialization left the national industrial bourgeoisie with no opening for either political domination or economic hegemony. Its position and privileges were always contingent on its ability to make alliances with other elite groups.

Failure to attain a hegemonic position should not be confused with passivity or lack of entrepreneurship. At least in cases like the Brazilian one, economic historians (cf. Graham, 1968; Dean, 1969; Queiroz, 1972) uniformly emphasize the role of local industrialists in embarking on new activities and contributing to accumulation at the local level. But if the past role of local bourgeois entrepreneurs in fostering accumulation is more usually underestimated, predictions of the demise of the local industrial bourgeoisie occur with even greater regularity.

Predictions of the imminent disappearance of the national bourgeoisie are based on two premises. One is that any local capitalist who enters into an alliance with international capital is transformed into a subordinate whose behavior must reflect the interests of his new boss. The second is that independent local capital has no chance of survival. Thus, Fernandez and Ocampo (1974:58) divide the local bourgeoisie into the national bourgeoisie which "suffers intensely from imperialist domination" and the big bourgeoisie who "serve the interests of imperialist countries." But this Dr. Jekyl and Mr. Hyde version of the local bourgeoisie caricatures both segments.

The "internationalized" bourgeoisie which is allied with international capital retains an interest in local accumulation despite their ties to the center. This is undeniable in the case of partnerships based on joint ownership of industrial firms, and may even apply in a restricted way to those who merely service the multinationals. The local bourgeoisie cannot afford to relinquish nationalism even if international capital has become their principal ally. Fernandes catches the ambiguity of their position when he describes them as having a status "in part mediator and in part free" and suggests that the maintenance of this dual status is the "fulcrum of the real internal power of the bourgeoisie" (1975:326).

The desperation of local capital unable to form alliances, like the disloyalty of the new members of the "transnational kernel," is exaggerated. While independent local firms may be disappearing from certain industries, the overall destruction of locally owned industry is usually asserted rather than established empirically. The progress of concentration may eventually wipe out small capital (which is to say local capital) on the periphery as it may in the center, but, if the experience of advanced capitalist countries is any guide, that progress is likely to be glacial rather than cataclysmic. In fact, the local bourgeoisie may have a "comparative advantage" in certain industries, or at least there may be certain roles necessary to accumulation at the local level that multinationals or their indigenous employees cannot perform as well as members of the local owning class.

Fascination with the power of the multinationals has tended to distract attention from the power of local capital to either maintain a degree of bargaining leverage while entering into alliances or discover niches in the economy where the multinationals are less likely to penetrate. Dispassionate examination of the economic bases of the survival of the national industrial bourgeoisie is one of the most obvious requirements for any empirical analysis of dependent development.

The political position of the national industrial bourgeoisie is at least as ambiguous as its economic position. As a class that never achieved a hegemonic political position and never really had a "project" (cf. Cardoso, 1971:194), it is easy to relegate the dependent national bourgeoisie to the status of the nineteenth-century French bourgeoisie as described by Marx (cf. Evans, 1974), a class which was forced to admit that "in order to preserve its social power intact, its political power must be broken" (Marx, 1963:67). Some instances of dependent development may indeed follow a "bonapartist" political model, insofar as groups outside the bourgeoisie (such as the peasantry in France of 1852) have substantial political leverage. But, in cases where the political exclusion of subordinate classes is thoroughgoing, as in O'Donnell's (1973) description of Brazil and Argentina, post-Peron bonapartism is not an apt label.

Since the political power of local capital cannot flow from its dominant role in the process of accumulation, it must depend on the nature of its ties to the "technobureaucracy" that staffs the state apparatus. Estimates of this relation vary. Cardoso and Faletto (1973:136) come close to suggesting a bonapartist model when they argue that under conditions of dependent development (the internationalization of the market) the bourgeoisie does not have any political organizations at its disposal and consequently its control over the state is "purely 'structural.' " The technobureaucracy goes its own way unless its policies "conflict with the mechanisms of capitalist accumulation." This seems more reasonable as a description of the political strategy of the multinationals than of local capital.

Fernandes suggests a different interpretation of the political situation of the bourgeoisie. He argues (1975:308) that precisely because of the economic weakness of the national bourgeoisie, "state power emerges as the principal structure and real dynamo of bourgeois power" and that therefore dependent development involves the "modernization and rationalization of the articulation" between the dominant segments of the bourgeoisie and the state. Fernandes's model of "bourgeois autocracy" may underestimate the possibility of conflict between the "technobureaucracy" and private capital but, for most instances of dependent development, it is more plausible than a bonapartist model.

The bonapartist state executive meditating the interests of opposing classes is replaced under bourgeois autocracy by a state apparatus which brooks no opposition from subordinate groups when the interests of the bourgeoisie as a whole are in question. Yet still local capital is not hegemonic. The "national industrial bourgeoisie" must be seen as a class "fraction" or "segment"[5] whose ability to control the state becomes ambiguous when the

---

[5] The usefulness of the idea of "class segments" in the analysis of dependent development is nicely illustrated by the work of Zeitlin and his colleagues on the Chilean dominant class (Zeitlin, Ewen, and Ratcliff, 1974; Zeitlin and Ratcliff, 1975; Zeitlin, Neuman, and Ratcliff, 1976).

interests of the multinationals are at stake or when the interests of entrepreneurial groups within the state apparatus itself are involved.

The State

Regardless of ambiguities in its relation to the national bourgeoisie, the centrality of the state to accumulation on the periphery is incontrovertible. Imperialism as a process and the multinationals as organizations concentrate accumulation at the center of the international system. The local owning class has failed to achieve domination over local industry even in the most advanced peripheral countries. Unless the state can enforce a priority on local accumulation and push local industrialization effectively, there is no effective sponsor for peripheral industrialization.

The centrality of the entrepreneurial state to economic development is neither a novel phenomenon nor one peculiar to dependent capitalist development. From Gerschenkron's (1952) classic work on the role of the state in late European industrialization to Trimberger's (1972) analysis of entrepreneurial state bureaucrats in Japan and Turkey, comparative historical analysis has demonstrated the importance of "taking the state seriously as a macrostructure" (Skocpol, 1979). If Polanyi's (1944) questioning of the myth of the "laissez faire" state and Wallerstein's (1974a) emphasis on the strength of the early English state are correct, the state also played a central role in the original industrial revolution.

Even given the importance of the state in other instances of industrialization, the centrality of the state in dependent development is special. The disarticulated nature of the dependent social structure makes bureaucratic roles more independent of the dominant class. As Amin (1976:202) says, "The mutilated nature of the natural community in the periphery confers an apparent relative weight and special functions upon the local bureaucracy that are not the same as those of the bureaucratic groups at the center." At the same time, the penetration of the local economy by the multinationals means that the state's traditional role of dealing with the external environment has an internal economic dimension which demands as much attention as normal "statecraft."

The problem is to redirect the global rationality of the multinational when it conflicts with the necessities of local accumulation. The state must continually coerce or cajole the multinationals into undertaking roles that they would otherwise abdicate. The power and flexibility of the multinationals suggest that making the returns to desired local investments more attractive is the least problematic way of assuring a response, but this pure incentive method has other costs. It usually means shifting some of the local surplus to the multinationals at the expense of either the national bourgeoisie or the state itself. Relying too heavily on coercing multinationals is also costly. Not only are they likely to withdraw from entrepreneurial ventures, but they are also likely to try to mobilize political opposition both internally and externally. Achieving an effective blend of coercion and incentive is not likely to be easy.

The state apparatus must be willing to oppose the multinationals when questions of local accumulation are at stake. Supine compradore states are excluded from the game. Even the most militant state needs some chips to bargain with. A peripheral society that lacks valuable natural resources, an extensive local market, or an exploitable labor force is hardly in a position to bargain. The capacity of the state apparatus is also important. States must have control over a sufficient segment of the surplus so that they can offer incentives as well as support their own activities. Finally, technical expertise and control over relevant information play a role.

Relations between states and multinationals have been the

focus of some of the best recent empirical work in the dependency theory tradition. Moran's (1974) work on copper in Chile and Tugwell's (1975) study of oil in Venezuela have demonstrated the usefulness of examining the course of the bargaining over time. Their work indicates that at least in these industries there was a secular shift over the course of the last fifty years in the direction of an improved bargaining position for the state. This shift seems to be rooted both in the increasing political decentralization of imperialism and in a gradual process of learning within the state apparatus itself. In each case the state combined incentives and threats and ended up with a greater share of the returns.

While the same scenario may well apply to the evolution of state-multinational relations with respect to manufacturing industries, it is harder to document. Moran (1975) has suggested that the state stands the best chance of improving its position in industries involving extraction of raw materials, where technology is stable and fixed investment large; whereas in industries where intangible capital is more important and continual product innovation the rule, the multinationals have a stronger position. If he is correct, then any thoroughgoing analysis of state-multinational bargaining will have to take into account the spectrum of industries over which the bargaining is taking place as well as the overall capacities and resources of the state.

Simple bargaining is, of course, not the only alternative open to the state. In both Chile and Venezuela the end of the bargaining process was takeover of the industries in question by the state. State enterprise may also be the result of failure to convince the multinational to undertake a new venture, as in the case of the Brazilian steel industry. Whatever their origins, state enterprises add a new dimension to state-multinational bargaining. They can be used to provide extra incentives to the multinationals in the form of low cost inputs. Or, they may threaten the recalcitrant multinational with a new source of competition, vastly stronger than local private capital. The creation of state enterprises does more, however, than simply increase the capacity of the state to bargain. Just as the existence of multinationals changes the effects of imperialism, the creation of state enterprises changes the institutional nature of the dependent capitalist state.

In Latin America, and to a lesser degree in the former colonies of Asia and Africa, state enterprises have existed for a long time. Traditional infrastructural activities or in a few cases production of raw materials have been their main activities and they have behaved more or less like other parts of the bureaucracy. New state firms, created on the model of modern private corporations and engaged in export and directly productive activities previously reserved for private capital, exhibit a more entrepreneurial approach. It has even been argued that they signify a "change from a classical administrative bureaucracy into a state bourgeoisie" (Amin, 1976:346; see also Cardoso, 1974).

Once the concept of the "state bourgeoisie" has been introduced, new possibilities emerge for describing the interaction of the state and the multinationals as well as the state and the national industrial bourgeoisie. If it exists, a state bourgeoisie would be the most natural agent of local capital accumulation. Hampered neither by the necessity of tending to international concerns that distracts the multinationals nor the resource limitations that constrain local private industrialists, a state bourgeoisie might take over the role of the "conquering bourgeoisie." But can there be a "state bourgeoisie"? A bourgeoisie by definition appropriates surplus to itself; yet as part of the state apparatus, managers of state enterprises are supposed to be directing the process of accumulation in the general interests of capital as a whole, and not in their own particular interests.

If a state bourgeoisie is directing accumulation, then the natural movement of the industrial structure should be in the direction of state capitalism. Yet, what is the political base of these state managers if not the support of the local private bourgeoisie? It seems unlikely that the managers of state enterprises should be so disconnected from the bourgeoisie as a whole that they would push "state capitalism" to the detriment of local private capital. Amin (1976:347) takes this view when he argues for the coexistence of state and private bourgeoisies, saying that "state bourgeoisies have never eliminated private bourgeoisies but have been satisfied with absorbing them or merging with them." Likewise, while the state enterprises may try to squeeze multinationals, they are more sensitive than other parts of the state apparatus to the importance of not losing the inputs that multinationals have to offer.

Rather than see the state bourgeoisie as a replacement for the national industrial bourgeoisie, we may consider it a sort of class "fraction" which participates in a common project with both the multinationals and local private capital. Each group may view the project as subject to different constraints and each may have particular interests that contradict those of the others, but they all have an interest in a high rate of accumulation at the local level.

The image of the dependent capitalist state cannot be based simply on its role as an agent of accumulation. It is also an agent of social control. As Skocpol (1978:33) says, "The state first and fundamentally extracts resources from society and deploys these to create and support coercive and administrative organizations." The extremely exclusionary nature of dependent capitalist development accentuates the coercive aspects of the state just as the necessity of coping with the multinationals accentuates the entrepreneurial side. In the context of European industrialization, it seemed even to Lenin that representative democracy was the "best possible political shell" for capitalist growth. In the context of dependent development, however, the association of bourgeois democracy and capitalist accumulation no longer holds. As Florestan Fernandes (1975:312, 316) puts it, the dependent bourgeoisie has been forced to "revise and redefine the ideologies and utopias assimilated from the bourgeois-democratic experience of Europe and North America." Instead they must "support the hardening of bourgeoisie domination and its transfiguration into a specifically authoritarian and totalitarian social force," that is, "bourgeois autocracy."

The tendency toward repression stems in part from the economic rationale of exclusion. Any rise in the wages of the work force threatens the attractiveness of a given peripheral country as a site for export-oriented routine manufacturing activities. At the same time, concentration of income enhances the market for luxury consumer goods, which is the most dynamic part of the domestic market. Because of the disarticulated nature of the local economy, "the existence of an objective relation between the rewarding of labor and the level of development of the productive forces is completely absent" (Amin, 1976:192).

Repression is especially necessary in those countries which have passed through the phase of "easy import substitution" and are trying to push the process of dependent industrialization further. Guillermo O'Donnell (1973:53) has illustrated this nicely by contrasting Argentina and Brazil in the late sixties with some less developed Latin American countries. In the more advanced areas of the periphery, the coercive apparatus must be "geared to exclude the *already activated* urban popular sector." The aim is to return the working class to the political position it held before it became urbanized and organized (albeit organized only partially and under the wing of the state). Repression is the only way to enforce such a step backward.

In the context of dependent development, the need for repression is great while the need for democracy is small. One of the functions of parliamentary regimes is to provide a forum for the resolution of differences among the bourgeoisie. During the original industrial revolution a degree of political consensus among the members of the owning classes was essential to carrying out their "class project" of capital accumulation. But when accumulation depends on the triple alliance of multinationals, state enterprises, and their local private allies, parliamentary means of achieving consensus are inappropriate. Neither the multinationals nor the state bourgeoisie are likely to be politically represented in proportion to their economic importance. For the local private bourgeoisie the disproportionate (relative to their economic position) representation of small capital could be a real problem. The lack of representative political bodies may make it harder for the local private bourgeoisie to forge an internal political consensus, but, since its role in accumulation is ancillary rather than dominant, an overall consensus is not crucial.

When repression of the urban working class, effective bargaining with the multinationals, and entrepreneurial initiative on the part of the state bourgeoisie are the critical components of capital accumulation, then imperative control, not consensus building within the bourgeoisie, is the response. There emerges, in Fernandes's words (1975:292), "a strong *rational* association between capitalist development and autocracy." To complement the state bourgeoisie in the economic sphere a professional bureaucratic group is required to staff the coercive apparatus, and the military are the obvious candidates.

Military rule is not only a good choice because the military are the immediate wards of the state's monopoly on violence; they are also an apt choice because the dependent capitalist state, despite its disavowal of popular mobilization, is likely to be nationalist. Like repression, nationalism is useful both in promoting accumulation and in maintaining order. Nationalism provides the ideological basis for giving priority to local accumulation and is therefore useful in arguments with the multinationals. It provides a legitimation for the activities of the state bourgeoisie in the eyes of private capital. It is also the only basis on which the state can claim common ground with the mass of the population, especially as "developmentalist" promises of future material rewards begin to lose their credence (cf. Portes, 1977).

The contradictions of dependent development are reflected in the paradoxical nature of the dependent capitalist state. It is a nationalist state whose strategy of accumulation is conditioned by its relation to the international economy and depends in the first instance on the cooperation of the multinational corporation. It is a state whose repressive protection of the interests of the dominant class is blatant, yet it excludes most of the national bourgeoisie from political participation just as it excludes the mass of the population. Nonetheless, despite or perhaps because of the contradictions it contains, the state has been a key instrument in fostering dependent development.

The Analysis of Dependent Development

Imperialism remains the frame for the analysis of dependent development. Except for the inroads of socialism or state collectivism (cf. Amin, 1977a), the international economy is dominated more thoroughly than ever by capitalist relations of production and exchange. Control of capital internationally is still concentrated in a few industrialized countries of the west (and Japan). Production in both center and periphery is still directed toward the accumulation of capital, particularly capital controlled by center country corporations. The political and military resources of center states are still used to preserve and maintain capital invested in the periphery. Despite all that has changed, the essential features of imperialism as it was described by Hobson and Lenin remain.

Throughout the analysis of the Brazilian case, imperialism will be used to refer to the worldwide system of capital accumulation, both to its abstract logic and to the concrete relations among nations and social groups that it entails. Dependency complements the idea of imperialism by focusing on the consequences of a specific subset of the relations created by imperialism—those which tie peripheral countries to center countries. The principal contribution of dependency theory has been to provide an analysis of how imperialism affects the internal social structures of peripheral countries. In doing so, dependency theory has directed attention to variation among countries in the periphery and to the analysis of dependent development, which is a special instance of dependence. While any peripheral country not experiencing stagnation or devolution might be considered to be undergoing "dependent development," the term has been reserved here for cases of capital accumulation at the local level accompanied by increasing differentiation of the economy, which is to say by some degree of industrialization.

A focus on dependent development, rather than simply on dependence or imperialism as a whole, means that the crucial cases are few. Chad, Nepal, and Paraguay are of only indirect interest. The larger and more advanced countries of the third world are the testing ground: clearly Brazil and Mexico, probably Nigeria, Indonesia, and Iran, and perhaps India and Zaire are the countries exploring the consequences of capitalist development in the periphery. They illustrate the conditions, both institutional and contextual, that make dependent development possible. It is also these countries that will define the limits of dependent development.

Each case has a distinctive position within the international economy and is shaped by the specific circumstances of its historical development. Brazil is notable for its tremendously favorable combination of large size, low population density, and rich endowment of natural resources. Geographically, Brazil resembles the United States or the Soviet Union more than it does most other third world countries. In this sense it is the ideal case for testing the limits of dependent development. Brazil should be able to push industrialization as far as any country of the "semiperiphery" can. Using Brazil to estimate the limits of dependent development is, however, only a secondary objective here. The principal aim is to delineate the institutional arrangements that underlie dependent development, especially the internal structure of the dominant class.

Citing recent literature on dependency and imperialism, a model of the social structural basis of dependent development has now been presented. Since several of the important contributors to that literature, such as Fernandes and Cardoso, are Brazilians, the model should apply to Brazil if it applies anywhere. Its central premise is that an alliance which includes the multinationals, the state, and the local industrial bourgeoisie is a necessary condition for dependent capitalist development.

The dominant class in the semi-periphery is seen as composed of three interdependent partners who have a common interest in capital accumulation and in the subordination of the mass population, but whose interests are also contradictory. This view stands in contrast to versions of dependency theory that see conflict within the dominant class as a primary feature of dependent development. The present version assumes no irreconcilable differences between local industrialists and the multinationals or between the state and the multinationals. The contradictions between the global rationality of the multinationals and the interests of the local bourgeoisie and the state are seen as potentially resolvable, provided that the overall conditions under which the alliance operates are not too unfavorable to continued capital accumulation in the semi-periphery.

Viewing the internal structure of the dominant class as a triple alliance also means rejecting the notion that dependent development represents the capitulation of local capital to imperialism. The dominance of the multinationals within the partnership is not taken for granted but seen as varying from industry to industry and over time. Nor is the subordinate position of local capital taken for granted; rather it is assumed that the local industrial bourgeoisie has certain economic and political advantages that give it leverage in its bargaining with the multinationals.

Analysis in terms of a tripartite alliance goes against binary models of the dominant class, whether they are based on two-sided conflicts or two-partner alliances. If there is a triple alliance, then splits in the dominant class can not be reduced to either the national bourgeoisie (state and private) versus the multinationals, or to statism versus private capital (local and multinational). Nor can the partners be reduced to two, either by dropping out the local bourgeoisie as inconsequential or by assuming that the state is simply the instrument of the local bourgeoisie.

Accepting the idea that the carapace of dependent development is formed by an alliance of multinational, state, and local capital provides an orientation distinct from a number of other existing perspectives on dependence and industrialization. But what exactly is meant by "alliance" remains to be defined. It is clearly an ambivalent alliance, but the balance between antagonism and cooperation is yet to be explored. There is a division of labor among the three allies, but it needs to be specified. There must be continual bargaining among the partners, but the terms of the bargaining have not been spelled out. All of which is as it should be. Abstract analysis of such relations quickly reaches the point of diminishing returns.

In the chapters that follow, the ideas presented so far will be filled out, refined, and modified by their confrontation with the Brazilian case. The aim is to move from a discussion of dependent development that must, like any model stripped down to bare essentials, seem overly abstract and mechanistic, to an analysis that captures some of the richness of a concrete historical situation. Adding a sense of movement and change will be even more important than further specifying the current nature of the alliance. Here the processes of change that connect the different structural phases of dependence have been given only passing attention. The chapters to come will try to show that the class structures that sustain dependent development are in flux, on their way to taking a new form, still carrying with them the mark of earlier periods.

Brazil appears today as a paradigm of dependent development, an ideal case by which to explore the dynamics of capitalist expansion in the periphery. But it was once a sprawling impoverished country that seemed perfectly suited to the classic peripheral role of exporting primary products and importing manufactured goods. The roots of the current alliance go back to those days when Brazil was a collection of regional attempts at agriculture. Getting some sense of how this underprivileged coffee producer was transformed into an exemplar of dependent development is the first step in taking hold of the Brazilian case.

2.

From Classic Dependence to
Dependent Development*

BAGS of coffee, loaded onto ships docked in the port of Santos, were Brazil's link to the international economy of the late nineteenth and early twentieth centuries. International trade of unparalleled dimensions was coupled with capitalist accumulation on an equally unparalleled scale in the center countries of the system. Countries at the periphery helped support this accumulation of capital by producing primary products and by consuming manufactured goods turned out by the factories of the center. Few played this role better than Brazil.

The construction of this international system was a unique achievement for which British ingenuity deserves considerable credit. The power of the British navy helped maintain the peace that made trade possible. British banks kept the capital flowing and maintained the gold standard. Even British economists helped, providing, in the form of the theory of comparative advantage and other neoclassical theoretical formulations, important pieces of the ideological superstructure. Britain was not without competitors for its position of preeminence, but the center of the system was unquestionably the City of London.

Britain and Brazil together provide a concrete example of what center and periphery mean in the context of this system. In the

* An earlier version of this chapter was published under the title "Continuities and Contradictions in the Evolution of Brazilian Dependence," in *Latin American Perspectives*, 3(2):30-54. I am grateful to the editors and especially John Meyer for his useful comments on that version.

late nineteenth century Brazil had hardly begun to mill its own wheat or make its own lard. Anything manufactured was likely to come from the factories of Britain and be paid for with the proceeds of Brazilian agriculture. There is no better way to gain an understanding of the structure of classic dependence than by looking at the relations between Brazil and Britain prior to the First World War.

Classic dependence worked well for the British and for the Brazilian coffee planters, but despite the wealth, power, and ingenuity of its beneficiaries, the system could not be preserved. Its own development created forces of production and social groups that eventually transformed it into a very different kind of political economy. Fifty years after World War I first disrupted the international system that the British had constructed, Brazil was producing most of its own manufactured goods. Brazilians were selling more and more of their manufactures on the international market, while the British were having increasing difficulty finding buyers for theirs. Dependence in its classic form had been superseded and dependent development was under way.

As classic dependence matured and the nature of dependence began to change, the triple alliance also began to take shape. At the beginning of the period none of the three actors had learned their contemporary roles. International capital was wary of manufacturing endeavors. Even the largest center country firms had still not developed the organizational techniques necessary to take full advantage of direct investment possibilities on the periphery. Local industrialists had neither the economic strength nor the self-awareness that might justify calling them an "industrial bourgeoisie." They relied more on the support of the exporters and agrarian capitalists than on alliances with international corporations or the state. The state apparatus was the home of traditional bureaucrats rather than a technocratic "state-bourgeoisie," and the oligarchic political structure of the old Republic provided no basis for moving beyond traditional kinds of investment in infrastructure.

As the internal structure of the Brazilian productive system and Brazil's relation to the international economy changed, local capital, the multinationals, and the state changed also. They shaped the transformation and were shaped by it.

Classic Dependence

The surplus created by the production of coffee for the international market may have ended up in large measure in the City of London, but coffee also provided Brazil with the means for the accumulation of capital locally. The growth of the coffee economy in the latter part of the nineteenth century was truly impressive. The increase in real income per capita in Brazil in the second half of the nineteenth century was greater than growth of real income per capita in the United States during the same period (Furtado, 1965:163-164). The value of Brazil's exports expanded two-and-a-half times between the founding of the republic in 1889 and the First World War (Villela and Suzigan, 1973:439). In São Paulo, coffee exports from Santos quadrupled between 1892 and 1912 and the population of the state quadrupled along with them (Dean, 1969:4). For Brazil, classic neocolonial dependence was anything but stagnant.

Being primary producers of an export crop with a growing market was a fine place in the international division of labor as far as the Brazilian oligarchy was concerned. For the elite families who owned the large coffee plantations, coffee was profitable and provided them with income sufficient to buy all the goods they needed from Europe. Though reports of profits as high as 80% annual return on capital are probably exaggerated (see Dean, 1969:6), the returns were certainly substantial. Brazil's balance of trade was always favorable. Between 1890 and 1930, there was no decade in which the median annual trade surplus was less than 15% of imports. During the period 1901-1910, the apogee of classic dependence, the median annual trade surplus was 50% of imports (Singer, 1975:351). Running an import/export economy had the additional advantage of funneling the exchange of goods through a few ports where they could be easily taxed. Duties on imports consistently provided the federal government with 60-70% of its revenues in the period from the founding of the republic to the First World War (Villela and Suzigan, 1973:418-421).

However profitable, the dependent economy was still vulnerable. Brazil's was an agricultural economy in which two-thirds of the agricultural production was exported as late as 1907 (Villela and Suzigan, 1973:68). Not only was most agricultural production exported but exports were concentrated in a very few products. Coffee never accounted for less than half of total exports from 1889 to 1913. Coffee and rubber together never accounted for less than three-fourths of the exports. And 95% of the exports were made up by these two plus half a dozen other primary products, like sugar and cacao (Villela and Suzigan, 1973:20). In short, the prosperity of most of the Brazilian economy depended on the international market for a few agricultural commodities.

Brazil's vulnerability was illustrated in the 1890's when economic crisis in the United States drove the price of coffee down from over four pounds sterling a bag to less than a pound and a half. Being at the mercy of changes in the international price, however, was not totally devastating as long as the demand for coffee was rising rapidly. Brazil produced 5.5 million bags of coffee in 1890 and by 1901 was able to export just under 15 million bags (Furtado, 1965:193-194). Real crisis for the dependent economy required falling prices combined with a stagnant market, which is what was in store for Brazil in the thirties.

What happened in the thirties provides the best illustration of the dangers of dependence. Between 1929 and 1931 the New York price for top grade Brazilian coffee dropped by 60%. This time there was no possibility for recouping the price losses by increasing output, as the market for coffee was no longer expanding as it had been in the late nineteenth century. In addition, new competitors forced Brazil to face the prospect of a declining share of the world market. Brazil's total export income (measured in pounds sterling) declined from a 1928 high of almost 100 million to a 1935 low of 33 million pounds. After World War II both price and quantities of coffee exports picked up, but the coffee market never again boomed as it had earlier. Average exports of coffee in the 1950's were a little under 15 million bags, exactly their 1901 level. If Brazil had remained tied to the economic pattern of classic dependence, it would have had to face more than periodic crises. It would have had to face periodic crises and long-term stagnation.

Reliance on a single export product was one of the defining features of classic dependence. Extreme reliance on imports was an equally central feature. Brazil's attachment to the international market placed it in the curious position of being an agricultural country that had to import food. While two-thirds of its total agricultural output was exported, it had to import large amounts of beans, rice, and all of the wheat it consumed. Agricultural imports were, however, minor items in comparison to the imports of industrialized products.

It is an understatement to say that the economy was "oriented to the exterior." Warren Dean (1969:19) summarized the situation by saying, "The coffee economy was at first destitute of the industrial capacity to feed or clothe itself." Most of the imports came, of course, from Great Britain. As the coffee economy prospered, British imports grew from 16 million pounds sterling in 1850 to over 40 million at the beginning of the twentieth century. The French, North Americans, and Portuguese were also important trade partners but their efforts combined barely matched those of Britain on its own. As the historian Richard Graham (1968:81-82) put it, ". . . every member of society from the slave wielding an iron hoe to the planter installing coffee hulling equipment, from the city worker who bought cheap cottons to the gentlewoman who used fine soaps, all were touched by English imports. In no other way was Brazil's dependence on the British economy more marked."

Behind the extreme reliance on imported goods lay a lack of local industry, and behind both of these lay the distribution of income generated by the primary export economy. The major difference between the incomes of the immigrants who worked the coffee plantations and the slaves that had preceded them was that the immigrants received their incomes in cash. They were pushed as close to subsistence as possible, so close that many of them decided to return home. Dean (1969:7) summarizes the situation politely by saying, "The demand of so depressed a mass market was restricted in volume and narrow in range." As long as the planters could afford to buy their luxuries from Europe and the workers could hardly afford to buy at all, there was little room for industrial profits. At the same time, the growth of industry and a more diversified internal economy seemed to be the only way to escape from excessive reliance on the external market.

Classic dependence restricted the possibility of industrial growth because it created such a poor domestic market and also because it left a large part of the surplus from the booming primary exports in the hands of the British. The British, however successful they may have been at industrial entrepreneurship at home, showed little inclination or aptitude for it in Brazil. In the late nineteenth century, Rio Flour Mills was apparently unique in being a profitable, British owned and managed manufacturing operation (Rippy, 1959:154-58). British attempts to manage sugar processing plants in the northeast were "universally a failure" and the apparent reason was "gross mismanagement of their affairs by the directors and local managers" (Graham, 1968:153-54). Given these difficulties it is not surprising that only 2% of total British investment in Latin America on the eve of World War I was in manufacturing (ECLA, 1965:17).

The British might have been more motivated to overcome the difficulties of managing manufacturing operations in a strange environment if there had not been so many other profitable roles for them in the dependent economy. They not only sold manufactured imports, they also operated the leading import/export houses. Even though the coffee was shipped to the United States, British firms controlled much of the trade. The British also controlled a large part of Brazilian shipping. Given the prominence of the British in the import/export complex it is not surprising that they might be accused by Brazilian industrialists of trying to "smother and demoralize national industry" (Graham, 1968:86). It is certainly not surprising that they did not form the spearhead of a drive toward industrialization.

The predilections of British capital and the perverse effects of income distribution on the internal market were forces locking Brazil into the pattern of classic dependence, but there were also forces disrupting the stability of the system. Brazil was more fortunate than many dependent nations. Its major export crop, coffee, was in the hands of local rather than foreign capital (cf. Cardoso and Faletto, 1973:39-51). Local ownership of the plantations not only provided some degree of local autonomy, but more important, the possibility of local capital accumulation. A substantial part of the profits from the coffee trade found its way into the development of infrastructure and later into the process of industrialization itself. Even Richard Graham, an admirer of the British, considers it "doubtful that the British—had they owned most of the plantations themselves—would have followed the same course" (Graham, 1968:79). Brazilian planters with capital to invest could not buy mills in Manchester. Some of them continued, of course, to keep their money in coffee plantations, but others became the allies of the commercial and industrial bourgeoisie that was gradually forming in the shadow of the coffee economy.

Surplus capital was not the coffee economy's only contribution to the genesis of the industrialized economy that would succeed it. To get the coffee to market railroads were necessary. The growth of railroads in the latter part of the nineteenth century was as spectacular as the growth of coffee exports. Between 1880 and 1890 twice as much railroad mileage was constructed as in the entire previous history of Brazil. Railroads continued to be built at an accelerated pace throughout the period of classic dependence. By 1915, Brazil, which could boast of only 750 kilometers of track in 1870, had over 25,000 kilometers (Graham, 1968:30).

The railroads were built because the export economy needed them, but fledgling manufacturers also made good use of them. Having delivered coffee to the port of Santos, the São Paulo Railway could return with coal, iron, and other imported raw materials, inputs that early manufacturers needed. Railroads also made possible a wider distribution of manufactured goods once they were produced. In all, they are the best example of how the coffee economy provided, as a consequence of its own natural development, important parts of the "economic and social overhead necessary to make domestic manufacturing possible" (Dean, 1969:8).

Given their central position in the export economy it is not surprising that the British played an important role in the creation of the new rail net. From the late nineteenth century until the First World War, roughly two-thirds of British capital invested in the private sector was involved in railroads (ECLA, 1965:10). Most of these proved very profitable. The São Paulo Railway, which ran between Santos and São Paulo, paid 11% a year to its owners from 1876 until the depression (Rippy, 1959:154-58). In addition to accounting for the bulk of British direct private investment, railroads were also an important part of British portfolio and public investment. A 1.5 million pounds-sterling loan from London was crucial to getting the federally owned Estrada de Ferro Dom Pedro Segundo into the Paraiba Valley. Almost 5 million pounds sterling were loaned to private railroad companies in Minas Gerais (Graham, 1968:52-54).

The British provided equipment, engineering expertise, and

technicians along with their capital. Their contribution to the construction of the rail net is undeniable. Yet, as in the case of manufacturing, their contribution was not particularly pioneering or entrepreneurial. In the 1850's when Brazil was looking for capital to push a railroad into the original coffee areas of the Paraiba Valley, British capital was too cautious to come in, even with a government guarantee that the interest on the loan would be paid. The federal government itself, finally, had to provide the capital. In the case of the São Paulo Railway, which eventually proved so profitable for its British owners, it was only the "continued enthusiasm and gullibility" of a Brazilian entrepreneur, the Visconde de Mauá, that kept the funds necessary to complete construction flowing and made the railroad possible (Graham, 1968:62).

The interplay of foreign capital and the local bourgeoisie within the structure of the dependent economy was important to its transformation in general just as it was important to railway construction. Despite a clear vested interest in the status quo, the British played a central role in creating the preconditions for a new structure in which they would eventually play only a marginal role. At the same time, local entrepreneurship was critical. If the Brazilian economy had been forced to rely on foreign capital to undertake risks and open up new areas of enterprise, the dynamics of change within the dependent economy would have been very different.

The combination of factors that allowed Brazil to move out of the coffee exporting economy in the direction of industrialization was very special. Earlier export booms in primary commodities like sugar, cacao, or even gold, did not produce the same effects. Other economies experiencing export-oriented growth in the same period, such as Cuba, found no connection between export-oriented growth and subsequent industrialization.

If classic dependence had managed in Brazil, as it did elsewhere, to preserve itself intact, the results for the Brazilian economy would have been disastrous. The effect of the great depression on an economy totally dependent on export agriculture would have been to drive it back toward subsistence agriculture, just as the population of the northeast was driven back to subsistence during the crisis in the sugar trade at the end of the seventeenth century (Furtado, 1965:69-70). But this is not, of course, what happened. The first tentative encroachments of industrialism appeared in the coffee economy before it had even matured. From the beginning, change, in the direction of industrialism, marched along, giving every appearance of being inexorable rather than founded on a delicate combination of social forces and historical circumstance.

Internalizing the Process of Production

"Industry on the periphery is unnatural" was the message of the Portuguese mercantilists and the British free trade advocates (Frank, 1967:161-63). A large part of the Brazilian political elite believed that they were right. Throughout the nineteenth century the dominant ideology held that industry was "entirely artificial in Brazil, surviving only at the expense of excessive monetary devaluation and tariff protection" (Villela and Suzigan, 1973:37). Despite this prevailing ideology, industry began to spring up even during the period when imports of manufactured goods from Britain were at their peak. Evidence of early movement in the direction of industrialization can be seen in the changing composition of British imports (Graham, 1968:330-32). In the 1850's, 70% of the goods imported from Britain were textiles. Other nondurable consumer goods accounted for a large share of the remainder. By the 1890's, imports of textiles had doubled, but they represented less than half of Brazil's imports from Britain. Imports of iron, hardware, tools, coal, and other intermediary or capital goods had all increased more than imports of consumer goods. In the case of machinery, the increase was twentyfold. Brazil was still dependent on British products, but the content of the imports increasingly foreshadowed local production.

In the decades since the turn of the century, the structure of Brazil's external trade had continued to provide one of the best indicators of internal changes. Exports have been diversified, with coffee accounting for a smaller share of the total and manufactured goods for an increasingly larger share. The shift in the structure of imports, with consumer goods accounting for a smaller and smaller proportion, has continued. There has been a diversification both of suppliers of imports and customers for exports. All of these changes together spelled the end of the old structure of dependence; yet they left Brazil tied to international capitalism at least as tightly as before.

Just after the turn of the century exports and imports probably amounted to about a quarter and a fifth of the gross domestic product respectively. Over the course of the next sixty years the proportion of each gradually declined, until by the beginning of the seventies imports and exports were a much smaller proportion of Brazil's total output than they were for countries like France, Britain, or Germany. The evolution was not, of course, either smooth or autonomous. As Table 2.1 indicates, external disturbances, particularly the depression and World War II, cut down the proportion of imports sharply and exports almost as dramatically. Conversely, the spree of buying that accompanied the end of World War II brought Brazil back to pre-World War I levels of imports and exports. In general, years of stagnation, like 1965, were years of low imports and exports, whereas both increased as the economy began to grow more rapidly in the early seventies. Nonetheless, despite the fluctuations, there was a clear long-term trend toward diminished overall involvement with the international market.

As overall reliance on imports and exports was diminishing, exports were becoming more diversified. Both the great depression and the two world wars stimulated diversification (see Table

TABLE 2.1 Exports and Imports as a Proportion of Gross Domestic Product, Selected Years 1907-1972

Year	Exports (%)	Imports (%)
1907*	24.9	18.7
1920	11.6	13.8
1930	10.9	8.8
1934	9.5	6.9
1939	12.7	11.3
1944	8.5	6.5
1947	14.0	15.2
1951	7.8	11.4
1954	8.6	8.9
1960	7.0	8.5
1965	5.7	4.1
1970	6.3	6.7
1972	6.6	7.7

* Estimated from Villela and Suzigan, 1973:68.
Sources: Villela and Suzigan, 1973:436, 440; Baer, 1965:226; ECLA, 1974:51.

2.2). The proportion of coffee dropped during World War I, then rose again in the twenties. Despite the government's coffee support program (Furtado, 1965:203-13), an even larger drop in coffee's share accompanied the great depression and World War II. A rise in the proportion of coffee followed World War II, but the long-term downward trend continued. Coffee declined from almost three-quarters of exports during the heyday of "export-oriented growth" in the twenties to less than a quarter of exports by the early seventies. Most other exports continued to be primary products, such as manganese, hematite, meat, and sugar. There was, however, an impressive growth in the export of manufactures. By the early seventies manufactured goods represented a greater proportion of exports than coffee. The structure of Brazil's exports is still not that of a typical center country, but the single crop model of classic dependence has clearly been left behind.

The structure of imports changed more quickly than the structure of exports. By the 1920's, when coffee was still king among

TABLE 2.2   Distribution of Brazil's Exports

Year	Coffee (%)	Other Primary (%)	Other (%) Manufactures (%)
1898-1910	53	47*	
1914-1918	47	53	
1924-1929	73	27	
1934-1939	48	52	
1940-1945	33	68	
1946-1948	38	56	6
1960-1962	53	44	2
1965-1969	42	51	7
1970	36	53	11
1971	24	62	15
1972	25	46	29

* Until the post-World War II period manufactured exports are a tiny proportion of total exports and have not been categorized separately.
Sources: Villela and Suzigan, 1973:70; Bergsman, 1970:16; Baer, 1973:5; IBGE, Sinópse Estatística, 1973:245.

exports, nondurable consumer goods had dropped to about 10% of the imports. The bulk of imports were divided among capital goods and raw materials and intermediary products. There had already grown up within the export-oriented economy a considerable amount of "import-substituting industrialization." By the early sixties, after import substitution had become official policy, imports of durable as well as nondurable consumer goods had been cut down (see Table 2.3).

Just as the changes in the import structure began earlier than the changes in exports, they also began to encounter resistance earlier. In the late sixties and early seventies, exports were still moving dramatically in the direction of increasing the proportion of manufactured goods. It was hard to see how imports could change further. A large part of the imports of raw materials and intermediary products was dictated by demand for locally unavailable resources, like coal and petroleum. Capital goods, the other major segment of imports, seemed equally difficult to eliminate. It has been obvious since the early sixties that the next

TABLE 2.3   Distribution of Brazil's Imports

	1901-1907 (%)	1919-1923 (%)	1929 (%)	1937-1938 (%)	1948 (%)	1955 (%)	1961 (%)
Consumer goods	36.9	19.9	18.7	13.3	17.3	9.3	7.4
(durable)			(7.5)	(6.2)	(9.8)	(1.7)	(1.2)
(nondurable)			(11.2)	(7.1)	(7.5)	(7.6)	(6.2)
Capital goods	7.1	11.5	26.7	23.7	39.3	27.2	31.6
Raw material and intermediary goods*	55.1	68.6	54.6	63.0	43.4	63.5	61.0

* Includes fuels and lubricants.
Sources: Villela and Suzigan, 1973:72; ECLA, 1965a:16, 22.

major project for import substitution would have to be in the capital goods sector. Yet, while local manufacture of capital goods has increased, the share of capital goods in total imports has not declined. In 1971 capital goods made up about 38% of total imports (Baer, 1973:5), the same as their share in 1948.

Changes in the commodities of commerce were accompanied by important changes in Brazil's trading partners. At first the decline of Britain and the rise of the United States increased the concentration of Brazil's trade. With the increasing importance of U.S. imports, Brazil's most important customer also became her most important supplier. Brazil thus became dependent not just on the international market in general, but on a particular center country, the United States. Despite the clear-cut ascendance of the United States relative to Britain, however, competition among the center countries persisted. In the period before the Second World War the Germans presented a clear threat to U.S. dominance of Brazil's trade. Germany was the second largest market for coffee and potentially the best customer for Brazil's cotton exports (Wirth, 1970:20). Germany also became, just before World War II, as important as the United States and much more important than Britain as a supplier of Brazil's imports (see Table 2.4). If the violent conflict of World War II had not been substituted for commercial competition, the hegemony of the United States would have been severely threatened.

TABLE 2.4   Origins and Destinations of Brazil's Foreign Trade* (principal countries)

	1938		1948		1958		1965		1971	
	Exports (%)	Imports (%)	Exports (%)	Imports (%)	Exports (%)	Imports (%)	Exports (%)	Imports (%)	Exports (%)	Imports (%)
U.S.A.	34	25	43	52	44	36	33	30	26	29
Europe	52	53	33	26	36	32	45	30	38	41
(Britain)	(9)	(10)	(9)	(10)	(4)	(3)	(4)	(3)	(4)	(6)
(Germany)	(19)	(25)	(1)	(0)	(6)	(10)	(9)	(9)	(9)	(13)
Latin America	6	16	12	16	13	24	12	26	13	10
Japan	0	0	0	0	2	2	2	3	5	7
Other	7	5	12	6	4	5	8	11	18	13
Total	99	99	100	100	99	99	100	100	100	100
($US billions)	(0.289)	(0.295)	(1.158)	(1.120)	(1.243)	(1.353)	(1.595)	(1.096)	(2.903)	(3.701)

* Imports refers to "general imports c.i.f." for 1933, 1948, and 1958 and "special imports c.i.f." for 1965; exports refers to "national exports f.o.b."

Sources: United Nations, Yearbook of International Trade Statistics 1953, 1958, 1965, IBGE, Anuário Estatístico, 1972:279-81, 296-98.

North American dominance appeared most secure immediately after World War II, when the United States was supplying 50% of Brazil's imports and buying over 40% of its exports. By the beginning of the seventies, however, this position had been severely eroded. Competition among the center countries was by then clearly reflected in the division of imports and exports, with Europe as a whole much more important than the United States both as a customer and a supplier. Germany and Japan were accounting for an increasing share of trade. New markets were being opened up for Brazil's exports, and by 1971 the Communist countries of Europe were in combination a more important customer than Britain, and Africa was a more important customer than Portugal (IBGE, 1972:279-81). While the United States remained Brazil's most important single customer and supplier despite all, competition among the center countries was an established pattern by the early seventies; hegemony by a single center country was clearly a thing of the past.

Trade statistics provide a convenient window on the changing nature of dependence, but concentrating on them may leave the impression that the dynamic of change was all in the external sector, the international market, and relations among center powers. This was not the case. Changes in the nature of trade would have been impossible without a fundamental reorientation of the internal economy. Internal and external changes reinforced each other.

Dividing the value of Brazil's output of goods between agriculture and industry, Villela and Suzigan (1973:241) estimate that in 1907 agriculture accounted for four-fifths and industry only one-fifth. The proportion remained unchanged during the first two decades of the century, but then the balance began to shift in favor of industry until, by 1939, the proportion was closer to two-fifths industry and three-fifths agriculture. Throughout the period, of course, a large part of the total domestic product remained involved in commerce, trade, government operations, and various service producing sectors. The share of tertiary has remained relatively constant up to the present, but the balance between industry and agriculture has continued to shift until, by 1973, the share of industry in the gross domestic product was twice that of agriculture (see Table 2.5).

TABLE 2.5   Changes in Sectoral Composition of GDP (percent distribution at current prices)

Year	Agriculture (%)	Industry (%)	Service* (%)
1939	25.8	19.4	54.8
1949	26.0	26.2	47.8
1959	20.2	30.1	49.7
1966	19.1	27.1	53.8
1973	15.3	33.3	51.5

* Service includes government, transport and communication, financial intermediaries and rent, as well as commerce.
Source: IBGE, 1972:516; 1976:466.

The growing importance of industry was accompanied by equally important changes within the industrial structure itself. In 1920, when the first real industrial census was taken, food and textiles, the first areas of import substitution, accounted in combination for almost 70% of the total value added in manufacturing. By 1968, two industries that were too miniscule to be counted as late as 1940, transportation equipment and electrical equipment, accounted between them for 15% of the value added in manufacturing. Combined with metal fabrication, chemicals, and machinery (sectors that also increased dramatically in importance), these new industries came to represent the central core of the industrial structure just as textiles and food had in the earlier era (see Table 2.6).

The rise of new industries was intimately associated with diminished dependence on foreign manufactured goods. In 1949 Brazilian imports of transportation equipment were more than

TABLE 2.6   Changes in the Distribution of Industrial Output,
1920-1968 (% of total value added in manufacturing)

	1920 (%)	1940 (%)	1950 (%)	1960 (%)	1968 (%)
Metal Fabrication	4.3	7.7	9.9	11.9	11.4
Machinery	2.0	5.8	2.2	3.5	6.0
Electrical Equipment	—	—	1.7	3.9	6.3
Transportation Equipment	—	—	2.3	7.5	8.6
Chemicals and Pharmaceuticals	6.0	10.4	9.4	13.4	17.6
Total "Modern" Industries*	12.3	23.9	25.5	40.2	49.9
Food, Beverages, and Tobacco	32.0	29.6	25.5	21.2	17.0
Textiles, Footwear, and Apparel	37.2	27.6	24.4	15.6	12.9
Timber and Furniture	7.8	5.1	5.6	5.4	4.2
Leather Products	2.4	1.7	1.3	1.1	0.6
Total "Traditional" Industries*	79.4	64.0	56.8	43.3	34.7
Paper and Paper Products	1.5	1.4	2.1	3.0	2.7
Rubber Products	0.2	0.7	2.1	2.3	2.0
Nonmetallic Minerals	4.7	5.3	7.4	6.6	5.8
Printing and Publishing	—	3.6	4.2	3.0	3.0
Miscellaneous	1.9	1.1	1.9	1.6	1.7
Total Other Industry	8.3	12.1	17.7	16.5	15.2

* "Modern" here means simply those industries which have increased their share
of the market, "traditional" means those industries which have shrunk. The industries defined as "modern" also happen, however, to be characterized by
higher amounts of capital per worker and higher productivity (Singer, 1971:83).
Sources: Baer, 1965:269; Newfarmer, 1975:33.

four times greater than local production on a value added basis,
but by 1962 imports were only 12% of local production (Bergsman, 1970:94). In electrical machinery, imports went from over
five times local production in 1949 to less than a quarter in 1962;
in chemicals, from almost nine times local production to about a
third. Since these three categories of imports accounted for almost half of Brazil's manufactured imports in 1949 (Tavares,
1973:92), the necessity of their internal development to the strategy of import substitution is obvious.

    As the nature of industrial output changed, the nature of pro-
duction changed also. Up to the Second World War, while tex-

tiles and food were still dominant, the growth of the industrial plant seems to have been mostly in quantitative expansion. In the most advanced industrial area, São Paulo, between 1920 and 1940 the number of industrial establishments increased at about the same rate as the labor force, which is to say that the average size of each establishment remained about the same (Dean, 1969:117). In the next two decades, however, the average size of establishment quadrupled (*Survey*, 1965:99). During the same period manufacturing output per worker employed increased fourfold in the economy as a whole (Baer, 1965:263; Singer, 1971:64, 66). Industry had not only taken over the predominant position previously held by agriculture, it had also been transformed.

By the early seventies, Brazil's industrial establishment was already of dimensions that precluded considering it as a peripheral agrarian nation. The point is made most simply by comparing Brazilian outputs of a few industrial commodities with the outputs of her old supplier of manufactures, Britain (see Table 2.7). In the early sixties, Brazilian outputs were still only a small proportion of British. By the early seventies, they were a substantial proportion. More important, projecting the relative growth rates over the next two decades produces Brazilian outputs equal to or greater than British outputs in all six commodities.

Since the period from 1963 to 1972 included the stagnation of the mid-sixties as well as the "miracle" of the late sixties and beginning of the seventies, the prediction that Brazil will surpass Britain in the production of basic products such as crude steel and cement by 1990 is probably not unreasonable. Looking only at quantitative changes in the production of a few basic products misses, of course, the differentiation and introduction of newer, more sophisticated kinds of products that is the essence of development in an industrial structure. The figures do indicate, however, that the correspondence between development and industrialization has become more complex. When steel factories on

TABLE 2.7   Brazilian and British Outputs of Some Industrial
Commodities (Brazilian output as a percentage of British)

	Year			
	1963	1972	1981*	1990*
Commodity	(%)	(%)	(%)	(%)
Pig Iron	14	37	98	258
Crude Steel Ingot	12	26	56	122
Cement	37	63	107	183
Passenger Cars	6	22	81	246
Tires	19	34	61	109
TV Receivers	19	33	57	100

* Based on a simple linear extrapolation of trends from 1963 to 1972.
Source: United Nations, Growth of World Industry, 1974.

the periphery rival the output of those in the center, then the old
definitions of center and periphery need revision.

Brazilian industrialization has been impressive. It is nonetheless clear that the end of classic dependence has not meant escape from ties with center countries, or even the loosening of
these ties. As industrial production moved from the center to the
periphery, the relations of production that had characterized the
old system were not overthrown; they were extended. Instead of
being connected to the center primarily in terms of the exchange
of commodities, the periphery became part of an integrated system of industrial production whose ownership continued to remain in substantial measure in the center. The obverse side of
industrialization on the periphery was the insertion of foreign-
owned enterprise squarely in the middle of the industrial order
that was created. Brazil had reached Cardoso and Faletto's stage
of the "internationalization of the domestic market." Or, to put it
another way, imperialism was internalized.

The Changing Face of Foreign Capital

The intimate association between the internalization of industrial production and the growth of foreign investment is evident

even in aggregate statistics. The four industries in which most foreign investment was concentrated in 1973 accounted for 62% of Brazil's imports of manufactured goods in 1949. At the other end of the scale, the five industries which had the smallest amounts of foreign investment in 1973 accounted for less than 1% of manufactured imports in 1949 (see Table 2.8). Much of this investment was made in the context of protective legislation that penalized importers whenever there was a locally produced "similar" available. In all, it is hard to disagree with Alvaro Pigna-

TABLE 2.8 Import Substitution and Direct Investment

	% of Manufactured Imports 1949	% of Foreign Direct Investment 1972 in Manufacturing
High Investment		
Chemicals and pharmaceuticals	22	29
Transportation equipment	19	17
Electrical equipment	7	11
Metallurgy	14	9
Total	62	66
Low Investment		
Furniture	0	0
Leather	0.3	0
Apparel and Footwear	0	0.3
Printing and Graphics	0.4	0.2
Wood Products	0.2	0.2
Total	0.9	0.7

Sources: Tavares, 1970:92; Pignaton, 1973:95.

ton's conclusion (1973:14) that "these companies made their investment decisions with the objective of maintaining a market that offered good prospects and would have become inaccessible."

Because of the association between industrialization and the dramatic growth of foreign direct investment, it is tempting to argue that industrialization was *caused* by foreign direct investment. Such an argument is not only implausible on theoretical grounds; it is also hard to support on the basis of aggregate statistics. Foreign investors moved in to protect markets that they might otherwise have lost to local capital or to more adventurous foreigners. There is little evidence to support the view that the foreign manufacturer was at the forefront of industrialization. The absence of any extensive British involvement in manufacturing during the heyday of classic dependence has already been noted. A look at United States investment in Latin America shows no great interest in manufacturing at the time industrialization was first getting underway. As late as 1919, three-fourths of all United States investments in Latin America was in the primary sector and less than 4% in manufacturing (ECLA, 1965:16).

Brazil did, however, have an advantage as far as U.S. investment was concerned. The United States was never heavily involved in the primary sector in Brazil. In 1929 when three-fifths of American investment in all of Latin America was in extractive industry, only an eighth of the American capital invested in Brazil was in these industries. United States investors were not even heavily tied to the old export complex through investments in railroads. The small amount of U.S. direct investment in Brazil was mainly in public utilities. As the United States gained preeminence, Brazil had the good fortune of not being under the domination of a center country whose investors had a heavy stake in the maintenance of "export-oriented growth." The distribution of U.S. investment gave Brazil a strong advantage over countries like Cuba where North American investments were directly linked to the primary production-export syndrome of classic dependence.

In contrast to the rest of Latin America, manufacturing was an important part of U.S. investment in Brazil as early as 1950. By this time, the pattern of investments in Brazil was already beginning to be more similar to the European pattern than to other countries of Latin America. The trend toward a concentration of U.S. investment in the manufacturing sector has continued until, in 1973, almost 70% of all U.S. direct investment was in manufacturing (see Table 2.9). Never having been involved in extractive investments, the United States apparently found it easy to go along with industrialization.

The fact that the hegemonic center power during the period of industrialization had not been the mainstay of the classic system of dependence probably made it easier for Brazil to industrialize. To place undue emphasis on this element, however, would be to underestimate the flexibility of foreign investors. European investors also found it profitable to participate in the process of industrialization; so much so, in fact, that European investments are currently at least as heavily concentrated in the manufacturing sector as are North American investments (Pignaton, 1973:95).

Along with the shift from British to North American predominance and from nonmanufacturing to industrial activities, the pattern of investment changed along a third dimension that was equally important. British and other European investment during the "golden age of foreign capital" before the First World War tended on the whole to be "portfolio" investment. Stocks or bonds for Brazilian companies were sold on the London Exchange, but foreign ownership of these assets did not necessarily imply the ability to control what went on in the Brazilian company, as many British bondholders found out to their chagrin (see

TABLE 2.9 Sectoral Shifts in United States Direct Investment, 1929-1973

	1929 Europe (%)	1929 Latin America (%)	1929 Brazil (%)	1950 Europe (%)	1950 Latin America (%)	1950 Brazil (%)	1973 Europe (%)	1973 Latin America (%)	1973 Brazil (%)
Extractive and Primary (mining, petroleum, and agriculture)	17	61	12	26	53	17	23	35	12
Manufacturing	47	7	24	54	18	44	56	35	69
Commerce, Service, and Other (includes trade, public utilities and other)	36	32	64	20	29	39	21	30	19
Total	100	100	100	100	100	100	100	100	100
($US millions)	(1,353)	(3,519)	(194)	(1,733)	(4,445)	(644)	(37,218)	(18,452)	(3,199)

Sources: Pizer and Cutler, 1957:161, 1960:93, 91; Survey of Current Business, vol. 54, no. 8 (August 1974):18-19.

Rippy, 1959). As long as investment was primarily portfolio, dependence on foreign capital implied only a diffuse control of Brazilian enterprise by foreigners.

United States investment, unlike the capital flows associated with classic dependence, involved the creation of subsidiaries under the specific organizational control of a parent company. Direct investment, that is, investment that implied organizational control over the Brazilian enterprise, was the chief form of North American investment from the very beginning. Sometimes the supply of American capital seems to have exceeded the ability of organizations to expand, as in the twenties, and the proportion of portfolio investment rose. On the other hand, portfolio investment, more sensitive to hard times (see Hirschman, 1970:233), declined relative to direct investment during the depression and World War II. Thus the proportion of direct investment rose to over 90% just after World War II. But in general direct investment maintained itself at about 80% of total American investment (see Table 2.10).

TABLE 2.10   U.S. Direct Investment as a Proportion of Total U.S. Long-term Investment in Latin America

Year	Total U.S. Investment (in millions of current $US)	Direct Investment	Direct Investment as a Proportion of Total Investment
1897	304	304	100%
1908	1,063	749	70%
1914	1,641	1,276	78%
1919	2,396	1,978	83%
1929	5,370	3,646	68%
1946	3,603	3,045	85%
1950	5,143	4,735	92%
1956	8,203	7,408	90%
1960	9,850	8,365	85%
1966	12,294	9,826	80%
1973	23,029	18,452	80%

Sources: ECLA, 1965:14; Pizer and Cutler, 1957:111; Survey of Current Business, 1961, 1967, and 1974.

Direct investment implies an increase in the control by center-based corporations over what goes on in enterprises on the periphery. Bondholders or shareholders have influence, and the international commodity market shapes the domestic economy as well as the export sector, but the direct investor is *inside* the peripheral economy. The direct investor has power over where equipment and inputs are bought, what products are produced, how the process of production is organized, where and to whom goods are to be sold, and so on. This power is exercised through the authority channels of hierarchical bureaucratic organizations, and is therefore much more thoroughgoing than earlier forms of influence.

The degree of foreign involvement implied by the growth of direct investment becomes even more impressive when we examine the extent to which multinationals have penetrated the domestic market in Brazil. Estimates based on the sales of U.S. affiliates in Brazil put the multinationals' share of total sales in manufacturing at between 35% and 50%. The magnitude of these percentages is, in a way, ironic. Villela and Suzigan's estimate (1973:68) of the percentage of manufactured goods supplied by foreign firms via importation in 1907, during the period of classic dependence, is of about the same magnitude.

If these estimates can be relied upon, then the transformation of dependence is really best characterized as the internalization of imperialism. Read in conjunction with the changed nature of Brazil's exports, they imply an increased foreign presence since 1907. In 1907, at least the coffee plantations were almost entirely Brazilian owned. In 1969, Fajnzylber estimates (1971:209), foreign firms accounted for over 40% of exported manufactured goods. And so, again ironically, as Brazil succeeds in increasing the proportion of manufactured goods among its exports it will be moving further away from one sort of dependence only to become even more deeply embedded in a different sort of imperialist structure.

The internalization of international capital makes imperialism a central fact of the domestic market as well as the international one, and gives foreign owners increased power to shape what goes on within the peripheral economy. Yet at the same time, the internalization of foreign capital gives the local bourgeoisie, and more particularly the local state, power that it did not have before. The peripheral nation is dependent on the multinational in new ways, but the multinational is also dependent on the domestic market of the peripheral nation to a much greater degree.

If the Ford Motor Company were exporting 100,000 cars a year to Brazil, and it were, for one reason or another, to lose the Brazilian market, it would have the unpleasant job of finding somewhere else to sell its cars. If, on the other hand, Ford has manufacturing facilities in Brazil capable of producing 100,000 cars, it can be affected even more seriously by what happens in Brazil. An untoward turn of local events can render its capital incapable of producing a profit, which is to say useless. This can happen because the market collapses or is taken over by someone else. It can also happen because the cost of inputs—raw materials, subcontracted parts, or labor—gets too high in relation to the price of cars. In theory, it could happen because the state decided to take advantage of its monopoly on force and simply not allow Ford to produce cars. Losing a market is a threat but losing capital is a more severe threat.

In Brazil, the new dialectics of power produced by the transformation of dependence are further complicated by shifts in the national origins of international capital. During the first phase of the internalization of manufacturing, Brazil became increasingly dependent on a single country, the United States. From the late fifties onwards, however, it became clear that North American firms were no longer competing so much with a declining British empire as with a rising combination of Japanese, German, and other European firms.

The rough outlines of the changes over the past fifty years seem relatively clear (see Table 2.11). Before World War II the British held about half of all direct investment. The rest was split

TABLE 2.11   Distribution of Foreign Investment by Country of Origin

	1914 (ECLA) (%)	1930 (Whyte) (%)	1950 (Baklanoff) (%)	1959 (Baklanoff -Banas) (%)	1972 (Pignaton) (%)
North American	4	25	71	56	46
(U.S.)	(4)	(21)	(48)	(38)	(37)
(Canadian)	—	(4)	(23)	(18)	(9)
European	96	72	25	36	42
(British)	(51)	(53)	(17)	(7)	(8)
(French)	(33)	(8)	(3)	(5)	(5)
(German)	*	*	—	(9)	(11)
(Other)	(12)**	(11)	(5)	(15)	(18)
Other	—	3	4	8	12
(Japanese)	—	(1)	—	(2)	(6)
Total	100	100	100	100	100

* Included in Other European.
** Other may include some non-European investment.
Sources: ECLA, 1965:17; Whyte, 1945:154; Baklanoff, 1966:109; Pignaton, 1973:98.

between the United States and continental Europe with the share of the United States growing steadily. In the post-World War II period the United States started out with a very dominant position. If Canadian investments are assumed to be split between the United States and Britain in terms of ultimate ownership, then the United States seems to have controlled about three-fifths of all direct investment in Brazil immediately after World War II. Since then the North American (U.S./ Canadian) share has declined. The British share has eroded further, and the European share is growing along with Japan's.

Because the European share is split among a number of different countries, the overall result of the evolution is to make dependence less a question of a relationship with a particular country and more a question of a relationship with the multinationals as a collectivity. The tendency toward dispersion of the origins of direct investment parallels the tendency toward the dispersion of imports and exports, and, since exports and imports are increasingly transactions between different parts of multinational firms, the two tendencies probably reinforce each other.

The result of dispersion is to give the Brazilian state increased maneuvering room. There is no longer a single hegemonic power standing behind foreign capital. Any U.S. efforts to protect foreign capital through political or military action would be protecting capital that was about 60% non-U.S. No single European power has a sufficiently strong interest to take over the U.S. role. Furthermore, any single power entering into direct conflict with the Brazilian state would risk prejudicing its own capital relative to that of the other center countries. In short, while the multinationals can obviously count on political support from their home countries, support is likely to be limited.

The weakening of relations between the multinationals and their home states flows both from their increasing involvement in the internal organization of the Brazilian economy and from increasing competition among investors of different foreign origins. Once the multinationals no longer feel securely sheltered by the umbrella of political control exerted from their home states, local allies become a necessity. The internalization of their own productive operations within the Brazilian economy makes local allies even more essential. The creation of alliances, however, also requires the existence of local elites who have an interest in capitalist accumulation as well as sufficient political and economic power to make them interesting as allies.

The Changing Role of the State

The economic efforts of the state during the period of classic dependency (that is, during the old republic) have been characterized as "incidental" (Rezende et al., 1976:83). And well they

might have been. The politics of the central government reflected the general economic strength of agrarian landholders
who, of course, had little interest in breaking free of the export-
oriented model of expansion. In addition, regional cleavages
made the agrarian oligarchy suspicious of granting power to the
federal government at all. Despite these limitations, however,
the "incidental" involvement of the state was not inconsequential.

As early as the 1850's the state found itself compelled to
counter the reluctance of international capital to invest in the development of Brazil. The rate of return on British money invested in railroads, for example, was guaranteed by the government, first at 5% and then at 7%. Government expenses from
these guarantees reached 6% of the value of imports by the
1880's (Villela and Suzigan, 1973:396). Later the government
suspended its guarantees and acquired direct ownership of the
railroads, and by 1929, two-thirds of them were state-owned.
The government also subsidized various navigation companies at
the end of the nineteenth century but these were not consolidated into a state-owned company until after 1930 (Rezende et
al., 1976:82).

In other areas of infrastructure the main activity of the state
was granting "concessions" to local and foreign capital to operate
public utilities. Concession hunters like Percival Farquhar (see
Singer, 1975:377-89) were alert to the lucrative possibilities represented by state-granted monopolies over electricity or trolley
service to Brazil's expanding urban areas. Since 64% of all U.S.
investment was still in commerce and services, including public
utilities, at the end of the old republic (see Table 2.9), Paulo
Singer (1975:376) may well be correct in arguing that these concessions "constituted the most important form of penetration of
capital from industrialized countries" as far as the domestic side
of the Brazilian economy was concerned.

In addition to infrastructure, the oligarchic state was involved in finance. The Bank of Brazil and the Caixa Economica both date back to the days of imperial Brazil. But neither in finance nor in transportation did the state give much evidence of trying actively to shape the process of capital accumulation. A more passive kind of support of foreign investors and the export complex in general seemed to be the aim. Concessions and interest guarantees were services to foreign capital. The provision of railroad transportation was more a service to the general export complex.

The emergence of a self-consciously interventionist and entrepreneurial approach required a restructuring of the political basis of the state. In 1930, along with the international economic crisis, came an internal political upheaval that opened the way to a transformation of the state's role. The revolution of 1930 and the ascendance of Getulio Vargas were the foundations of a central government capable of playing a direct role in capitalist accumulation.

The state in the old republic was dominated in theory by the coffee planters, yet it was characterized by what Boris Fausto (1970) has called "a split between the dominant class and its political representatives." President Washington Luis refused to support the price of coffee after the crash of 1929 even though he was a planter and a Paulista (Martins, 1976:102). The government of the state of São Paulo was willing to support coffee prices, but the federal government was not prepared to take an active interventionist stance even in behalf of the economically hegemonic group it supposedly represented.

If its inability to deal effectively with the economic problems that beset the export complex helped undermine the old political apparatus, it was failure to abide by the rules of the oligarchic game that provided the immediate cause for the demise of the regime. When it looked as though control over the federal executive was not going to be rotated from São Paulo to Minas or Rio Grande do Sul, a takeover seemed legitimate even to members of the oligarchy. Had Washington Luis been willing to support the price of coffee, the Paulistas might have felt more like opposing Vargas and the "revolutionaries" (see Rowland, 1974:15); but as it was, their opposition did not gel until two years after Vargas's takeover. Thus the oligarchic state fell, mostly of its own weight.

What came to power was a peculiar coalition of landholders and others, like the "tenentes," who were more technocratic in their orientation (see Martins, 1976:96-101). Two things seem clear about the political nature of the Vargas regime. First, it was by no stretch of the imagination controlled by the industrial bourgeoisie, and second, it represented a crucial step on the path toward greater penetration and control of society by the central state apparatus.

On coming to power, Vargas had a vision of Brazil's economic future exactly as one would have expected from the large land-owner. Industrialization was seen as creating disequilibrium and social disorder (Rowland, 1974:21). "Artificial industries" (industries that did not use local raw materials) were castigated by Vargas as "raising the cost of living in order to benefit privileged industrialists" (Dean, 1969). Vargas saw the fact that Brazil was "an excellent market for imports" as an advantage, not a disadvantage, since it would, he thought, improve the treatment afforded Brazilian agricultural products in the customs schedules of center countries (Rowland, 1974:21).

Despite the desire of Vargas and many of his supporters to preserve Brazil's traditional place in the international division of labor, his rule was pivotal in creating a state apparatus able to participate in the process of accumulation required by dependent development. Corporatism was primarily an ideology of social control, designed to integrate Brazilian society from the top down (see Schmitter, 1971), but it also had implications for the state's role in the process of accumulation. From Vargas's initial ascent to power, the state approached the economy with an attitude of "conscious interventionism" (Rezende et al., 1976:85).

The price supports for coffee that Washington Luis would not provide were brought in by Vargas (Martins, 1976:111). A National Coffee Council was set up in 1931 to regulate the coffee economy. At the same time, the Institute for Cacao in Bahia was established, and later the Institute of Sugar and Alcohol was added. Along with a willingness to intervene in the operation of the economy there was a nationalist side to the economic initiatives of the Vargas regime that put the state in the position of acting as a counterbalance to the power of foreign capital. In 1931, Vargas gave the state-owned navigation companies a special break on port fees, placing them in an advantageous position vis-à-vis foreign shipping companies (Bandeira, 1973:230-31). The 1934 mining code restricted foreign ownership of mineral assets (Wirth, 1970:83). Later, after the imposition of the Estado Novo in 1937, the government claimed the right to regulate the foreign-dominated petroleum industry and demanded that refineries be owned only by Brazilian nationals (Martins, 1976:288).

Intervention by means of regulation was a characteristic of the Vargas regime from the beginning and continued into the Estado Novo. But, state entrepreneurship began with the Estado Novo itself. The state-owned shipping lines were consolidated into Lloyd Brasileiro; VASP, the state-controlled airline of the state of São Paulo, was created; the government took over the administration of a number of ports; and the Bank of Brazil took on the powers of a central bank (see Rezende et al., 1976:84). Perhaps most important, however, was the evolution of the state's role in the steel and petroleum industries.

In the later thirties, Percival Farquhar, who had been so successful as a "concession hunter" under the old regime, found that Brazil was making new demands on foreign capital. Vargas had declared when he first came to power that national security demanded that the country not "remain at the mercy of foreigners" in its steel industry (Martins, 1976:188). There was soon pressure on Farquhar to combine the export operations of his Itabira Iron Company with a local steel mill, but his efforts to comply were unsuccessful. He was unable to secure the cooperation of any major North American or European steel company. In the view of historian John Wirth (1970:78), the major companies "seemed to have acted in unison to discourage the founding of new plants in steel-importing countries that, in their opinion, did not enjoy 'natural' conditions for a steel industry."

Nationalist pressure finally resulted in the cancellation of the Itabira Iron Company's concession in 1939, and was also responsible for the government's refusal of Dupont's steel project in 1937 (Baer, 1969:97). An attempt to put foreign and local capital together behind an undertaking that would have been controlled by U.S. Steel was impeded by nationalist opposition, especially from within the army. Vargas was willing to accommodate to the demands of the American conglomerate despite the opposition, but his concessions came too late. In January 1940, the finance committee of U.S. Steel decided to abandon the Brazilian project (Wirth, 1970:112; Baer, 1969:101).

Brazil remained, at the beginning of the Second World War, dependent on a foreign company, Belgo Mineira, for the majority of its steel production and dependent on imports for a major part of its consumption. Belgo Mineira was "unable or unwilling" to expand its capacity (Baer, 1969:95). Yet without rapid growth, steel would either become a bottleneck to development or a major problem in the balance of payments. The situation was unsatisfactory even for those who were simply interested in pushing industrialization, with or without foreign capital. Direct involvement by the state was one answer, and the conflict between the United States and Germany made it possible to get foreign support for this solution.

Vargas managed to convince the American government that if they did not participate, the Germans would. A few months before Pearl Harbor, the Import-Export Bank promised to provide the Brazilians with 20 million dollars worth of credits to finance the purchase of equipment for a steel plant. In April 1941 the

Companhia Siderúrgica Nacional (CSN) was officially founded. A year later the state complemented its initiative in the steel industry by creating the Companhia do Vale do Rio Doce to mine iron ore.

Two things about the CSN should be emphasized. First, pressure from the military dating back to the formation of the National Steel Commission by war minister Leite de Castro in 1931 was the most important single factor leading to the creation of the CSN (Baer, 1969:94). Second, while the CSN was clearly a state enterprise, private Brazilian capital was never excluded. The first president of the CSN, Guilherme Guinle, made every attempt to get private Brazilian capital involved in the operation (Baer, 1969:103). From the beginning, state technocrats attempted to draw the national bourgeoisie into state-sponsored industrial projects.

The Second World War also stimulated the founding of the Fábrica Nacional de Motores (FNM) and the Companhia Nacional de Alcalis. In both cases, the companies were formed in order to make sure that products considered essential to continued industrial operation would not be cut off. As in the case of steel, "since no foreign or domestic private enterprise was in a position to establish such an undertaking, a government firm was found to be the only solution" (Baer et al., 1973:25). By the end of the war a "Conference of the Productive Classes" recommended that certain key industries should be more directly subject to state action, especially where "private initiative showed itself to be lacking or incapable" (Cohn, 1968:75). Yet there was still considerable ambivalence over the role of the state, as the postwar debate over petroleum would show.

Between 1930 and 1945, when Vargas was turned out, the role of the state had changed dramatically. The construction of a centralized state bureaucracy had moved significantly forward, and direct intervention of the state in economic affairs had accompanied it. Nowhere along the way is there evidence that the expansion of the state role was undertaken as part of a "developmental project" of the local industrial bourgeoisie. They appear to have remained more as bystanders, pleased by the regime's ability to maintain control over the working class, sympathetic to the nationalist elements in the program, yet ideologically opposed to "statism."

In contrast to the industrial bourgeoisie, the army was more concerned with "national security" than with statism. In the thirties it had been the army, specifically General Horta Barbosa, that had led the search for a solution to the problems created by Brazil's lack of petroleum. The National Petroleum Council, founded in 1938, was the precursor of Petrobrás. As in the case of steel, the army felt that local availability of petroleum was essential to national security. General Horta Barbosa was impressed with Argentina's state-owned oil company (YPF) and did not entirely trust even Brazilian industrialists. A statist solution was his preference (Wirth, 1970:139, 145), an arrangement that did not fit very well with the ideological climate in the immediate postwar period.

In 1945 Vargas was overthrown by the military, who were to bring a "return to democracy." Statism was associated with the Estado Novo and fascism in general. Vargas's successors were pro-American and in favor of economic liberalism. One of the first steps of the National Petroleum Council after Vargas's departure was to open bids to private Brazilian companies for the construction of refineries. The results were not encouraging. They ended up with bids for two 10,000 barrels-a-day refineries. At this time Brazil's oil consumption was already 50,000 barrels a day and growing at a rate that would bring it to almost 100,000 barrels by 1950 (Cohn, 1968:102, 130). One of the problems of local companies was the difficulty getting foreign firms to sign long-term contracts assuring them of supplies of crude oil. Private nationalist development of the oil industry would have required strong initiatives from local capital coupled with willingness on the part of major international oil firms to play a supportive, but not dominant, role. Neither was forthcoming, and the debate between those who wanted to let foreign firms in and those who wanted the state to take over began in earnest.

The chief argument for allowing foreign (North American) participation in petroleum development was simply that without it Brazil did not have the ability to take advantage of its petroleum reserves. The Security Police even went so far as to say that the communists were opposing cooperation with foreign firms because with Brazil able to take advantage of its petroleum reserves, the United States might be strengthened in its fight against the Soviet Union (Cohn, 1968:120). More moderate arguments were provided by those like Odilon Braga who tried to convince the nationalists that the Brazilian government with the support of Washington would be able to control the international firms involved and make sure that "abuses of an imperialist character" did not occur (Cohn, 1968:116).

The arguments of those who felt that private development of the petroleum industry could be achieved without risking foreign domination did not carry the day. The "O Petroleo e Nosso" (The Oil is Ours) campaign managed to put together a broad nationalist coalition which was successful in imposing nationalist restrictions on petroleum development. In the end nationalist solutions turned out to mean statist solutions. Even Oswaldo Aranha, an old friend of the United States, decided by 1949 that despite all his liberal economic training, he could see only one viable direction. "There is only one conclusion," he said. "To the State and only to the State belongs the role of exploiting this wealth" (Cohn, 1968:170).

The election of Vargas in 1950 was a repudiation of the liberal internationalist policies of Dutra, and smoothed the way toward a nationalist/statist solution to the petroleum problem. By October 1953 Decreto Lei No. 2,004 was passed granting the state a monopoly over the exploration and refining of petroleum and setting up Petrobrás to exercise the monopoly. Of all state enterprises, this was the most important. Petrobrás gave the state a powerful lever with which to shape and direct the process of accumulation. At the same time, Petrobrás was not easily controlled from the outside, even by the federal bureaucracy.

Another state enterprise created in the early fifties, much less controversial than Petrobrás but also extremely important, was the National Development Bank (BNDE). Its establishment was recommended by the Brazil-United States Mixed Commission. Again there seemed to be no way to provide the financing for needed improvements of Brazil's infrastructure other than by action of the state. The BNDE eventually came to control important holdings in a variety of industries, yet it was created as an auxiliary to a plan for liberal, private enterprise-oriented development. Through the BNDE the federal government became the dominant stockholder in the new "mixed-enterprise" steel companies formed in the fifties, Usiminas and Cosipa. Petrobrás and the CSN opened the possibility of the state operating as an industrial entrepreneur, the BNDE gave it the chance to operate as a financier.

A third area in which the growth of state projects in the fifties was particularly impressive was the generation of electrical energy. Like petroleum and steel, electricity was an obvious potential bottleneck in Brazil's postwar industrialization. As in these other cases, the reluctance of international companies to make major investments, combined with and reinforced by nationalism, resulted in a statist solution (Tendler, 1968). Rate increases by foreign power companies were resented. Lacking confidence that their rate increases would be accepted and generally dubious about their future security, the foreign companies would not increase their capacity. Industry suffered, and factories had to build their own generators. The first state company, the CHESF, was established in the late forties. It was joined by a whole barrage of state-owned generating companies. FURNAS and

CEMIG were formed in Minas Gerais in the fifties, CESP in São Paulo in the sixties. Eventually, after the American and Foreign Power Co. was nationalized, Electrobrás was created as a holding company. The other companies became subsidiaries or associates of Electrobrás, and state control over the generation of electrical energy became almost as complete as state control over petroleum. The state's involvement in electricity generation can be regarded as a traditional public sector investment in infrastructure and therefore not an expansion of the state's role. In any case, the hydroelectric schemes gave the government experience in organizing massive and technologically difficult construction projects, and in confronting some formidable engineering problems.

The ascendance of "desenvolvimentismo" as an ideology in the late fifties increased the state's general involvement in the economy. The state's share of gross fixed capital investment rose from 25% in the 1953–1956 period to 37% around 1957 and to 48% by the end of the decade if the investments of state enterprises are included (ECLA, 1964:162, 178). By 1964 ECLA summarized the state's role as follows: "Brazil's public sector owns and directs the country's maritime inland waterway and rail transport facilities and its facilities for the production of petroleum and atomic fuel, controls most of the steel making capacity and is rapidly becoming the principal electrical energy producer . . . it is also the principal iron ore producer and exporter."

The effects of the military takeover of 1964 on the role of the state paralleled in many ways the effects of the revolution of 1930. As in 1930, the necessity of making the revolution from above before someone else succeeded in starting one from below was a compelling motivation. As in 1930, there was a disjunction between the ideology which the new regime espoused and the direction in which it reshaped the economy. In 1964, it was not a case of championing agriculture while taking actions that moved the economy in the direction of industrialization, rather it was a case of espousing liberal free enterprise while acting to increase vastly the economic role of the state, both regulatory and entrepreneurial.

While Schmitter's (1971) contention that the post-1964 regime represented primarily a return to the "Getulian system" may understate the differences, it is nonetheless true that during the thirties and forties the foundations were laid that would enable the state to play its role in the triple alliance of the sixties and seventies. Without these foundations, the military's pursuit of dependent development would have been a much more formidable task.

The Dialectics of Dependence

The classic model of dependence proved to have within it forces that made for its own metamorphosis. Far from being a stagnant or self-reproducing system, it was a self-transforming one. The export of primary products and import of manufactured goods did more than evolve in a quantitative way. In its own terms the system was revolutionary, at least insofar as it changed itself into something quite different from what it had been. The future structure of Brazil's political economy is without doubt being generated inside the present structure, just as the current structure was created within the system of classic dependence. The pressure for change is certainly as strong as ever. Industrialization proved to be no panacea. Industrialized dependent development not only left unresolved the fundamental problems of classic dependence, it did not even offer any obvious route to their resolution. The new political economy created new social groups with new demands. It left the mass of the population as excluded as it had been from the export economy, more so in relative and psychological terms.

One of the reasons for rejecting the agricultural mode of production that predominated under classic dependency was that it did not use the human resources of the society as productively as industry could. Industry was supposed to provide productive employment for the masses and thereby create an internal market sufficient for self-sustaining economic growth. As Celso Furtado described the potential of an industrialized Brazil, "Each new impulse would mean an increasing structural diversification, higher productivity levels, a larger mass of resources for investment, a quicker expansion of the internal market, and the possibility of such impulses being permanently surpassed" (quoted in Hirschman, 1970:87).

The actual configuration of the industrialism that came out of dependency was less lyrical. In fact, the majority of the population did not participate in the growth of industry. While industry grew primarily on the basis of increased output per worker, agriculture grew primarily on the basis of extension. Average yields for major crops remained stagnant (Baer, 1965:256-59), and increased output resulted mainly from increased acreage. Consequently, agriculture continued to absorb a large proportion of the work force but the productivity of agricultural jobs stayed low. In the late sixties, the productivity of agricultural workers was just over 20% of the productivity of workers in industry (Singer, 1971:72).

Most of those who moved out of agriculture found jobs not in industry, but in the tertiary sector. The heterogeneous nature of the service sector makes it hard to characterize the fate of these workers in aggregate terms. Lumping a few thousand lawyers, doctors, and other highly paid professionals together with the millions of workers who fill marginal urban jobs, work as domestic servants, and so on, produces meaningless income statistics. Nonetheless, there is no real disagreement that most who have been forced to work in the tertiary sector receive wages that, relative to the cost of living in an urban situation, are almost as close to subsistence as those of the agricultural labor force.

A look at the changes in the structure of the labor force that have accompanied the internalization of manufacturing production serves to summarize the situation. Of the 20 million workers added since 1920, only one-sixth joined the industrial labor force. One-third joined agriculture and almost half joined the tertiary sector. This sector doubled its share of the work force despite the fact that its share of total output was roughly the same in 1970 as it had been before the Second World War (see Table 2.12).

Nothing indicates the divergence between the benefits expected from industrialization and the actual results better than the changes in Brazilian income distribution between 1960 and 1970 (see Table 2.13). In a decade during which the production of television sets tripled and the top 5 percent of the population almost doubled their average income, the 80 million on the bottom remained stagnated at incomes averaging below $200 a year.

Further indication of the disjunction between human benefit and industrial performance within the Brazilian model can be gleaned from the statistics on infant mortality. The rate of infant mortality in São Paulo, one of the most modern and heavily in-

TABLE 2.12   Structure of the Work Force in Brazil, 1920-1969

Work Force	1920	1969
Primary (principally agriculture)	67% (6.4 million)	43% (12.5 million)
Secondary (principally manufacturing and construction)	13% (1.3 million)	19% (5.5 million)
Tertiary (principally services)	20% (1.9 million)*	38% (11.1 million)
Total	100% (9.6 million)	100% (29.1 million)

* Includes 450,000 working in "poorly defined occupations."
Source: Singer, 1971:63, 67.

dustrialized cities in the world, was 84 per 1000 live births in 1969 (IBGE, 1972:87), about a third higher than the rates for the entire nation of Argentina. The rate for Recife, the largest and most advanced city in the northeast, was 263.5 per 1000 in 1971 (IBGE, 1972:87), about 60 percent higher than the rate for the rural population of Chad, which was the highest national rate recorded by the United Nations (UN, 1968). Even more discouraging is the fact that Recife's rate of infant mortality is apparently no lower than it was a generation ago (Villela and Suzigan, 1973:258).

The income distribution accompanying industrialization cannot help but have consequences for the shape of the industrial structure as well as for the lives of workers. A domestic market for industrial products has been created, but it is a market that must be dominated by luxury goods rather than by wage goods, given the distribution of income. The growth of the automobile industry is of course the most important example, but it is not an isolated one. During the height of Brazil's recent "miracle" from 1970 to 1973, production of consumer durables grew two-and-one-half times as fast as production of consumer nondurables. The nature of the output in turn affects the kind of inputs that industry requires, both in terms of capital goods and in terms of intermediary products. There is more than a coincidental con-

TABLE 2.13   Changes in Brazilian Income Distribution (percent of total income received) 1960-1970

	1960 (%)	1970 (%)	Change in share 1960-1970 (%)
Richest 1%	11.7	17.8	+ 6.1
Next 4%	15.6	18.5	+ 2.9
Total Top 5%	27.3	36.3	+ 9.0
Bottom 80%	45.5	36.8	− 8.7

Source: Singer, 1972:65. Calculations are from 1970 census and were done by José Carlos Duarte.

nection between the failure of industrialization to speak to the needs of Brazil's population and the fact that it has also left Brazil dependent on foreign goods in ways that are as vexing as the dependence of the classic model.

The new industrial establishment is anything but autarchic. Import substitution has meant changing from one kind of imports to another. Machinery and equipment, fuels and intermediary inputs have been required by manufacturers in steadily increasing amounts. All the impressive increases in exports of manufactured goods have been necessary just to cover the increasing needs of the manufacturers themselves for imported equipment and intermediary inputs.

The comfortable positive trade balances of classic dependence are a thing of the past. Rising exports failed to balance the need for imports in 1971 and 1972 even before the cost of imported services was included (ECLA, 1976:77). Once the price of oil tripled, deficits in the simple balance of trade became even harder to avoid, and over and above the question of balance of trade there were the growing costs of servicing internalized foreign capital. Repatriated profits, interest payments, fees, royalties, and technical assistance payments grew along with imports. There was a continual need for new loans to make up for deficits in the current account. As fast as exports rose, Brazil's demand for new loans rose even faster. While exports tripled between the beginning of the sixties and 1972, the amount of foreign loans went up over 1,300%. Exacerbated by the rise in the price of oil, Brazil's foreign debt was between $25 and $30 billion by the end of 1976 (Aronson, 1977:13)

The most disturbing aspect of the new balance of payments problems was that the only way to solve them seemed to be to slow down industrialization. In years when capacity is not fully utilized, such as 1964 and 1965, Brazil's current account balance was favorable; but as the economy began to operate at full capacity the balance of payments problem worsened. Analysis by

Edmar Bacha indicates that the trade-off between growth and balance of payments stability has been getting progressively worse since the end of World War II. Bacha's data show that a deficit amounting to about 30% of exports seemed to be necessary in order for the economy to reach its potential output in the period 1947-1957. In the period 1966-1974 the required deficit was 58% of exports (Bacha, 1975:16). The only alternative to continuing balance of payments deficits and spiraling foreign debt seemed to be stagnation. By creating an industrial structure whose requirements for imported goods and services exceeded the market for the goods it produced for export, even when exports were heavily subsidized and the international market was not in crisis, the new system, like the old, seemed to have created pressures that could only be resolved by its transformation.

Brazil in the seventies had not escaped the problems associated with dependence. On the contrary, it illustrated beautifully the extent to which disarticulation (epitomized by the growing need for imported capital and intermediary goods) and exclusion (exemplified by the changes in income distribution between 1960 and 1970) could persist despite dependent development. It showed the tremendous amount of growth and structural change that could be fostered by the new system. But, it showed equally well that the contradictions created by dependent development are at least as severe as those which confronted the country during the period of classic dependence.

Looking over the transition from classic dependence to dependent development also reinforces Cardoso and Faletto's point (1973:140) that relations of dependency "are made concrete possibilities through the existence of a network of interests and interactions which link certain social groups to certain other social groups." Without a particular configuration of class alliances within Brazil, classic dependence would have persisted or been transformed in a different way. Likewise, the statistically observable characteristics of the current model of dependent development do not arise simply from the operation of external factors or "objective conditions"; they arise from the concrete interaction of social groups and classes.

The state, the multinationals, and local capital developed their contemporary strategies in response to external and "objective" factors, just as they developed them in response to the actions of the Brazilian working class. Nonetheless, the pattern of alliance that emerged could not have been mechanically predicted on the basis of either the internal economic context or the pressures of the working class. Interaction among the dominant elites shaped the transition from classic dependence to dependent development, and, in the same way, the interaction of the state, the multinationals, and local capital will shape the response to the contradictions of dependent development.

3.

Local Capital and the Multinationals*

BY 1890 Francisco Matarazzo had become so successful at buying pigs and selling lard that he decided to move from the small town of Sorocaba to the state capital of São Paulo. In Cleveland, Ohio, at about the same time, the National Carbon Co. had also developed into a successful enterprise, manufacturing carbon elements to light the streets of the growing cities of the United States. Eighty years later the companies that grew out of these disparate enterprises were both major participants in the chemical complex burgeoning in São Paulo. Union Carbide, the multinational descendant of the National Carbon Co., was São Paulo's largest producer of polyethylene. Indústrias Reunidas F. Matarazzo, founded by Francisco Matarazzo, was a diverse conglomerate producing hundreds of products from polyvinyl cloride resins to cellophane.

Looking at Paulo Figuereido and Antonio de Abreu Coutinho, one would probably not find anything to indicate that one worked for Union Carbide and the other for the Matarazzo empire. Both have the reputation of being sophisticated men, with long expe-

* The analysis of "Grupos Econômicos" which appears in this chapter is built on years of work by Professor Maurício Vinhas de Queiroz and his colleagues at the Instituto de Ciências Sociais in Rio de Janeiro, as well as on our work under a grant from the Brazil office of the Ford Foundation at the Universidade de Brasília in 1974. A Portuguese version of the analysis is available in Queiroz and Evans, "Um Delicado Equilíbrio: O Capital Internacional e o Local na Industrialização Brasileira" in Queiroz et al., 1977. This chapter also contains material that appeared in my dissertation and in my article on the pharmaceutical industry, "Foreign Investment and Industrial Transformation: A Brazilian Case Study," which appeared in the *Journal of Development Economics* in 1976, 3(4):119-139.

rience in large-scale enterprise. Probably neither would consider himself an "entrepreneur," since neither is the final arbiter of what goes on in his company. Both are Brazilians, but more important, both are professional managers. One must answer to the family that owns his company, the other to a board of directors that meets in New York City. Yet both of them must turn a profit or lose their jobs.

Should Paulo Figuereido, president of Union Carbide do Brasil, and Antonio de Abreu Coutinho, financial vice-president of Indústrias Reunidas F. Matarazzo, be considered simply as two representatives of the "industrial bourgeoisie"? Should they be considered as members of two antagonistic fractions of a class— one a representative of the "national bourgeoisie," the other an agent of international capital? Looking at the individuals, there is no reason to believe they could not exchange roles, Paulo Figuereido managing an enterprise owned by Brazilians and Antonio de Abreu Coutinho working for a multinational enterprise. The two corporations, however, are not so interchangeable. For Union Carbide, Brazil is an important market but still represents less than 5% of worldwide sales. For the Matarazzo empire, exports to the world market are a valued source of profits, but what happens in Brazil determines the future of the enterprise. They are two different kinds of capital, despite similarities between the men who run them.

The historical relation between these two kinds of capital has already been sketched out in crude aggregate form. At this level it appears that extensive involvement of international capital in Brazilian manufacturing operations did not come until the transition from classic dependence to dependent development was well underway. The relative absence of "pioneering" by foreign capital has led Brazilians to view the entry of such capital in terms of "denationalization." Foreign manufacturing capital plays the role of the cuckoo, laying its eggs in nests constructed by others. Local capital, having gotten industrialization going, is pushed aside by the more powerful outsiders. To see the role of foreign capital in terms of denationalization is not consistent with the model of dependent development proposed in Chapter 1. If denationalization were the central thrust of the relation between foreign and local capital, then the supposed alliance between them would be simply a facade to gloss over the growing domination of the foreigners. If the evolution of the industrial structure could be summarized in terms of denationalization, then Cardoso's image of dependent development as entailing the "simultaneous and differentiated expansion" of different kinds of capital would not apply. Yet the data show a tremendous growth of direct investment in manufacturing from World War II to the present. It is implausible that this investment was purely complementary to the Brazilian industrial establishment that had grown up between the wars.

The aim of this chapter is to show how the relation between foreign and local capital has encompassed both denationalization and "simultaneous and differentiated expansion." To do this it is necessary to move from an examination of the growth of foreign investment in toto to an analysis of different branches of industry and the relations between foreign and local capital within them. Two specific industries have been chosen for special attention, pharmaceuticals and textiles.

The form that collaboration between foreign and local capital is likely to take depends on the kind of leverage that is available to each within a given branch of industry. But local capital cannot be assessed as a homogeneous category. Averitt (1968) and others have argued for making a categorical distinction within the U.S. domestic economy between "center" and "periphery" firms. This terminology is confusing when applied to local capital within Brazil, but to make the distinction between large and small capital is even more important there. The fate of local capital that has attained the scale and sophistication necessary to become part of the "internationalized bourgeoisie" has to be distinguished from the lot of smaller local capital.

Large capital is, of course, much easier to discuss than small capital. The ties of "elite" local capital to the multinationals in the contemporary period will be examined concretely by looking at the ownership, local, foreign, and joint, of the very largest manufacturing corporations. Ties between smaller local capital and the multinationals will be examined only for pharmaceuticals and textiles. Statistical data provide some basis for commenting on the contemporary situation of local capital in other branches of industry, but evidence on longer term trends is restricted to the largest firms.

The Creation of the Brazilian Industrial Establishment

In the period of classic dependence, the intense involvement of British capital in the export complex lent credence to the charge that the British tried to "smother and demoralize national industry." Nonetheless, even in this early period, the relation between foreign and local capital was collaborative as well as antagonistic. It was, after all, a British banker who supported Francisco Matarazzo in his efforts to gain credit for the construction of his first flour mill (Martins, 1973:30). British technicians also made a contribution to the early surge of Brazilian industrialization, and there were even a few British firms that successfully entered the manufacturing arena.

Incipient alliances notwithstanding, the vast majority of firms entering textiles, food and beverages, and other industries that formed the core of early manufacturing were Brazilian-owned. The industrial census of 1920 counted 14,000 industrial establishments (Baer, 1965:13). Only 600 of them had been in existence thirty years earlier, and with a few exceptions these were owned by Brazilians. The exceptions should not, however, be overlooked; they were among the largest, most successful and longest lived of the early firms. Nonetheless, even when one examines long-surviving large firms, it is clear that at the earliest stages of the development of Brazilian manufacturing foreign capital was by no stretch of the imagination preeminent.

The most extensive research on the largest Brazilian firms has been done by Maurício Vinhas de Queiroz and his associates at the Instituto de Ciências Sociais of the Universidade Federal do Rio de Janeiro (Queiroz, 1965, 1972). What follows here relies very heavily on this seminal work. The unit of analysis is an "economic group," defined as a set of companies connected by links of shared ownership or multiple interlocking directorates (Queiroz, 1962). When the foundation dates of the largest groups are examined (see Table 3.1) it is clear that, while the largest foreign groups were established in Brazil earlier than the general range of industrial subsidiaries, the earliest large-scale enterprises were predominantly locally owned. Almost two-thirds of the largest local groups were founded before the First World War.

Of the foreign groups that entered Brazil before 1914, the majority were not engaged in industrial activities when they first entered. Among the five pre-World War I entries, two were simply distribution organizations of the major petroleum companies (Esso and Shell). Another, Brazilian Traction and Light Power Co., was a public utility growing out of the electrification of the

TABLE 3.1   Foundation Dates for Largest Economic Groups and American Subsidiaries

	Pre World War I	1914- 1929	1930- 1945	Post-World War II	Total	
Largest Locally Owned Economic Groups*	64%	28%	8%	0%	100%	(25)
Largest Foreign-Owned Economic Groups*	20%	37%	17%	27%	101%	(30)
American Subsidiaries of Industrial Firms	0%	11%	21%	68%	100%	(131)

* The two groups classified in the original study as mixed have been classified here according to the origin of the currently dominant partner. One (Bethlehem/Antunes) is considered local; the other (Union Carbide/White Martins) is considered foreign.
Source: Evans, 1971:33, 36, 39.

trolley system in Rio de Janeiro. Of the two that could legitimately be called "industrial" at the time of their inception, only one, a subsidiary of the British Match Corporation called Fiat Lux, was really an example of industrial entrepreneurship coming from the center to the periphery. The other, Bunge & Born, was an Argentine company that had built itself into a giant grain-dealing establishment in Argentina and moved into flour milling in Brazil soon after the turn of the century (Queiroz, 1972:170-71). It was only during and after the First World War that foreign industrial entrants really began to appear. British American Tobacco started making cigarettes, General Electric light bulbs, Rhone Poulenc sulphuric acid and other chemicals, and Schneider steel.

Even when foreign entries might be considered pioneers, their activity was often based on the acquisition of existing Brazilian firms. Bunge & Born's entry into flour milling came when they bought some of the stock of the Moinho Santista, a local firm, albeit one founded by an immigrant (Queiroz, 1972:170). Fiat Lux (British Match) actually set up industrial operations from scratch at the end of the nineteenth century, before any local match industry existed. British American Tobacco, on the other hand, bought out a local manufacturer and their cigarettes bear his name, Souza Cruz, to this day. Schneider & Cie, the earliest foreign entry in steel, got into the industry when Brazilian entrepreneurs decided that their Companhia Siderúrgica Mineira would not survive without more capital and technology than they could provide (Queiroz, 1972:243).

The largest foreign groups played almost no role in the early history of the industry most central to the beginning of industrialization: the textile industry. Textiles were, however, the starting point for several of the largest local groups. Of the sixteen local groups founded before the First World War, roughly half were engaged in industrial activities, and of these, four were involved in textiles. Most of the others began, as might be expected, with the production of food products: flour, sugar, or beer. If the activities of the largest economic groups can be taken as an indication of the general distribution of foreign and local capital, then the core industries of the first phase of Brazilian industrialization were initiated primarily by local capital.

While the capital that created the first surge of industrialization did not take the form of center country corporations extending their operations to the periphery, the early phases of industrialization were hardly indigenous. The importance of immigrants in the early Brazilian entrepreneurial class is widely acknowledged (see Dean, 1969:49-67). Of "Brazilian" groups among the largest economic groups, at least 40% were founded by immigrants (Queiroz, 1965:57). Matarazzo is only the most famous example. One of Matarazzo's fellow immigrants in Sorocaba in the late 1880's was a Portuguese, Pereira Ignácio, who arrived with no capital but went on to found a group of industrial companies even larger than Matarazzo's. Hermann Lundgren, a shipwrecked Swedish sailor, arrived in Brazil twenty-five years before Matarazzo, founded the Pernambuco Powder Factory in 1866, and went on to head one of the biggest textile trading organizations in Brazil. Maurício Klabin left Lithuania, became a typographer in Brazil, and began Brazil's largest paper company. Eduardo Guinle, founder of the group that built its fortune around the Santos docks, was the son of a French immigrant. The two great Brazilian beer companies, Antarctica and Brahma, were also created by immigrants.

External capital and entrepreneurship were important in the early history of the largest "Brazilian" economic groups, but they did not create links to the center in the same way that later investments did. Perhaps the most interesting illustration of the contrast is the case of Luis La Saigne and Mesbla, the largest economic group based on retail trade. La Saigne was sent by a French department store to become manager of its Brazilian branch. He managed to take over the firm, wresting control from the French parent. It would be unimaginable for the current manager of Sears and Roebuck to attempt the same sort of coup. Half a century ago when La Saigne succeeded, foreign capital was more easily separated from its origins.

In addition to the foreign enterprises and entrepreneurs that were "Brazilianized," there were, of course, large economic groups founded by members of families that had been in Brazil for generations. Othon Bezerra de Melo, founder of one of the largest early textile empires, for example, came from a family of large landholders. Severino Pereira da Silva, like Bezerra de Melo, came from the interior of the state of Pernambuco. Although he did not have the advantage of being a member of the landowning class, he also went on to found a textile empire.

Whether established by immigrants or families long rooted in Brazil, one of the common features of the largest Brazilian economic groups is that they moved into industry via commerce (cf. Queiroz, 1972:90-93). If they had capital, like Othon Bezerra de Melo, they could begin with their own stores; if they did not, like Severino Pereira da Silva, they worked in other people's stores. Whether one began with textiles or with foodstuffs, it was natural to move from expanding commercial operations to manufacturing. Dean points out (1969:19-33) that many of the Paulista importing houses made this same sort of transition.

The use of commerce as a route to industrial entrepreneurship is another indication of the way in which the classic pattern of dependence based on the export of primary products and the import of manufactured goods helped create the conditions of its own overthrow. The commercial capitalism that grew up under the reign of classic dependence provided a seedbed for entrepreneurs who eventually moved into manufacturing. At the same time, the resistance of foreign corporations to making the transition from trade to manufacturing is another indication of the significantly different roles played by local and foreign capital in the early stages of industrialization.

Bunge & Born, the Argentine grain giant, moved, like Matarazzo, from buying and selling flour to milling flour, to making flour sacks, to textile manufacture. Corporations from the center countries, with a few exceptions like Coats and Clark and United Merchants, seemed reluctant to follow up their exports to Brazil with local manufacture of textiles. As late as 1924, the Rio representative of a North American hosiery company, himself an American, told a visiting reporter plaintively:

"Will you look up Mr. So and So, the president of our company, when you get back to New York, and do me the favor of telling him the truth about the situation down here? I've been telling them for a long while that what they need to do is set up a few knitting machines down here, import their regular silk yarn from the United States and make the hose down here. I have built up a big volume even in the face of this tariff. If they will begin to make the goods here, of exactly the same quality as before, we can sell any amount of it, at a better profit. But they think I'm crazy." (Murphy, 1924:645).

For those on the scene, manufacturing looked like a good investment, whether they were Brazilians or not. But for those who made the decisions back in the center, the tendency was to send goods from the center to Brazil as long as possible, whether or not manufacturing in Brazil itself might produce more profits.

By the end of the First World War the foundations of an industrial economy had been created in Brazil. Coffee still dominated, but investment in industry began to look less adventurous. The pace of foreign entries increased. The largest foreign groups entering at this time (with the exception of Swift/Armour), were not, however, involved in either textiles or food. Ford and General Motors followed the lead of the major oil companies in setting up organizations to handle distribution of their cars. Dupont, Imperial Chemical Industries, and Remington joined together to make shells and gunpowder. Pirelli started making copper cable. Philips began making radios and the great Unilever soap combine set up a Brazilian subsidiary.

The local groups that were established in this period were also mainly in industries other than textiles and foods. Monteiro Aranha started producing glass. Pignatari and Cicillo Matarazzo (who split off from the branch of the family headed by Francisco) began large projects in metallurgy. Carlos and Luis Villares began manufacturing elevators. There were also a number of local companies in the textile and food products industry formed after the First World War, but all of the textile groups among the "grupos multibilionários" date from before it. Conversely, only one group which is primarily industrial but not engaged in either food or textiles was founded before the war.

By the end of the war local groups based in food and textiles were no longer the spearhead of industrialization. The newly formed groups were more likely to be foreign and almost certain to be in other industries. Both of these trends were accentuated after 1930. Only two new local groups were formed and one of these was a joint venture. The entry of foreign groups, however, continued apace. Alcan came in to produce aluminum. Ciba/ Geigy and Union Carbide entered the chemical industry along with Solvay and Cie. St. Gobain, Pittsburgh Plate Glass, and Corning joined together to work in glass.

The "grupos multibilionários" formed after World War II were almost exclusively foreign. The development of the automobile industry was to foreign groups in the fifties what textiles and food products had been to local groups in the pre-World War I period. Of the six foreign groups that entered in the fifties, three of them, Volkswagen, Mercedes, and Willys, were involved in the production of cars, trucks, or buses. In addition, Ford and General Motors, who had been engaged mainly in the sale and distribution of cars, along with some final assembly, became involved in integrated local production.

As new industries took a central role in Brazil's industrial growth, foreign groups gained prominence and began to take on the "pioneering" role that they had avoided in the earliest, pre-World War I phase. Foreign firms could take credit for introducing the local manufacture not just of automobiles and tires, but also of refrigerators, locomotives, radios, and washing machines. The rise of foreign industrial capital was a reflection of the rise of new industries in which local capital was not prepared to compete, and was not caused by the displacement of local groups from industries in which they had previously been active. Or at least this is the conclusion that might be drawn from focusing on textiles and autos. If the focus is on other industries the situation is quite different.

As foreign groups began to enter a variety of new industries in the thirties and forties, some local groups were beginning to diversify. The result was, in some cases, direct competition. In aluminum, for example, the Votorantim group headed by José Ermírio de Moraes moved from textiles to aluminum manufacturing in 1941 and began competing with Alcan. Two local groups, Votorantim and Villares, both entered the steel industry in the late thirties and created new competition for the foreign-owned Companhia Siderúrgica Belgo-Mineira. As locals entered industries where they were in competition with foreigners, foreign penetration of traditional industries increased. Anderson Clayton is perhaps the best example. Founded in 1934, Anderson Clayton and Cia. Ltda. first moved into the production of cotton seed oil and margarine, an area previously dominated by local groups like Matarazzo. Later, in the fifties, it became one of the major coffee exporters, moving in alongside groups like Almeida Prado, which had entered the coffee export business much earlier using capital acquired by previous generations of coffee plantation owners.

In some cases foreign capital displaced local capital directly. The glass industry provides a good example. In 1903 Antonio da Silva Prado incorporated the Companhia Vidraria Santa Maria, founding what was to become Brazil's largest producer of glass. In 1917 the Monteiro Aranha group founded what was to become the second largest glass producer. Then, during the Second World War, the initiation of protective tariffs increased foreign interest in the glass industry. Santa Maria was bought by Corning in 1945 and eventually became a joint venture split among Corning, Pittsburgh Plate Glass, and St. Gobain. Later, Owens Illinois acquired a controlling interest in the glass company owned by the Monteiro Aranha group. The history of glass production in Brazil is a history of denationalization, the displacement of local groups by foreign ones.

In other cases, local and foreign capital entered the same industry on the basis of collaboration rather than competition or displacement. Mining is one example. By associating himself with the Bethlehem Steel Company, Augusto de Azevedo Antunes turned what had been a minor mining company into the biggest mineral-based empire in Brazil. Mourão Guimarães, which started out with a base in textiles, moved into the mining of magnesite in a venture that included equity participation by the Schneider (French) steel producing group. The Martins family, which had been one of the pioneers in the local manufacture of oxygen and acetylene, and also owned one of Brazil's largest textile companies, brought Union Carbide into its chemical business. The results of collaboration were very different in the three cases. Bethlehem and Antunes are still partners. The foreign partner eventually dropped out of the magnesite venture, leaving it a Brazilian-owned enterprise. Union Carbide became the owner of the oxygen and acetylene business, leaving the Brazilian group with its textile holdings.

Competition and collaboration complicate the differentiation of capital by industries. Differentiation is partially explicable in historical terms. Local groups pioneered in the expansion of some industries and still dominate them; other industries were created by foreign groups, and local capital never managed to gain entry. But local and foreign capital have worked together in a number of industries. In some of these, local capital has been displaced; in others it has survived. The patterns of displacement and survival must be explained, not simply in terms of historical conjuncture, but also in terms of the structural characteristics of the industries involved.

The Contemporary Pattern of Differentiation

Every Brazilian businessman knows that foreign capital is strong in some industries and local capital is strong in others. Translating this impression into quantitative estimates of the importance of foreign and local capital in various industries is not easy, but a number of estimates are available. The data on which they are based come mainly from large firms and may thus lead to an underestimate of the amounts of local capital involved in the myriad tiny enterprises that populate the fringes of each industry, but the picture they provide is a good representation of the "commanding heights" of Brazilian industry.

The four estimates of ownership by industry shown in Table 3.2 are consistent enough to provide a rank ordering of the importance of foreign capital, even if the actual percentages cannot be considered exact. In four industries (transportation equipment, rubber products, pharmaceuticals and tobacco) foreign capital is dominant. In another six (leather products, printing and publishing, apparel and footwear, wood products, paper products and nonmetallic metals) local capital holds the predominant position when the industry is examined as a whole. In three other industries (food and beverages, textiles, and metal fabrication), local capital still accounts for the majority of the sales and assets among the largest firms of the industry, but foreign capital also plays a major role. Finally, there are three industries in which foreign capital is predominant but local capital plays a significant role (chemicals, machinery and electrical machinery).

To begin interpreting the pattern of differentiation found in Table 3.2, it is necessary to consider the relative importance of

TABLE 3.2 Estimates of the Distribution of Foreign and Local Capital by Industry

| Industrial Categories[1] | Type of Estimate (all %'s represent percentage foreign-controlled) | | | |
	Top 300 Manufacturers Assets[2] (Newfarmer and Mueller) 1972	Ownership of Brazilian[3] Economy (Jasperson) 1969	Top 500 Corporations[4] (Fajnzylber) 1968	Sales-1970[5] (Pignaton-U.S. Tariff Commission)
Local Predominance				
Leather products	N.A.[6]	37%	N.A.	N.A.
Printing and publishing	N.A.	0%	0%	2%
Apparel and footwear	N.A.	0%	N.A.	N.A.
Wood products & furniture	N.A.	0%	N.A.	N.A.
Paper products	29%[7]	12%	5%	24%
Nonmetallic minerals	22%	21%	N.A.	25%
Local Predominance with Significant Foreign Capital				
Food and beverages	32%	53%[8]	40%	8%
Textiles	44%	29%	44%	29%
Metal fabrication	25%	38%	44%	54%
Foreign Predominance with Significant Local Capital				
Chemicals	65%	76%	60%	44%
Machinery	74%	61%	56%	71%
Electrical machinery	78%	49%	68%	62%
Foreign Predominance				
Tobacco	N.A.	91%	N.A.	N.A.
Rubber products	100%	82%	94%	58%
Pharmaceuticals	100%	94%	87%	N.A.
Transportation equipment	84%	100%[9]	92%	90%

[1] I have used the IBGE's (Instituto Brasileiro de Geografia e Estatística) industrial categories as the basis of my classifications by industry. Despite its problems, this set of categories offers greater comparability across sources than any other. The authors cited here have sometimes used different sets of categories in which the statistics for a given industry are not separately calculated. Even when the IBGE set has been used by an author, industrial categories have sometimes been collapsed leaving no separate calculation for a given industry.

[2] Newfarmer and Mueller (1975:108) base their analysis on *Visão's* list of the largest Brazilian firms in 1972—"Quem é Quem na Economia Brasileira" (August 1973). Their judgments as to ownership were, however, based on other sources.

[3] Jasperson's estimates come from a document prepared for the U. S. Department of State and are cited in Newfarmer and Mueller (1975:112). They do not cite the sources of his data.

[4] Fajnzylber's estimates are from a study done under the auspices of a research organization connected to Brazil's Ministry of Planning (IPEA/INPES) with the cooperation of CEPAL. The estimates (1971:45) are based on data from *O Dirigente Industrial* and the Brazilian Central Bank.

[5] Pignaton's (1973:109) estimates are based on the U.S. Tariff Commission Report (1973) and data from the Brazilian Central Bank.

[6] N.A. signifies that the source cited does not separately calculate a percentage for the industrial category under consideration. As would be expected, given the interest of the investigators in foreign capital, this occurs most frequently in locally controlled industries.

[7] Newfarmer and Mueller's figure actually refers to wood products and paper products in combination, which suggests that their estimate of paper products alone might be somewhat higher.

[8] This figure represents a weighted average of two separate figures which Jasperson presents for food and beverages.

[9] Jasperson's figure does not include auto parts, which he estimates at 78% foreign-controlled.

the industries. Table 3.3 gives an idea of relative importance. The industries in which either foreign or local capital are clearly in control account for about one-third of the total value added in manufacturing. This fraction is split about evenly between locally dominated industries and foreign-dominated industries. About three-fifths of the value added in manufacturing is produced by industries in which there is participation by both local and foreign capital. Differentiation provides some refuges for local capital, but not large ones and, more crucially, not growing ones. The second column of Table 3.3 shows that most of the redoubts of local capital are shrinking relative to the totality of the industrial establishment, whereas most of the fastest growing industries are foreign-controlled. There are only two rapidly growing industries in which local capital predominates—paper products and metal fabrication. In the larger of these, metal fabrication, the local part of the industry is primarily the state-owned companies that dominate the steel industry.

While the industries controlled by local capital are relatively stagnant, penetration by local capital into industries now controlled by foreign capital is unlikely. Some of the reasons for this are indicated in Table 3.4 which provides a rough measure of the structural differences between foreign-controlled and locally controlled industries. Local preserves are typically less concentrated, characterized by small-scale plants and less capital per worker. They are also industries in which technology is relatively unimportant. The only locally controlled industry which is above the median on more than half of these measures is again the state-dominated metal fabricating industry.

The industries dominated by local capital in Brazil are the same industries where small businesses flourish in the United States. Leather products, furniture, and apparel/footwear, to take three examples from Brazil, are the three industries with the lowest amounts of investment per worker in the United States. (U.S. Dept. of Commerce, 1970). They are also among the least

TABLE 3.3 The Growth and Importance of Local and
Foreign-Dominated Industries

Industry	Importance (% of value added 1968)[1]	Growth (change in relative share of value added 1950-1968)[2]
Local Predominance		
Leather products	0.6%	46
Printing and publishing	3.0%	71
Apparel and footwear	2.8%	65
Wood products and furniture	4.2%	75
Paper products	2.7%	129
Nonmetallic minerals	5.8%	78
Local Predominance with Significant Foreign Participation		
Food and beverages	15.6%	63
Textiles	10.1%	50
Metal fabrication	11.4%	154
Foreign Predominance with Significant Local Participation		
Chemicals	12.1%	187
Machinery	6.0%	273
Electrical machinery	6.3%	371
Foreign Predominance		
Tobacco	1.4%	88
Rubber products	2.0%	95
Pharmaceuticals	5.5%	187[3]
Transportation equipment	8.6%	374

[1] Figures are from Newfarmer and Mueller (1975:116). They are based on Fajnzylber (1971) who in turn used the IBGE's 1969 *Produção Industrial*. Percentages are a fraction of all value added in manufacturing. They do not add up to 100% because 3.5% of total value added is produced by industries not on the table.

[2] Index numbers represent the share of total value added accounted for by the industry in 1968 as a percentage of the share of value added accounted for by the industry in 1950 according to Baer (1965:269).

[3] Pharmaceuticals are not considered separately from chemicals by Baer and therefore are given the same growth rate in this table. The real growth rate of pharmaceuticals in these terms is probably somewhat lower than that of chemicals as a whole.

TABLE 3.4 Comparative Indices[1] of the Structural Characteristics of Foreign and Locally Dominated Industries

Industry	Scale[2]	Concentration[3]	Capital Intensity[4]	Importance of Technology[5]
Local Predominance				
Leather products	52	70	56	43
Printing and publishing	46	79	68	86
Apparel and footwear	32	53	24	29
Wood products and furniture	52	37	58	100
Paper and paper products	100	109	100	114
Nonmetallic minerals	63	113	58	171
Local Predominance with Significant Foreign Participation				
Food and beverages	65	72[6]	102[6]	100
Textiles	49	70	60	43
Metal fabrication	185	126	104	100
Foreign Predominance with Significant Local Participation				
Chemicals	345	126	186	471
Machinery	63	100	114	400
Electrical machinery	122	121	98	542
Foreign Predominance				
Tobacco	190	126	62	100
Rubber products	552	184	132	229
Pharmaceuticals	154	44	80	1042
Transportation equipment	530	144	182	314

[1] All figures are relative to the median figure for all industries on a given measure, with the median considered as 100 and the figure for an individual industry on a measure treated as a ratio to the median.

[2] The measure of scale used here is Fajnzylber's "characteristic size" of establishment in terms of value of production (1971:57). It is derived from IBGE's 1967 *Produção Industrial*.

[3] The measure of concentration is from Fajnzylber (1971:95) and is based on the percentage of production in an industry that is accounted for by the top four firms.

[4] The measure of capital intensity is Singer's estimate of capital per worker (1971:83) and is based on the 1960 industrial census.

[5] "Importance of technology" is based on the importance of technology to the industry in the U.S., not Brazil. The measure is research and development scientists and engineers per 1,000 employees, taken from National Science Foundation (1974:Table B-30). The use of U.S. data is more appropriate in this case, since any measure internal to Brazil is distorted by the use of center country technologies by multinationals. Brazilian data are also of course much less reliable.

[6] Food and beverages are treated separately by both Fajnzylber and Singer (1972), and the index represents the average of the two weighted according to their relative contribution to value added in 1968.

concentrated of North American manufacturing enterprises. Unconcentrated industries with small-scale establishments are not choice sites for capital accumulation either in the United States or in Brazil. They are likely to be competitive and consequently to enjoy neither monopoly power nor monopoly profits. The areas in which the multinationals predominate are, quite the contrary, precisely those in which there are likely to be high barriers to entry and consequently high profits for those who operate in them.

Transportation equipment is the obvious example. It involves large-scale plants, capital intensive processes of production, and high profits. American multinationals in the Brazilian transportation equipment industry reported about 19% return on equity to the Senate subcommittee on multinationals (Newfarmer and Mueller, 1975:140). Even tobacco, which does not appear to have important barriers to entry in terms of either capital intensity or the importance of technology, is an industry in which product differentiation based on large-scale advertising ensures protection against competitive pressures that would drive down profits.

Half of the Brazilian affiliates of United States multinationals reporting to the Senate subcommittee on multinationals admitted to controlling 25 to 100% of the markets in which their principal products were sold. Market control was associated in turn with high profit rates. Affiliates controlling at least 25% of their markets averaged about 20% return on equity (Newfarmer and Mueller, 1975:133, 143). As Connor and Mueller (1977:19) point out, the overall profit rates of Brazilian affiliates are substantially higher than general profit rates for large American domestic manufacturing corporations—16.1% as opposed to 10.5%. Given these levels of profitability, the motivation to increase control over the Brazilian domestic market is obvious.

Examination at this gross level of aggregation leaves a pessimistic picture of the prospects for local capital. Looking at the aggregate data, it seems that denationalization is the inevitable consequence of the evolution of the industrial structure. As industry moves toward more capital intensive, technologically based production, the differentiation of capital will leave local capital increasingly marginalized. This is, of course, the conventional view of the relation between local and multinational capital.

Unfortunately, differentiation as it emerges at the aggregate level leaves most of the industrial order unexplained. Three-fifths of the value produced in industry comes out of industries containing significant amounts of both local and foreign capital. Local capital in significant amounts has found its way into "modern" industries. There remains, however, a question. Has this capital discovered, within these industries, sub-areas in which small-scale, competitive production is still possible? The presence of foreign capital in "traditional" industries like food products and textiles raises a complementary question. Are there high-profit sub-branches within these industries that have been taken over by foreign capital? In short, does the structure of differentiation within industries replicate the structure of differentiation between industries?

Another question that appears difficult to answer on the basis of aggregate data is the question of change. Newfarmer and Mueller (1975:108-110) and Pignaton (1973:109) both supply estimates of the increase of multinational predominance in the late sixties, but while they both agree that the strength of multinationals has increased in manufacturing as a whole, their estimates for individual industries are often contradictory. Pignaton finds a dramatic rise in foreign sales in textiles; Newfarmer and Mueller find a slight decline in foreign control of assets in textiles. Newfarmer and Mueller find a fall in the foreign share of the machinery industry, while Pignaton again finds a dramatic increase. The only industry in which they both find a substantial decline is food and beverages, which is curious since this is a locally controlled industry in which foreign firms appear impressionistically to have increased their participation recently. The data is inadequate. Four to six years is too short a period over which to assess trends in ownership, and there is no good data covering a longer time span.

Only within industries can the processes of competition and displacement be examined. Likewise, it seems that the most important kinds of symbiosis, complementarity, and collaboration between local and foreign capital exist within rather than between the major industrial categories. Each industry cannot be analyzed individually here. We will examine only two industries in detail—pharmaceuticals and textiles. Pharmaceuticals provides the classic case of denationalization, but it is also an interesting example of symbiosis and complementarity. Textiles is an industry in which local capital still predominates. Both the strengths of local capital and the degree to which such capital is threatened even in its traditional strongholds are well illustrated by textiles. Both industries are important because they yield clues to the situation of small capital.

Displacing the National Bourgeoisie: The Case of Pharmaceuticals

The pharmaceutical industry has been used as the archetypal example of denationalization. For some, the lesson of denationalization was that "many Brazilian firms, which might have evolved and grown larger, were abandoned by the Government." In addition, they say, "the 'arbitrary and unjust' price controls which the industry suffered in the past had grave consequences and one of them was 'denationalization' " (Banas, 1969:177). Others try to show their fellow Brazilians, "how we are unmercifully exploited by the international trusts and cartels of the [pharmaceutical] industry which dominate the Brazilian market in the elevated proportion of 90%" (Pacheco, 1968:1). Agreement exists on all sides that the pharmaceutical industry has been effectively "denationalized."

From the perspective of the foreign-dominated pharmaceutical industry of the seventies, to envision the Brazilian industry as a flourishing indigenous institution on a pharmacological footing equal to its American counterpart appears more an exercise in fantasy than historical reconstruction. Yet, in the late nineteenth and early twentieth centuries the two countries possessed very similar pharmaceutical industries. Enterprising individuals in either place fortunate enough to create compounds whose purported medicinal properties were not disconfirmed by the experiences of their customers were able to build flourishing firms.

In Greensboro, North Carolina in 1875, Lunsford Richardson founded the Vick Chemical Company to satisfy a growing demand for Vick's Vaporub. Lunsford's sons would be able to watch the transformation of the Vick's Vaporub factory into one of the biggest pharmaceutical companies in the world, with sales in the hundreds of millions of dollars. In Minas Gerais in the early 1900's, a young pharmacist called Cândido Fontoura developed something he called Biotônico. It too proved to be an eminently saleable product and the basis of one of the most successful pharmaceutical companies in Brazil. Neither Richardson nor Fontoura could have foreseen that one day major policy decisions regarding the future of the companies they had founded would be made from offices located within a few blocks from each other in New York City.

Companies selling patent medicines began to emerge in Brazil as early as the mid-nineteenth century (cf. Oliveira and Ayres, 1949). They bore names like *Elixir de Inhame* or *Saude da Mulher* (Woman's Health), and were probably neither more nor less scientific or efficacious than Bristol's Pills, Carter's Little Liver Pills, Mother Seigle's Curative Syrup, or other popular American products. The American consul reported from Brazil in 1898 that, while Brazil had an important advantage in being the exclusive world source of Ipecuanha root, American patent medicines were also imported and sold there (U.S. Bureau of Foreign and Domestic Commerce, 1898).

The pharmaceutical industry took on a more scientific tone in the 1930's when sulfonamides were discovered in Germany (cf. Davis, 1967:1-22). The importance of science to medicine was reinforced by the advent of penicillin during World War II, and the general upsurge of scientific remedies stimulated the formation of new firms in Brazil. A few of the older companies that had previously specialized in popular medicines succeeded in moving into the rapidly expanding ethical drug market, but in general the change in the nature of the industry was accompanied by a turnover in the firms themselves. A sample of the larger pharmaceutical firms as of 1969 (see Table 3.5) shows that most of them were not formed in the early days of patent medicines, but rather in the thirties and forties when the industry started to become scientific. Several local firms were formed during World War II. A strong market had been built up for penicillin, especially as a cure for syphilis, but prices were still high enough to support small-scale production and the war disrupted the flow of imports. World War II was the "golden age" of the local pharmaceutical industry.

TABLE 3.5   Formation of Local Firms and Entry by Multinationals in the Pharmaceutical Industry

		Pre-WWI	1914-29	1930-39	1940-49	1950-59	1960-69	Totals
Entry of Foreign Firms	Number	1	5	5	9	13	6	39
	Cum. %	3%	15%	28%	51%	84%	100%	
Foundation of Locally Owned Companies	Number	3	5	6	9	2	0	25
	Cum. %	12%	32%	58%	90%	100%		

Source: Evans, 1971: Tables 3-I, 3-II.

As new products derived from research and development became increasingly central to profits in the fifties and sixties, the
situation for Brazilian firms became more difficult. A comparison
of the entry of foreign firms and the formation of local firms in the
fifties and sixties gives stark evidence of the growing problems of
the local bourgeoisie in the pharmaceutical industry. The formation of new local firms dropped off dramatically, while the formation of subsidiaries peaked. The fifties were as much a golden age
for the multinationals as the forties had been for the locals. Since
a goodly proportion of the foreign companies entered the Brazilian market by acquiring local firms, denationalization was the result.

Without the change in the technical nature of the industry,
pharmaceuticals never would have provided such a good case
study of denationalization. If it had been more like the chemical
industry, which from its beginnings relied on a high level of new
technology, there would not have been so many thriving Brazilian firms to be bought out. If technological innovation had not
come to be so important after World War II, the advantage of the
international firms relative to their Brazilian competitors would
not have been so overwhelming.

The contemporary industry is a blend of technology and commerce. The commercial skills basic to success in the days of patent medicines are still crucial. Because most discoveries of new
drugs take place in the center countries, the "marketing" aspects
of a company's operations are more critical in Brazil. According
to the most thorough piece of recent research on the cost structure of the Brazilian pharmaceutical industry, only about one-
third of total costs are "industrial costs" and of these, the major
part, more than 50% in the case of foreign-owned companies, is
accounted for by the cost of raw materials (CEME, 1973:62, 65).
Of the two-thirds of total costs that are "non-industrial," roughly
three-quarters represent commercial expenses.

The actual process of industrial production is the phase of the business least likely to present critical problems for the company. The critical phases are *before* the product is produced, at the stage of technological innovation, and *after* the product has been produced, at the stage of commercialization. While success in product innovation is usually associated with large size, operations that focus more on the commercial phase may be profitable even if pursued on a relatively small scale. The continued importance of the commercial side of pharmaceutical operations helps explain the ability of local firms to survive into the sixties.

The rhythm of foreign purchases slowed down in the early sixties, but there was no complementary upsurge in the locally owned segment of the industry. Hard economic times and the political uncertainties of the early sixties were much more devastating for locally owned firms than for foreign subsidiaries. According to some estimates, as many as seventy-five firms disappeared from the industry between 1960 and 1962, but all of the major foreign subsidiaries remained in operation. After the military coup of 1964, the rhythm of takeovers began to pick up again. In the period from 1966 to 1969 five of the largest remaining Brazilian pharmaceutical firms were bought out by international companies.

Studies at the end of the sixties (Evans, 1971; Bertero, 1972) looked at the pharmaceutical industry as a case in which denationalization was an accomplished fact. In 1072 Bertero wrote, "Actually 'denationalization,' in terms of non-Brazilian owned company's market share, was already completed around 1960." Hopes of reversing the trend toward foreign control seemed in retrospect completely quixotic. Yet at the same time it was clear that local capital would probably always have a place in the industry. I wrote at this time (Evans, 1971:107): "The prognostication that there will continue to be small, marginal locally owned firms appears as secure as the prediction of continued foreign predominance in the upper reaches of the industry . . . the industry will never be 100% foreign. There will always be a number of locally owned firms sufficiently vital and well-managed to survive, but still too small to be of interest to would-be foreign entrants." By the end of the sixties, the question was no longer whether foreign firms would dominate the industry; it concerned the terms on which local firms would be able to survive. There were still a number of local firms with good reputations and well-known product lines, operating at a profit, and not in any immediate danger of being eliminated by competition from the international companies. Bertero (1972:71), discussing a sample of the larger local firms, said, "Strange as it may seem these companies seemed relatively well situated financially. . . . These companies were successful within the Brazilian pharmaceutical industry and, to judge by their accounting reports were doing well."

Perhaps even more surprising than the ability of the remaining Brazilian firms of reasonable scale to survive financially, was the extent to which they continued to compete even in new products. While international companies had an indisputable advantage in technological terms, the efforts of the larger Brazilian firms were impressive. According to my assessment (Evans, 1972:200), "In their estimation of the sophistication of the Brazilian market, as well as their willingness to undertake local technological work, locally-owned firms often seemed less 'traditional' than foreign subsidiaries. A small locally-owned pharmaceutical firm was the first to make an 'antismoking' pill in Brazil . . . Likewise it was a locally-owned firm that was first to successfully introduce an artificial sweetener in the Brazilian market." Other assessments of the larger Brazilian subsidiaries during the period (cf. Bertero, 1972:209-211) generally agree that, while they were not engaged in basic research, Brazilian companies were technologically progressive within the limits of their resources.[1]

---

[1] See Chapter 4 below for a more detailed discussion of multinational and local attitudes toward product innovation.

In the early seventies the idea of dislodging foreign firms from their dominant position had all but disappeared. The rhythm of denationalization in the pharmaceutical industry continued apace. At least four firms that were among the largest of the locally owned companies that had survived and prospered during the hard times of the sixties were foreign-owned by the mid-seventies. In some sense it is surprising that the process of denationalization could continue. In 1969 it seemed as though all the major European and American firms were already installed in Brazil. Nonetheless, there were still new buyers looking for pharmaceutical firms to purchase in the 1970's. Newer North American firms—like International Nuclear Chemicals or Syntex—not so well established in the North American market, but growing rapidly, were anxious to get into Brazil. Likewise, foreign firms operating in the Brazilian market on the basis of manufacturing or marketing contracts with third parties (Smith Kline and French, for example) wanted to set up their own operations. Both sorts of firms provided buyers for Brazilian firms interested in selling out.

The decline in the number of new local entrants and the continued interest of foreign buyers are complementary trends that are made more severe by the reluctance of foreign companies to set up joint ventures. Not only is all the stock (or almost all the stock) retained by the international firm but the local entrepreneur is almost always removed from the management. The local owner may be retained during a period of transition, but almost invariably after a year or so he is replaced by someone who is more clearly an employee.

A third aspect of denationalization is slightly more subtle. It has to do with the transformation of the role played by the local firms that remain in the industry. While there are no Brazilian firms left among the top twenty firms or even the top thirty firms, there are a half dozen among the top fifty pharmaceutical firms even now. Some of them are growing more rapidly than their larger foreign competitors. But the firms that are left are different from those which led the locally owned segment of the industry in an earlier epoch. The first Brazilian firms to be bought out tended to be those with the most respected "scientific traditions." For the foreign purchaser, the better the reputation among the medical community the more useful the firm would be in securing quick acceptance of the buyer's own product line. Most purchasing international firms continued to sell the products developed by the firms they bought. The locally owned firms that were bought out in the fifties, and to some extent even those bought out in the next twenty years, were strong technologically as well as commercially.

The larger Brazilian firms that remain seem to be successful mainly because of their commercial and marketing organizations. They make no pretense of trying to develop "original" products and are perfectly willing to admit that their product lines consist of "similars," that is, products originally developed by other companies. Even among leading local firms of the sixties orientations have changed. Companies that talked of developing their own products in 1969 had given up these aspirations by 1974. Looking at the spectrum of locally owned firms in 1974 it was much more difficult to believe, as I did in 1969, that "when technological activities within Brazil are in question, the local entrepreneur appears more aggressive than subsidiary managements."

To say that local entrepreneurs have come to rely on their commercial ability rather than on technological competition is hardly to condemn them. They have discovered where their "comparative advantage" lies. The shift in the character of the largest local firms does, nonetheless, undermine the vestiges of the image of "the national industrial bourgeoisie as hero of development." The remaining local entrepreneurs are good businessmen. That they continue to survive in an industry where so much militates against their survival is proof of their skill. But to argue as Pacheco did in 1962 that the local entrepreneur represents the best hope for a *"tecnologia própria"* (indigenous technology) would seem absurd in the context of the current situation in the pharmaceutical industry. The disappearance of those few local firms which might some day have been able to claim a place in the industry on the basis of their own technological discoveries constitutes the most important effect of denationalization.

As far as the increase of the foreign share of the market is concerned, the progress of denationalization has been gradual. If accurate data for market shares were available for earlier periods we would probably be able to show that Bertero (1972:41) is correct when he claims that denationalization in the sense of the increasing market share controlled by foreign firms "began at the end of WWII and reached its peak in the 1950s." By the time denationalization became a public issue, the market share of local firms had already fallen to somewhere around 20%, and the takeovers of the sixties and early seventies seem to have had only a marginal negative effect on this figure. As Table 3.6 shows, however, the number of local firms among the top thirty-five dropped dramatically during the exact period when denationalization was an issue.

The effect of denationalization is not to eliminate local participation in the market but to transform that participation. Local capital has gradually become relegated to relatively small firms that survive by their commercial acumen rather than by industrial or technological innovation. Local capital no longer threatens, even vaguely, the most important source of the multinationals' profits (their monopoly on technological innovation), and the role of local capital becomes ever more complementary to the role of foreign capital.

Just as the local capital that stayed in the pharmaceutical industry tended to gravitate toward a role that differentiated it from foreign capital, the local entrepreneurs that left the industry

TABLE 3.6   Participation of Local Firms in the Brazilian
Pharmaceutical Industry, 1957-1974

	1957	1961	1965	1969	1974
Estimated Percentage of Total Sales	20%[1]	19%[2]	18%[2]	17%[3]	17%[4]
Number of Local Firms among the Top 35 Firms (according to sales)	11[5]	6[6]	4	3	1

[1] Based on data from Taques Bittencourt, 1961, but adding 1.6% of the market to his estimate to represent the share of small local firms, since his data do not go beyond the top 40 firms.

[2] These percentages are simply linear interpolations between Taques Bittencourt's estimate for 1957 and Bertero's for 1969.

[3] Bertero (1972:63) based on data from ABIF (Associação Brasileira da Indústria Farmacêutica).

[4] Market research estimates obtained from confidential sources.

[5] From Taques Bittencourt, 1961.

[6] From 1961 onwards the data is based on confidential market research sources.

Source: Evans, 1976b.

tended to reinforce the pattern of differentiation. Though systematic evidence is lacking, impressionistic data suggest that local entrepreneurs who remained in manufacturing moved into exactly the sort of industries whose smaller scale, lesser degree of concentration, and lesser capital intensiveness make them strongholds for local capital in general. One family, for example, decided to sell its pharmaceutical firm in order to concentrate its holdings in printing and publishing. Another entrepreneur took the generous price he received for his pharmaceutical company and entered the construction materials industry. Still a third family decided to use the commercial and industrial expertise it had gained in the pharmaceutical industry to produce and sell a line of specialty foods that had been previously a sideline to the pharmaceutical business.

In other cases denationalization means that local capital shifts from an entrepreneurial to a rentier role. If the owners of the local pharmaceutical firm are older and do not already own other promising industrial ventures, they are likely simply to invest their capital in other people's companies. Here again, they remove themselves from competition with the multinationals and play a complementary role, perhaps even helping to provide a little additional capital for the futher expansion of multinational enterprises within Brazil.

In the case of the pharmaceutical industry, denationalization and differentiation take on a different image from the one that emerges from an examination of the aggregate data. In pharmaceuticals, differentiation is based on increasing reliance on commercial strategies among local firms. It has allowed some local firms to remain in this "modern" and foreign-dominated industry, but it has meant that they are destined to play a marginal role. A symbiosis has evolved, but it is no more encouraging for local capital than the kind of differentiation that appears on the aggregate level. Still, the pharmaceutical industry is atypical. It is perhaps the only industry in which such an efflorescence of local enterprise has been followed by such thoroughgoing foreign domination. The textile industry is more typical and also offers the promise of answering the question, What is the attraction of a "traditional" industry for foreign capital?

Competition and Collaboration: The Case of Textiles

Denationalization is a reasonable label to apply to the evolution of pharmaceuticals; the textile industry is more difficult to characterize. Aggregate estimates (Table 3.2) show a continued predominance of local capital with significant foreign participation. It might be argued that since the industry was created by local capital, the amount of foreign participation that exists today represents denationalization over the long run. The label "denationalization," however, obscures the complex nature of the interaction between foreign and local capital in textiles.

The first step toward understanding the position of foreign and local capital in the contemporary industry is to get some picture of what has happened to the textile market since the beginning of the century, when local production began to supplant imports. For textiles, the "golden age" was from the turn of the century to the mid-twenties (Stein, 1957:98). By 1915, domestic production already accounted for 95% of internal consumption, but the industry continued to grow at an annual rate of 5% until 1923. It was during this "golden age" that most of today's leading local firms were established. After a period of decline in the late twenties, production rose gradually during the thirties. World War II was a boon to the textile industry just as it was to local capital in the pharmaceutical industry. "In 1946 the Brazilian textile industry was one of the largest in the world, supplying all domestic needs and exporting to various countries" (Bergsman, 1970:135).

By the end of the fifties, it was clear that the economic effects of World War II had been an aberration rather than a portent of the future. Production of cotton textiles in the late fifties averaged only about 35% more than average production in the thirties. In other words, production had increased more slowly than population growth. In 1959, the peak production of 1943 had still not been surpassed (Versiani, 1972:28). From the mid-fifties until 1970 the consumption of natural fibers was maintained at the same per capita levels (IPEA, 1973:25). Projections to 1980 showed prospects of a further growth of only 25% in the demand for natural fibers (IPEA, 1974:45). For firms engaged in the spinning and weaving of cotton, which is the traditional core of the industry, the market has been more or less stagnant ever since the end of World War II. The stagnation of the market is primarily responsible for the steadily declining share of textiles in total value of manufacturing.

The steady state of the market was reflected in plants and equipment. In the early sixties ECLA found about a third of the spindles and half the looms in the cotton sector too obsolete to be worth reconditioning. Setting a standard of productivity that represented about one-third of the production per man-hour of mills in the United States and that was considered appropriate for the "first stage of modernization of the industry," ECLA considered only 4.3% of the mills capable of meeting the standard. They attributed this inefficiency to obsolescent machinery and the poor quality of materials, but also to "deficient internal organization (administrative and technical)" (ECLA, 1963:42, 60, 2). Stanley Stein, author of the most extensive historical analysis of the industry also emphasized the "conservatism of the mill owners, their unwillingness to alter organization and administration" (1955:447). Reinforcing these patterns was the fact that the industry was protected by extremely high tariffs against imported textiles, about 280% in 1966, according to Bergsman (1970:137).

Antiquated, traditional, and inefficient may not have been an inaccurate way of characterizing a large number of the more than 4,000 textile plants that made up the industry as a whole in the mid-sixties. There were, however, tremendous differences between firms. While some cotton spinning mills had productivities of only 500 grams/man-hour and 80% of them did not surpass 2,500 grams/man-hour, there were mills with productivity levels of over 6,000 grams/man-hour (ECLA, 1963:60). If the inefficient mills were able to stay in business, then the most efficient mills should have enjoyed highly profitable operations.

An aggressive, efficient firm did not have to be limited by the growth rates of the domestic market. Exports were a real possibility, especially after the government began to develop export incentives. Locally grown cotton provided inputs at world market prices or better. Low cost labor, if combined with modern productive equipment, put Brazilian firms in a good competitive position. One Japanese subsidiary told me that they had been forced to compete with their own parent company to make a sale in Nigeria, but they had won. The possibilities are clear from the recent spectacular growth rates of exports, especially finished

products. Total exports of textile manufactures went from a value
of less than $10 million per year in the mid-sixties to $40 million
in 1970 to $325 million in 1973, becoming a substantial element
in Brazilian trade. Most impressive is the growth in the exports of
clothing which rose in value from about a third of a million dollars
in the mid-sixties to almost $100 million dollars by 1973 (Santista,
1973:8; IBGE, 1972:271).

Exports of cotton fabrics are not the only rapidly growing area
in the textile industry. Synthetic fibers, which cannot be exported because local raw materials costs are too high, have a
more than compensating advantage in the form of a steadily increasing share of the domestic market. Between 1960 and 1972,
production of nylon rose by 500% (IPEA, 1974:104). Production
of polyester rose from nothing in 1960 to match the output of
nylon by 1972. Cotton, which represented over 80% of Brazil's
fiber consumption in 1960, came to represent less than half by
1972. Synthetic fibers, which represented only about 1% of fiber
consumption in 1960, are taking an ever growing share of the
market. Projections of the synthetic fiber market show it more
than tripling between 1972 and 1980 until it comes to account for
more than one-fourth of fiber consumption (IPEA, 1973:31;
IPEA, 1974:45; ECLA, 1963:18). Thus, for companies in synthetic fibers, the domestic market is anything but stagnant.

Stagnation, like denationalization, is a misleading generaliza-
tion when applied to the textile industry. For some firms it does
not apply at all, either because they are engaged in a branch of
the industry that is growing rapidly, like the export of apparel or
the production of synthetic fibers, or because they are operating
with a plant much more efficient than those which characterize
the industry as a whole and are thus in a position to make good
profits and increase their individual shares of the market.
Analysis of the evolution of the industry as a whole does not il-
luminate the relation between national and international capital.
To understand how national and international capital fit together,

it is necessary to examine the leading firms in the industry, to see who owns them, what they do, and how they relate to each other. The distribution of foundation dates for a sample of the leading textile firms in 1973 (see Table 3.7) shows both local pioneers and

TABLE 3.7   Foundation and Entry Dates for Large Local and Foreign Textile Firms

	Pre-WWI	1914-29	1930-45	1946-64	Post-1964	Totals
Local	9 (45%)	4 (20%)	4 (20%)	2 (10%)	1 (5%)	20 (100%)
Joint Ventures				1 (33%)	2 (67%)	3 (100%)
Foreign	1 (12%)	3 (38%)	0	4 (50%)	0	8 (100%)

Source: Visão, 1974:265.

foreign newcomers among the top firms. About a third of the top textile firms are, in fact, local enterprises founded during the earlier phase of industrialization. In some cases they are even under the same management. While foreign entries form a larger part of the total entries after World War II, they never swamp local entries as they do in pharmaceuticals (Table 3.4) or manufacturing as a whole (Table 3.1). In the "grupos multibilionários" data (Table 3.1), groups formed after 1930 are over 80% foreign-owned. In the case of pharmaceuticals the turning point occurs around 1950, but the pattern of local formations being outnumbered by foreign ones is even more thorough. In textiles, it has not happened. If there is a trend, it is toward an increasing predominance of joint ventures.

New foreign entries after the Second World War are about half joint ventures. In contrast to their disappearance in pharmaceuticals, joint ventures appear to have become more popular among multinationals interested in breaking into the textile industry. Since multinationals do not give up control unless they get something in return, the growing popularity of joint ventures suggests that the continued presence of local companies is not just a historical holdover, but reflects persistent structural characteristics of the industry that favor local firms.

The data in Table 3.4 reinforce this view. Viewed in the aggregate, textiles are not capital intensive, nor concentrated, nor intensive in their use of technology, nor characterized by large-scale establishments. Viewed overall, the industry should be dominated by local firms. The degree to which individual local firms have an advantage depends, however, on the specific characteristics of the different sub-areas of the industry. As in the case of pharmaceuticals, the principal advantage of local firms is skill in commercial operations.

In some areas, spinning and weaving for example, commercial skill is not only essential but easier to apply on a small scale. Companies that produce cloth do not sell their product primarily to individual consumers; consequently the kind of mass advertising that is the key to commercial success in an industry like tobacco is not so important here. Spinning and weaving companies do sell their cloth to thousands of small retailers and apparel manufacturers. The network of customers must be continually expanded, especially since some old customers are likely to go out of business every year. Retailers and apparel manufacturers need credit, yet extending credit to customers who may go bankrupt is risky. Commercial success means having an extremely sensitive feel for which customers should continue to get credit and which are too shaky. A local firm with a carefully developed commercial network and a longstanding, intimate knowledge of its customers has a clear advantage over a foreign newcomer that is not so deeply embedded in the local market.

In the pharmaceutical industry, the commercial advantage of local firms appeared to be wiped out by the technological advantage of foreign firms. In textiles, technology is less important overall. It changes less rapidly because products change less rapidly. There are, of course, new weaves, new fabrics, and new fibers, but the connection between new products and profits is not so compelling as it is in pharmaceuticals. The nature of technological change in textiles is also significant. When technology is embodied in products, as in pharmaceuticals, then maintaining exclusive control over it is essential to appropriating the returns. Multinationals will keep their product innovations to themselves. If, on the other hand, technology is more a process technology, embodied in new capital goods, equipment manufacturers are anxious to sell it to as many firms as they can. It is in their interest to spread the new "product" rather than restrict its spread. In textiles, new technology is embodied in new machines (cf. Figuereido, 1972:288). Brazilian companies can, and do, order the latest Swiss looms, as long as they can find the money to pay for them and the markets to justify their purchase. Even if local firms choose to use less advanced technology than multinationals, they may well be able to lower their costs in other ways. The U.S. Tariff Commission reported, for example, that while multinationals in Brazil had average labor costs of about 29¢ per sales dollar, the general average for textile firms was only 13¢ per sales dollar, and this despite the fact that output per worker is much higher in multinationals (U.S. Tariff Commission, 1973:803, 765).

It is easy to see that the competitive advantage of a multinational is neither overwhelming nor assured, a situation exemplified by the lack of U.S. subsidiaries in the Brazilian textile industry. Of the top twenty American textile manufacturers only one, United Merchants and Manufacturing, has a subsidiary of any significance in Brazil. Once local firms and a few foreign ones, mainly European, became established, there was no superior leverage equivalent to the new drugs in the pharmaceutical industry that would enable multinationals easily to carve out new positions.

The commercial and technological nature of the textile industry makes the survival of local firms possible, but it does not make survival easy. Local firms must still compete with each other and with the multinationals for a market that, except in the area of exports and synthetic fibers, is not expanding very rapidly. The very features that make local survival possible also make it an unconcentrated industrial sector and therefore one highly subject to competitive pressures. According to the traditional lore of the industry, textiles fluctuate in an exaggerated way relative to the general business cycle. They are the first to enter a crisis and the last to get out of one, it is said.

Every time there is a contraction in the demand for textiles, more small local firms close their doors. Nor are problems of survival limited to small local firms. A quick look at the recent histories of companies that were ranked as the top five locally owned textile firms in terms of profits in 1949 is instructive.[2] They were, in order, América Fabril, Progresso Industrial-Bangú, Nova América, Brasital, and Deodoro Industrial. Deodoro Industrial was absorbed by América Fabril in 1968 (Banas, 1969:218). América Fabril entered on hard times and is no longer among the top 50 textile companies (*Visão*, 1974:265). Brasital is now controlled by Italian capital (*Visão*, 1974:263). Progresso Industrial-Bangú, went through an extremely difficult period in the early seventies and survived only with the help of financing from the federal government and a thorough reorganization undertaken in response to government pressures. Nova América is also reputed to have had financial difficulties and even rumored to have considered selling part of its equity to an American firm. Other large local firms have found survival equally difficult. Corcovado, ranked eighth on the 1949 list of local firms, has disappeared entirely. And, most recently, at the beginning of 1975 the Companhia Nacional de Tecidos in São Paulo announced that it was faced with $100 million in debts and would need emergency financial help in order to continue.

Alongside the local firms that have been driven into marginal positions or bankruptcy can be set other local firms that are Brazilian-owned, family-controlled, and highly successful. One

[2] This list is unpublished and was supplied to me by Professor Maurício Vinhas de Queiroz.

good example is Indústria Têxtil Hering. Founded in 1880 and still controlled by the Hering family (Banas, 1969:245; Visão, 1974:293), this is a vertically integrated company which does spinning and knitting and produces knitted apparel under its own nationally known brand name. Hering undershorts are as well known in Brazil as Jockey shorts are in the United States. Hering probably controls over 50% of the market in some lines of knit goods. Being a large-scale integrated producer gives them a clear cost advantage in this field where most producers are tiny. Technology is not a problem, since they are large enough to attract the interest of the foreign machinery salesmen. They have a well developed network of sales representatives. Overall, it is more likely that Indústria Hering will begin selling in other countries than that a multinational will be able to take their Brazilian market away from them.

Another large and successful company is Uniao Manufactora de Tecidos. Founded in the thirties, it was built around the manufacture and sale of jute bags to farmers and exporters (Banas, 1968:M-30). Again the construction of a strong network of sales agents has been crucial to success and again access to new technology has been no problem. In fact, União Manufactora has just added polypropylene bags to its line, based on technology acquired in Germany. While it is too specialized ever to become one of the top five or ten textile companies, it has a commanding position in the jute market and has had no difficulty maintaining its position among the top thirty companies.

Two other firms that have moved up into the top twenty in the last few years are Indústrias Paramount and Indústrias Reunidas Vicunha. Vicunha was formed after the Steinbruch family in 1967 purchased Lanificação Varam, a firm that had been in existence since 1896. Not only is Vicunha among the top twenty firms, but so is Textil Elizabeth which is also controlled by the Steinbruchs. These two, together with Fiação and Tecelagem Campo Belo, make the Steinbruchs one of the rising powers in the industry.

Their empire appears conventional in its strategy of expansion. Indústrias Paramount, on the other hand, has followed a rather interesting and unorthodox path of expansion. Founded before the turn of the century by Nasib Mattar, an immigrant from Lebanon, and still run by his sons, Indústrias Paramount decided in the late sixties that the best way to expand was through the export market and that the best product to export would be wool. Trips abroad led to the conclusion that Eastern Europe provided the best market. It was apparently difficult to convince Europeans that South America was a place from which to buy wool yarn, but the tactic succeeded and the firm is now in command of a rapidly growing export business. In the domestic market Paramount's focus has been on synthetics. Thus, it has stepped into the most dynamic sectors of the textile industry and has moved from being one of the top fifty firms in the late sixties to being one of the top twenty currently.

The success of local firms should not obscure the importance of foreign capital in the industry. The synthetic fibers market is thoroughly dominated by one foreign company, Rhodia. In a completely different branch of the industry, cotton sewing thread, another international firm, Coats Patons, maintains an equally impressive preeminence. Coats Patons has been manufacturing in Brazil since 1907; a recent annual report gives an indication of just how successful they are. The rate of profit relative to both sales and assets was about four times higher in South America than in the United Kingdom in 1973 (Coats Patons, 1973:7). The most interesting thing about their Brazilian operation is not, however, its high rate of profit but that it is competing successfully in an area with no obvious advantages for a multinational. Its sales are primarily cotton thread, sold retail. There is no arcane technology involved, and a tightly organized sales network is essential to success. Coats Patons is succeeding in precisely a line where local capital might be expected to have an advantage, and in doing so provides a good illustration of the fact that there are no safe preserves in textiles for local capital.

The ability of foreign firms to move into the "local" areas of the industry is shown even more dramatically by the successes of non-European, non-North American multinationals. The classic case here is the Argentine grain giant Bunge & Born. Having gone into textiles in order to provide sacking for their flour, Bunge & Born is now probably the biggest producer of cotton textiles in Brazil. Not only is their Tecidos Tatuapé one of the top five textile companies but S.A. Moinho Santista does a sizeable textile business in addition to its wheat business. When these two companies are added to Bunge & Born's new subsidiaries in the northeast, the result is a 100 million dollar textile business (Santista, 1974). One indication of the rate at which their growth is outpacing the growth of the industry as a whole is the recently inaugurated "Project Alpha," which at a cost of $54 million will increase Tecidos Tatuapé's output of cotton and blend cloth by 50%.

Recent Japanese entries also play a significant role. Toyobo do Brasil, for example, is already a major producer of cotton and blended cotton/polyester fabrics. Having entered Brazil in 1955 when it bought out a Brazilian firm to which it had been supplying technical assistance, Toyobo's expansion has been most impressive. From 1971 to 1974, the financial volume of sales increased fivefold and capacity in both spinning and weaving more than doubled. Both Toyobo, whose parent is one of Japan's largest textile producers (Toyobo, 1974), and Kanebo, which also entered Brazil in the fifties, are now among the top forty textile producers.

The growth of new foreign entries and the expansion of long-established foreign firms must come at the expense of other producers in a market that is not expanding rapidly overall. The most likely victims are smaller local firms, but no local firm, even a large one, can consider the textile industry a secure refuge from foreign competition. All local firms must consider their future problematic. Established multinationals are in a more secure position, but there are also, of course, a number of giant European,

American, and Japanese textile firms that are not yet established in the Brazilian market. For these firms, breaking into the market means engaging in an expansive and uncertain struggle with firms already established, a risky enterprise.

For multinationals asking "How can I get in?" and local capital asking "How can I survive?" the answer seems to be the same—a joint venture. Three major recent joint ventures provide interesting examples of the collaboration of local and foreign capital. All of them enabled local capital to get into synthetic fibers, an area in which the technological advantages of the multinational are greater. At the same time they gave foreign companies that are basically chemical companies a chance to take advantage of the long experience of local groups in the Brazilian market.

The first of these joint ventures was Companhia Brasileira de Sintéticos, which brought together Hoechst, one of the biggest German chemical firms, and the Klabin group, one of the strongest Brazilian groups though not one with great experience in textiles. Brasileira de Sintéticos is not producing on a scale comparable to Rhone Poulenc's Brazilian subsidiary, Rhodia, but it is still óne of a half dozen major producers of nylon and polyester fibers. Two other companies, which were scheduled in 1976 to be second and third after Rhodia in the production of polyester, are Polinor and Safron-Teijin, both associations between local capital and Japanese chemical companies. In the case of Safron-Teijin the venture gave the Safra group, which had previously been active only in the commercial side of the textile industry, a chance to get into the industrial side. Polinor brought together the textile experience of the Matarazzo group and the technology of the Japanese chemical firm Toray.

The associations in synthetic fibers are important because they represent the predominant strategy for recent foreign entries. Other more partial associations are also indicative of the tendency toward collaboration. Rhodia has developed close relations with a number of its customers. In one case, Filene, Rhodia ended up with a share of the equity after having supplied the company with nylon for fifteen years. In other cases the association has come in connection with developing export markets. Progresso Industrial provides a good example. The company's recent strategy of revitalization has included the formation of a joint venture with a Dutch apparel manufacturer and also an informal marketing arrangement with a Japanese trading company. Both of these have helped it to boost its export sales. Indústrias Hering has also recently entered into an association, with a small Italian company specializing in knitwear, and is exporting some of the products of this joint venture back to Italy.

There is little evidence that the continued survival of local capital in the textile industry is likely to produce a "national" bourgeoisie in the sense of a group of entrepreneurs isolated from and hostile to international capital. Joint ventures seem to be the wave of the future in the production of synthetic fibers. If the supportive relations that Rhodia has developed with its customers become typical of the new producers of synthetic fibers and their customers, the result will be more links between local and foreign capital. Further expansion into export markets is also likely to result in increasing collaboration between local and international capital.

The textile industry is not so much a scene of struggle between national and international capital as an arena in which big local firms are increasingly integrated with international capital, while small local firms are increasingly pushed into marginal positions. Viewed in this way, the textile industry reveals an alternative to the denationalization model illustrated by the pharmaceutical industry, an alternative that may well apply to a number of other industries.

The Situation of Elite Local Capital Groups

In the pharmaceutical industry, local capital has been moved out of a central position into a marginal role based mainly on commercial prowess. In textiles, a difficult struggle for smaller firms and the disappearance of some of the older leading local firms is counterbalanced by the expansion of certain local firms and successful collaboration between some large local groups and the multinationals. Textiles, like pharmaceuticals, can be seen as part of a pattern of increasing domination by international capital, but the textile example suggests that the rise of international capital does not necessarily mean the elimination of leading roles for locally owned industrial corporations.

In a few industries, the position of large local corporations is even stronger. Cement is one of the best examples. While it is not technologically sophisticated, the cement industry is also not "traditional" or stagnant. Its fortunes are tied to the growth of the construction industry, and cement consumption in Brazil almost doubled during the sixties. This area is clearly dominated by local companies. It is a relatively concentrated industry, and most of the companies are small and locally owned; even among the largest companies, local capital accounts for about two-thirds of total sales (*Visão*, 1974:137-141). The strength of local capital becomes most apparent when the ownership of the largest local companies is examined in detail.

The most important single local capital group in the industry is the Ermírio de Moraes group (Votorantim). Votorantim owns, in addition to its interests in steel, aluminum, metal fabrication, chemicals, and heavy machinery, six of the largest cement companies, stretching from Santa Catarina in the south to Ceara in the north. Thus, firms like Companhia de Cimento Portland Poty or Companhia de Cimento Portland Rio Branco are not competing simply as cement producers but as members of one of the largest and most diversified industrial conglomerates in Brazil. The Gastão Vidigal, Matarazzo, and Severino Pereira da Silva groups are also examples of diversified industrial groups that own local cement companies.

In addition to participation in the industry by the "grupos multibilionários" there are local capitalists who own several different cement companies. Seven of the largest companies are owned by

João Pereira dos Santos. They might also be considered parts of a conglomerate empire, since Pereira dos Santos has holdings in sugar and textiles as well as in cement. Finally, there is the Itaú group, which owns five cement companies, one of which is the largest in the industry. Itaú, Pereira dos Santos, and the three "grupos multibilionários" (Votorantim, Matarazzo, and Gastão Vidigal) own among them the majority of the top forty-five companies in the cement industry.

The foreign participants in the cement industry are a varied group. They come from several countries—Italy, Switzerland, France, the United States, Britain, and Portugal—and none of them owns more than two companies. With the exception of ITT and Union Carbide (and their holdings are small), they are not diversified industrial giants. They are either companies with a primary focus on cement like the Lone Star Cement Company or they are banks. No single foreign participant appears to have as strong a position in the industry as the biggest local producers.

Joint ventures are not characteristic of the cement industry, but even here, where local companies would seem least in need of foreign partners, there are two interesting examples of joint ventures. Both are associated with the Itaú group. Itaú's two largest companies have joined with a Swiss firm, Cementia: in the largest, Cementia is its only partner; in the second, Itaú and Cementia are joined by a British company, Associated Portland Cement, and a Swiss bank. Itaú also has a smaller joint venture with Gastão Vidigal in cement and a joint venture with BASF in fertilizers. Thus, while the older groups involved in cement, like Votorantim and Severino Pereira da Silva, have retained total control over their companies, Itaú (probably the most rapidly growing power in the cement industry) has adopted the strategy of trying to integrate itself with foreign capital. Competition is the primary relation between local and foreign capital in this stronghold of the national bourgeoisie, but Itaú represents a significant example of collaboration.

Variations on the themes of competition and collaboration

could be multiplied by examining other individual industries. But in elucidating the relationships between the "national bourgeoisie" and the multinationals, competition or collaboration within industries is only part of the picture. The relationships among the largest agglomerations of capital must be examined across industries as well. It is time to return to the "grupos econômicos."

Despite a decade of substantial changes in the Brazilian economy, the "grupos multibilionários" analyzed by Queiroz and his associates in 1962 still own the majority of Brazil's largest private companies. Analysis of the current position of these national and foreign groups, together with the other firms that have joined them among Brazil's top companies yields the best synopsis of current relations between the national bourgeoisie and international capital.

Table 3.8 provides a quick summary of what has happened to the fifty-five grupos multibilionários. The majority of the foreign groups have representatives among the top hundred firms and the majority of local groups do not. Among the top fifty firms the proportion of foreign groups represented is twice as large. These findings might be considered simply an artifact of the tendency for foreign groups to concentrate their assets in a smaller number

TABLE 3.8   Representation of 1962 "Grupos Multibilionários" among the Top 100 Firms of 1973 (according to *Visão* listing)

Representation in Top 100*	"Grupos Multibilionários"**	
	Local	Foreign
Top 50	4 (16%)	11 (37%)
Next 50	7 (28%)	8 (27%)
Total Representation	11 (44%)	19 (63%)
Nonrepresented Groups	14 (56%)	11 (37%)

* A group is defined as being "represented" among the top 50 or next 50 if it controls at least one firm in one of these categories according to the *Visão* listing.
** See note with Table 3.1 regarding the local/foreign classification.
Source: Visão, 1974:36-45.

of firms than local groups (see Queiroz, 1965:63). In fact, however, even if groups were compared on the basis of combined assets rather than as simply the largest firms, the proportion of local groups whose combined industrial assets were equal to those of the hundredth-largest firm on the *Visão* list would still be significantly smaller than the proportion of foreign groups.

It is instructive to examine the grupos that have "dropped out." In the case of the foreign groups, about half are not represented because they have changed ownership. The two utilities companies (AMFORP and Light) were bought by the state. Two of the industrial groups (Willys and Philco) were bought out by a third multinational, Ford. In one instance, a foreign group in a traditional industry (Swift/Armour) was bought out by the fastest rising of the local groups, Antunes, in combination with the remnant of the Light group, Brascan. Four of the five remaining unrepresented foreign groups remain under the same ownership without having individual firms among the top hundred, but are still important industrial powers. Two of them (Anderson Clayton and Unilever) just missed the top hundred, being ranked 102nd and 111th respectively. Two others (Ciba/Geigy and Dupont/Solvay/ICI) have combined assets that would rank them among the top hundred even though they do not have individual representatives there. Only Fiat Lux, the match company that was one of the first foreign groups to enter manufacturing, seems to have been marginalized by the evolution of Brazilian industrial development; it is currently ranked 274th by *Visão*. The last unrepresented foreign group (IBEC) was primarily involved in financial activities to begin with and remains so. IBEC's owners, the Rockefellers, have become, if anything, more powerful with the acquisition of Banco Lar Brasileiro, one of the largest commercial banks in Brazil.

The unrepresented local groups present a different picture. A number of them seem to have been prejudiced in their development because of their original commitment to "traditional" industries. Three of these are groups founded in the early burst of the textile industry—Mourão Guimarães, Severino Pereira da Silva, and Bezerra de Melo. Severino Pereira da Silva's Companhia Nacional de Estamparia is still one of the largest textile firms but does not rank among the top hundred or even among the top two hundred corporations. The Guimarães family's major textile company is not even among the top fifty textile companies and, despite the family's successful mineral operations, its industrial assets do not place it among the top hundred corporations. Bezerra de Melo's textile firms have also fallen from the top ranks. Diversification into the hotel business has been successful but not quite successful enough to produce a collection of assets that would rank the group among the top hundred corporations. A similar case is the Ometto/Dedini group whose enterprises were heavily involved in sugar and sugar machinery. Even though their Fazenda São Martinho is one of Brazil's largest agricultural companies and the Dedini steel company is one of the top twenty in the steel industry, the group's combined assets still do not put it among the top hundred corporations.

Other local groups that started out in modern industries have not succeeded in reaching the highest ranks. The metallurgy firm that heads the Cicillo Matarazzo group, for example, is among Brazil's largest but is not among the top hundred firms or even the top two hundred. The Pignatari group, which had interests in copper and metallurgy, has been unable to hold its own. The Novo Mundo group tried to get into the automobile industry on the basis of a joint venture with Auto/Union and ended up selling out to Volkswagen. The Simonsen/COMAL group tried to expand beyond commercial and financial activities by taking over Pan American's Brazilian subsidiary but was forced to give up the company as a result of charges of incompetent management and, eventually, state intervention (see Queiroz, 1972:203). The Capuava group and the Moreira Salles group lost control of their leading industrial firms (Refinaria União and Petroquímica

União)—also to the state. The Lundgren group remains one of the strongest commercial powers in the country but has no manufacturing company in the top two hundred firms.

Industrial activities have been hazardous for local capital. The difficulties of competing with foreign giants has led some groups to concentrate their activities in the financial sector. The Simonsen group, for example, still controls one of the top twenty commercial banks, as does the Moreira Salles group. Novo Mundo remains a strong financial group, despite its failure to break into the automobile industry. In addition, there are local groups like Faria and Quartim Barbosa that concentrated their activities in the financial realm from the beginning and continue to own banks which rank among the top ten. There are also groups like Gastão Vidigal which have retained industrial preeminence and have representatives among the top hundred firms but are, at the same time, powerful in the financial realm.

Small capitalists in the pharmaceutical industry were pushed in the direction of commercial emphasis or a rentier role. The pressures on large local groups run in the same directions. There is, of course, a difference between being a small rentier capitalist and owning a major commercial bank. The predominance of local capital in the financial sector might even be thought to give them an advantage over the multinationals. If multinationals were dependent on capital sources within Brazil, they would find only one foreign bank (First National City) among the top ten commercial banks, and that one ranked tenth (*Visão*, 1974:547). The importance of international borrowing for major industrial projects, however, complicates the picture and gives local bankers less leverage than they would otherwise have.

The problems confronting local "grupos multibilionários" trying to retain positions among the top industrial firms would not, in themselves, indicate a declining role for the national bourgeoisie within the industrial sector. It might be that they were replaced by other newer agglomerations of local capital, more dynamic and better able to compete with the multinationals. To some extent this is true. As Table 3.9 shows, there are almost as many local newcomers on the *Visão* list of the top hundred firms as there are local firms attached to the old "grupos mul-tibilionários." There are, in fact, more local newcomers than foreign newcomers. Overall, foreign firms retain a slim majority of private firms among the top hundred on the *Visão* list only because of the persistence of so many representatives of the old "grupos."

A closer look at the local newcomers suggests that the image of rising new local industrial firms must be treated with some skepticism. Nine of the twelve newcomers are construction companies. Of the other three, one is a sugar cooperative (Copersucar), one is a docking company (Estaleiro Mauá), and only one is primarily engaged in manufacturing (Companhia Suzano de Papel). The major implication of the *Visão* listing is not that there is an upsurge of local industrial corporations but, rather, an upsurge of a new sector—construction—in which local capital appears to have the upper hand.

One of the problems with using the *Visão* list to estimate the

TABLE 3.9   Affiliations of Private Firms[1] among the Top 100 Firms[2] (according to *Visão* listing)

| Represen-tation in Top 100 | Affiliations of Private Firms[3] | | | | | | |
| | Local | | | Foreign | | | |
	"Grupos"	Newcomers	Total	"Grupos"	Newcomers	Total	Total
Top 50	5 (28%)	2 (11%)	7 (39%)	11 (61%)	0 (0%)	11 (61%)	18 (100%)
Next 50	8 (23%)	10 (29%)	18 (51%)	11 (31%)	6 (17%)	17 (49%)	35 (100%)
Total	13 (23%)	12 (22%)	25 (47%)	22 (42%)	6 (11%)	28 (53%)	53 (100%)

[1] Firm rather than "economic group" is the unit, in contrast to Table 3.8; each firm is counted in this table even if a group is represented by more than one firm in a given category.

[2] About half the firms among the *Visão* top 100, and two-thirds of the firms among the top 50, are state-owned; these have not been included unless the state is a minority partner.

[3] Where firms are joint ventures, they have been assigned according to the majority of the equity.

Source: *Visão*, 1974:36-45.

current balance between local and foreign capital is that it is a ranking based solely on assets. An alternative list, which takes profits as well as assets into account, is provided by *Conjuntura Econômica*. Using this ranking, which is shown in Table 3.10, the number of foreign newcomers increases substantially. The relative lack of manufacturing firms among the local newcomers is as evident on the *Conjuntura* list as it was on the *Visão*. Five of the eleven local newcomers are construction companies; two of the others are engaged in retail commerce, a third is in publishing, and one is in shipping. Once again, Companhia Suzano de Papel is the largest manufacturing firm among the local newcomers, joined this time by one other manufacturing firm (Termomecânica).

Whether one starts from the original "grupos multibilionários" and looks at their current representation or starts from current rankings makes little difference. The emerging conclusions are similar, and consistent with both the earlier aggregate statistical analysis and the case studies of individual industries. Local firms, even relatively large and powerful local firms, have difficulty maintaining their positions within the modern manufacturing sector, but this does not mean that the "national industrial bourgeoisie" is in the process of being eliminated. Local capital remains strong in finance and in commercial activities and has found, in the construction industry, a new area for expansion.

TABLE 3.10   Affiliations of Private Firms* among the Top 100 Firms (according to *Conjuntura Econômica* listing)

Represen-	Affiliations of Private Firms[3]						
tation in	Local			Foreign			
Top 100	"Grupos"	Newcomers	Total	"Grupos"	Newcomers	Total	Total
Top 50	6 (24%)	1 (4%)	7 (28%)	15 (60%)	3 (12%)	18 (72%)	25 (100%)
Next 50	9 (23%)	10 (26%)	19 (49%)	8 (21%)	12 (31%)	20 (52%)	39 (100%)
Total	15 (23%)	11 (17%)	26 (41%)	23 (36%)	15 (23%)	38 (59%)	64 (100%)

* All notes to Table 3.9 apply to Table 3.10.
Source: Conjuntura Econômica, 1974:76-110.

The core of private manufacturing is increasingly foreign, but local capital retains an ample area of operation. This will become even clearer with the examination of a last set of "grupos."

The "drop outs" and the "newcomers" both help define the situation of local capital. But the most important representatives of local capital are the "stayers." There are nine locally controlled "grupos" that were among the "grupos multibilionários" in 1962 and still have representatives on both the *Visão* and *Conjuntura* lists for 1974. Three of them are firms in traditional industries for which the commercial aspects of their operations are the most important: the two beer companies (Antartica and Brahma) and Mesbla, the department store. The other six are more interesting. Five of them are diversified industrial groups whose interests are in manufacturing: Villares, Votorantim, Klabin, Matarazzo, and Gastão Vidigal. The sixth—Antunes—is primarily engaged in mineral extraction but is also involved in a variety of industrial ventures. To these six should be added the Monteiro Aranha group. Its majority-held industrial companies are not on the lists,[3] but it participates in the ownership of two companies that appear on both lists, one of which (Volkswagen) is the largest company on both lists.

If Brazil has a national industrial bourgeoisie, then these seven groups are its central core. What is most interesting about them are the varying degrees to which they have allied themselves with international capital. Two of the groups—Villares and Votorantim—have kept their partnerships with the multinationals to a minimum. Two others—Klabin and Matarazzo—have connected themselves with international capital only moderately. The last three—Gastão Vidigal, Antunes, and Monteiro Aranha—epitomize the new strategy whereby national capital

[3] Monteiro Aranha Eng. Com. Ind. S.A. seems to have been excluded from the *Visão* list somewhat arbitrarily, since *Visão*'s own estimate of its assets would justify its inclusion. This is probably because of its status as an "administrative" company.

can become an incorporated part of the structure of international capital. All seven groups are worth looking at individually.

The "grupo" Villares was one of the first Brazilian groups to begin producing machinery. The Villares brothers got into the elevator business in 1918 after returning from a course in engineering in Switzerland. Today, Indústrias Villares is second only to General Electric in the manufacture of electrical machinery in Brazil. During the Second World War, the family decided to enter the steel industry and started Aços Villares, which is now one of Brazil's largest private steel companies. Villares has managed to grow in two modern industries, competing directly against multinationals. Though there is some financial participation by the IFC in Aços Villares, the group's only joint venture is in a small auto parts company (Ferropeços Villares).

Like the Villares brothers, José Ermírio de Moraes was trained abroad at the time of the First World War; but, even more thoroughly than they the Ermírio de Moraes family has kept its holdings independent of the multinationals. M. V. Queiroz has called José Ermírio de Moraes the "exemplar of the national bourgeoisie"—looking at the history of his industrial empire, it is easy to see why. When Ermírio de Moraes returned from the Colorado School of Mines, his father-in-law, Pereira Ignácio, was already the owner of São Paulo's second-largest textile company, the Votorantim mill. Votorantim moved from cotton textiles into rayon in the thirties. Now, S.A. Indústrias Votorantim is second in assets only to Indústrias Reunidas F. Matarazzo among local, privately owned industrial companies. Even more impressive than the continued success of Votorantim was the aggressive expansion of the Ermírio de Moraes group into new areas. To support Votorantim's rayon business, Companhia Nitro Química do Brasil was created in 1937, first as a joint venture with the Klabin group and later in partnership with the Monteiro Aranha group. Nitro Química is still one of Brazil's top chemical companies and the fourth largest producer of rayon. In 1937, Votorantim moved into the steel industry, creating Siderurgica Barra Mansa, which is still one of the top five privately owned steel companies in Brazil. In 1941, at the beginning of the Second World War, José Ermírio created the Companhia Brasileira de Alumínio in direct competition with Alcan's new subsidiary. The company has done well and still shares the top position in the aluminum industry with Alcan. The forties also saw the expansion of Votorantim into the cement industry. Investments in cement were further expanded in the fifties, especially in the northeast. The Ermírio de Moraes group has also acquired holdings in the paper industry and in various companies involved in mineral products.

When the 1962 "grupos multibilionários" study was done, the Ermírio de Moraes group was the largest local enterprise in terms of the combined assets of the companies it controlled. It was also larger than any foreign group except the public utilities group, Light. On the basis of the assets of the group's companies listed currently in the *Visão* top two hundred, it is still the largest local group and the largest private one outside of Volkswagen. The most unusual thing about the group remains, however, its abstinence from association with international capital. It has few partnerships with local groups and no significant joint ventures with foreign groups. It has managed to combine strength in sectors that are traditionally dominated by local capital, like textiles and cement, with direct competition against the multinationals in steel and aluminum.

The Ermírio de Moraes group demonstrates that incorporation into the network of international capitalism is not an absolute necessity for survival as a major industrial power within Brazil, even in the modern manufacturing sector; but the group is almost alone in its success. The other important companies that have remained relatively independent of international capital operate only in a single industry—Indústrias Romi in machinery and Companhia Suzano de Cellulose e Papel in the paper industry, for example—but among diversified industrial empires, the Ermírio de Moraes group is almost unique.

The Matarazzo and Klabin groups provide the best examples of a more typical pattern of interconnection. In both cases, the lead companies of the group have been kept independent of foreign capital, but significant joint ventures have been set up in subsidiary companies and new enterprises. In the case of Klabin, Indústrias Klabin do Paraná de Cellulose has only a local partner, Monteiro Aranha. Metal Leve, the second-largest company in the group, has no major partners. In Papel e Cellulose Catarinense S.A., a major paper company that is small compared to Indústrias Klabin, there is participation by Monteiro Aranha and portfolio investment from Adela and the International Finance Corporation. Finally, there is the Klabin group's most important new investment, Companhia Brasileira de Sintéticos, the joint venture with Hoechst that has already been discussed in the context of the textile industry.

Like Klabin, the Matarazzo group has not relinquished control of its core companies. The keystone of the Matarazzo empire, Indústrias Reunidas F. Matarazzo, remains the property of the Conde Matarazzo's heirs. Indústrias Matarazzo do Paraná, which handles most of the group's textile business, is also the property of the Matarazzo family alone. The group has, however, been willing to bring in foreign capital in order to enter new areas of business. It formed early joint ventures with B. F. Goodrich and Union Carbide in order to get into the production of polyvinyl chloride and plastic casings. Its major joint venture in synthetic fibers, Polinor, has already been mentioned. In addition, the Matarazzos have combined with Teodore Wille and some other German capital in the creation of Cocam—Companhia de Café Solúvel e Derivados. Cocam is the major producer of freeze-dried instant coffee outside the United States and will also be a major producer of decaffeinated coffee and caffein. Finally, there is Sincarbon, a new joint venture that will produce carbon paper.

Matarazzo, like Villares and Klabin, has used the multinationals to further its expansion without allowing any foreign control of the central enterprises of the group. The last three groups to be considered exhibit a much more thorough integration with the multinationals. These groups—Monteiro Aranha, Gastão Vidigal, and Antunes—have expanded rapidly over the last ten years by associating with multinationals even in their most important industrial ventures.

Monteiro Aranha has retained control over the equity in a holding company, Monteiro Aranha Engineering and Construction S.A., and has a relatively large real estate company over which it has total proprietorship, but every major industrial company in the group is a joint venture. Owens-Illinois Glass has a controlling interest in the group's largest industrial venture, Companhia Indústrial São Paulo-Rio, which produces glass. The group's joint ventures with the Klabin and Votorantim groups have been mentioned earlier. In addition, Monteiro Aranha is connected to the IFC, Petrobrás, Halcon International (an American engineering firm), and the Peri Igel group through Oxiteno S.A., its newest chemical venture. The group has some interesting connections with Itaú (one of the largest and most successful locally owned commercial banks in the country) and a Portuguese financial group through Itaú's insurance company. It also has a small metallurgical company in which it shares ownership with Exxon. Most interesting of all is the group's connection to Volkswagen, which is reputed to amount to 10% of the stock of Volkswagen do Brasil (Queiroz, 1972:89).

The Monteiro Aranha group's success is due not so much to a flair for individual entrepreneurial ventures as to its ability to join with other large agglomerations of capital in mutually satisfying associations. Its partners are both local and multinational. Monteiro Aranha has become incorporated into a pattern of partnerships that link it indissolubly with the international capitalist community.

The Gastão Vidigal group has followed the same strategy. Its two major industrial ventures are Cobrasma and Braseixos Rockwell: Cobrasma deals in railway equipment and also produces auto parts; Braseixos Rockwell is Brazil's largest auto components company. Both are joint ventures, the first with American Steel Foundries, the second with North American Rockwell. Gastão Vidigal is also very strong in the financial sphere, and here too it is associated with multinationals. The group's leading commercial bank, Banco Mercantile de São Paulo, is in turn a leading stockholder in Finasa Banco de Investimentos, in which there is collected—together with Morgan Guarantee Trust and Barin Brothers—German, Japanese, and Swedish capital.

The final example of how local capital has become incorporated into the networks of international capital is the empire of Augusto Trajano de Azevedo Antunes. Antunes began his rise with the creation of ICOMI (Indústria e Commercio de Minerios, Ltda.) in Belo Horizonte during the Second World War. ICOMI might have amounted to nothing more than another small mining company except that it gained the right, in association with Bethlehem Steel, to exploit the massive deposits of manganese that were discovered in the federal territory of Amapa at about the same time. ICOMI is now the third-largest mining company in Brazil, but Antunes's other mining company, Minerações Brasileiras Reunidas, is even larger.

Minerações Brasileiras Reunidas (MBR) is in the process of beginning to mine and export some of the world's richest hematite deposits. Investments in the exploitation of the huge open pit mine of Aguas Claras are reputed to amount to $400 million. Iron ore is already second only to coffee and sugar among Brazil's export commodities, and MBR is contracted to start sending seven million tons of hematite a year to Japan alone. Antunes's major partner in Aguas Claras is the Hanna Mining Company. Antunes's holdings in MBR are, however, via Empreendimentos Brasileiros de Mineração. The other partners in EBM are several Japanese companies (including Mitsui), Daniel K. Ludwig, and his old ally, Bethlehem. By what amounts to pyramiding, Antunes has managed to retain control of EBM for himself even though the majority of its capital is foreign.

Mining is the keystone of the Antunes empire, but he has expanded far beyond minerals. He is involved with Anaconda Copper Company in a metal fabricating firm dealing with copper. He is also a part owner of one of Brazil's ten largest private steel companies, Aços Anhanguera, along with Bethlehem and the Swedish roller bearing giant, SKF. Scott Paper is his partner in a paper company, and he has joined together with the Dutch Bruynzeel in a timber venture. More recently, Antunes got together with Brascan (the investment group that is what remains of the old Light public utilities empire) to buy out Swift/Armour, thus becoming the only Brazilian group to buy out the holdings of a foreign "grupo multibilionário."

If José Ermírio de Moraes was the exemplar of the national bourgeoisie, Augusto Trajano de Azevedo Antunes is the exemplar of the new "internationalized" bourgeoisie. Antunes is not a pawn of international capital nor is he dependent on any individual multinational. Within Brazil, he has a more powerful position than any of his partners. In a struggle with any one of them, he would probably win. If any one of them tried to pull out, they could be replaced. Antunes needs the multinationals as a group, but individually they are dependent on him as well. If he had not formed his partnership with Hanna, for example, the rich deposits at Aguas Claras might have ended up in the hands of a state-owned company, like the Companhia do Vale do Rio Doce, instead of being available for private profits. Antunes's empire depends on his relations with the multinationals but, at the same time, international capital would be significantly weaker in Brazil without the connecting links that his empire provides.

Differentiation, Integration, and the Survival of the Local Bourgeoisie

Our picture of local capital is still partial. What may be the single most important source of bargaining power for local capital, its relation to the state, will be considered in Chapters 4 and 5. Even when the inquiry is restricted to the relations among private capital, however, certain trends are clear. First, local capital has clearly discovered the advantages of differentiating its role in accumulation from that of the multinationals. Differentiation is important for the survival of both large and small capital, but it is particularly important for small capital, which tends to populate locally dominated sectors such as leather goods where there is virtually no competition from the multinationals. Within sectors like pharmaceuticals and textiles, discovering differentiated niches has not only enhanced the survival chances of small local capital but also opened up the possibility of collaborative relations with the multinationals. The symbiotic ties between Rhodia and the local companies that buy its fibers are a prime example. Recently formed links between locally owned apparel manufacturers and international trading companies are another.

From industry to industry and within industries, the leverage of local capital is inversely related to the importance of scale and technology, but the leverage of local capital can be defined positively as well as negatively. A second common theme runs through instances of local strength. Across a range of instances where local capital is holding its own or expanding, the local bourgeoisie's success seems related to its ability to resolve what might be called "problems of integration."

The role of solidary, nonmarket ties among economic elites is still not well understood, but their apparent ubiquity is suggestive of their importance. From Ferdinand Lunberg to Digby Baltzell to William Dumhoff, center sociologists and others have noted the varieties of ties that bind dominant elites together in advanced capitalist societies. Kinship ties form a central part of the matrix. Friendships established at elite preparatory schools and universities are continued in select clubs. A social network constructed over several generations integrates the dominant class and stands behind more immediate and practical ties such as corporate interlocks.

The incapacity of multinationals to achieve the same sort of integration within peripheral social formations is related to the "disarticulation" (Amin) or "disintegration" (Sunkel) that characterizes the economies of dependent countries. To begin with, the multinationals converge from several different national origins. While they are hardly strangers to each other, they are not backed by a single, shared social network in the same way that corporations originating in a single society would be. For each subsidiary the most crucial links are those which bind them to the center. Until indigenous management becomes the rule rather than the exception, kinship ties and individual histories as well as organizational ties lead back to the center. The multinationals are, in short, much less thoroughly embedded in the dominant social class. This restricts their ability to deal with problems of integration. Members of the local bourgeoisie, who are both members of the dominant economic elite and embedded in the dominant social class, are much better equipped to play integrative roles.

One of the best illustrations of the integrative role of the local bourgeoisie comes from the work of Richard Newfarmer. Newfarmer (1977:163-180) studied the electrical goods industry, heavily dominated in Brazil by foreign capital. Seven firms based in four different countries control roughly 80% of sales assets and profits (GE, Westinghouse, Philco, Philips, Siemens, AEG, and Brown Boveri). These firms compete directly, and we know that in the United States the pressure of competition has been sufficient to drive members of the industry into explicit and even illegal collaboration (cf. Kefauver, 1965).

The necessity of cooperation is no less obvious in Brazil. Philco and Philips, for example, are two large multinationals from two different countries (the United States and the Netherlands) who each have about one-third of the television market. Cutthroat competition between them would be disastrous. But, how can cooperative links, such as interlocks, be established? Newfarmer (1977:228) notes that sitting on the board of both Philco and

Philips is one Luis de Franca Ribeira, of the law firm of the same name. He also notes that one J. P. Vieira, another member of the same law firm, is the lawyer for GE and sits on the board of two Westinghouse subsidiaries. Even more striking is the case of S. M. Durazzo, whom Newfarmer discovered on the boards of Brown Boveri, AEG, Westinghouse, and Siemens.

What is interesting here is not that interlocks exist among these companies. What is interesting is that in an industry dominated by multinationals, members of the local bourgeoisie are called upon to play such integrative roles. Westinghouse, Siemens, GE, and their confreres control the necessary technology and capital, but Luis de Franca Ribeira, J. P. Vieira and S. M. Durazzo constitute a different sort of resource that apparently is very useful to the multinationals. They are embedded in local networks in a way that the multinationals cannot be. Consequently they are able to perform integrative tasks for the multinationals better than the multinationals can perform such tasks for themselves.

Smaller local capital is not in a position to link together multinationals, but, as the discussion of the pharmaceutical and textile industries indicates, being embedded in local social networks is equally important for nonelite firms. In both pharmaceuticals and textiles, strategies of commercialization that involved the construction of a dense network of ties with buyers were a source of strength for local firms. Strength in this area helped compensate local firms for the power of the multinationals in both technology and marketing based on advertising.

Clearly there are niches for small capital even in the most advanced industrial societies. By this measure, dependent development would have a long way to go before small (local) capital was in danger of complete extinction. On the periphery small capital may be specially disadvantaged in terms of its access to technology. This analysis suggests, however, that the social embeddedness of local capital makes it particularly difficult for large capital (insofar as it is multinational) to dislodge small local capital from certain of its niches.

The integrative capacity of local capital helps explain its survival. It also helps in interpreting the role of large local capital. Like small local capital, large capital has sought to differentiate itself by seeking out branches of industry where it has a "comparative advantage." The cement industry, which requires smaller, geographically dispersed plants, seems to be one such branch. Large local capital has also, like small local capital, differentiated itself from the multinationals by gravitating from industrial to commercial and financial ventures. In some cases, large local capital has not chosen differentiation, but has managed to hold its own in more or less direct competition with multinationals, as in the steel industry. But the most interesting strategies of large local capital have been integrative ones.

The capacity of elite local groups like Matarazzo and Antunes to tie together diverse collections of foreign capital is what really defines the leg of the triple alliance that runs between local capital and the multinationals. This same capacity, of course, inextricably incorporates elite local groups into networks of capital that are international, not national, and makes the position of these groups ambiguous. Unless it is recognized that the role these groups perform would be quite difficult for the multinationals to perform for themselves, these local groups would appear simply dependent on foreign capital. The mutuality of dependence is obscured unless it is recognized that foreign groups with partners embedded in the local social structure have a special competitive advantage over those which lack such partners. The industrial order overall requires the existence of such integrative roles. When the roles are performed by individual members of the local bourgeoisie, these people are in a position to demand a share of the returns that accrue from cooperation. When integrative roles are played by owners of large-scale local capital they can go beyond that and participate not just in the returns but in shaping the process of accumulation.

4.

Multinational Strategies and Dependent Development

NYLON was the centerpiece of Dupont's corporate growth in the fifties, but they decided that Brazil was not one of the places they would develop nylon manufacture. By the seventies that decision looked lamentable from Dupont's point of view. Rhone Poulenc, starting with a license from Dupont, developed the nylon business in Brazil into something approaching $100 million dollars a year. By this time Dupont was making more adventurous choices, but the nylon industry was definitely lost. Dupont's decision not to develop nylon in Brazil had little effect on the country's industrialization. To Brazil it made little difference whether Dupont or Rhone Poulenc controlled nylon manufacture. But, if Dupont, Celanese, Rhone Poulenc, Hoechst, and ICI had all decided not to make nylon in Brazil, then Brazilian industrialization would have suffered and not just Dupont's profits.

If one multinational fails to engage in entrepreneurial behavior for idiosyncratic reasons, then its competitors will fill the gap. But if there are systematic similiarities among the multinationals, then their common logic has consequences for dependent development. The argument has already been made in general terms in the first chapter. Multinational managers are expected to make decisions that differ systematically from those which would be made by local capitalists.

It has already been suggested that foreign capitalists were unwilling to undertake the kind of entrepreneurial initiatives that were required for the transition from classic dependence to dependent development until they were prodded and enticed by the state. This chapter will try to show that dependent development has not eliminated the conflict between the global rationality of the multinational and a nationalist logic that places a primary emphasis on local accumulation. The issue of whether the multinationals are willing to engage in manufacturing operations has been replaced by other issues, but the tension persists.

One of the chief areas of tension in the context of dependent development is, not surprisingly, technology. Technology is what the multinationals have and what the countries of the periphery, especially dependent developing countries of the "semi-periphery," want. On the surface nationalists and the multinationals appear to be in agreement. The multinationals want to bring their technology to Brazil and the Brazilians want it implanted in their country. But underlying this apparent common interest are two quite contradictory interests. Both sides recognize that proprietary control over knowledge creates the potential for extracting monopoly rents. The multinationals want to be able to exercise that potential over the widest possible range. They are happy to bring their technology to Brazil as long as making it available does not jeopardize their monopoly. The Brazilians want just the opposite. They want to see the local utilization of the multinationals' technology precisely because they see local utilization as the first step toward local control. Ultimately, nationalists would like to be able to reap their own monopoly rents from locally generated knowledge.

In the initial discussion of the triple alliance, I tried to emphasize the continued existence of contradictions between the strategies of the multinationals and the priorities of local accumulation. Negative effects of multinational strategies on local capacities to generate new knowledge would be a good indication of these contradictions. This chapter employs a detailed examination of local product innovation in the pharmaceutical industry to get at the ways in which the centripetal logic of the multinational runs counter to the nationalist logic of local accumulation. The argument has two steps. First, the relative failure of multinationals to engage in local product innovation is described. Then rationales that might explain this behavior in "neutral" efficiency terms are examined and rejected, leaving the conclusion that failure to engage in local product innovation may be a "correct" decision in terms of the logic of a global corporation without being correct in terms of any geographically neutral economic logic.

If the argument stopped at the point of demonstrating a contradiction between global strategies and local accumulation, it would hardly support the idea of a triple alliance. Rather it would lead to a conclusion that conflicting interests separate the local bourgeoisie and foreign capital. So, having pointed out the tension, I then try to show how nationalist pressures have been able to modify the behavior of the multinationals, making it more compatible with the requirements of local accumulation.

Throughout the discussion it is important to keep in mind that "nationalist" logic is being narrowly defined. Nationalists in the broader sense (those whose concerns lie with the welfare of the entire citizenry) are likely to find the kind of local product innovation that the multinationals can be persuaded to do irrelevent or even pernicious. In the eyes of cultural radicals like Ivan Illich, for example, "the plows of the rich can do more harm than their swords" (1969:24). Questioning the substantive content of local innovation raises the issue of contradictions between the needs of the mass of the peripheral population and product innovation aimed at profitability. That issue is not discussed here. The nationalist is defined here simply as one with a primary interest in local accumulation, which in the context of dependent development means maximizing long-run rates of profit and investment within the local economy.

The crux of the argument is that there is tension between the multinationals and the nationalist even when nationalism is defined in terms of local profits. Once one has accepted the view

(Boulding, 1964:431) that rates of return on new knowledge are "substantially above the rates of return on investment in material capital," then multinationals and the nationalists must disagree on the issue of where innovative activities should take place, even when "nationalist" is defined simply as an interest in local capital accumulation.

As long as contradictory interests separate the multinationals and the nationalists, the issue of control will be central to the progress of dependent development. As long as the multinationals can maintain control over their enterprises and investments within Brazil, decisions will be made according to their own global rationality, and considerations of local accumulation will take second place. Raising the issue of control means evaluating the possibility that the multinationals can be constrained to place a higher priority on local accumulation even at some sacrifice of their own global strategies.

The degree of divergence between global strategies and local accumulation, as well as the chance of modifying the former in favor of the latter, depends on the context. The less well endowed the peripheral country in question and the less favorable an "investment climate" it offers, the greater the contradiction between the global rationality of the multinationals and local nationalist logic. The tension is obviously much less severe for the countries undergoing dependent development than for other peripheral countries. Among such countries, Brazil has been something of a limiting case, especially in the late sixties and early seventies when most of the decisions discussed in this chapter were made.

Brazil as an Investment Climate

The fact that Brazil's "economic miracle" made it "the Latin American darling of the international business community" (*Business Latin America*, 1972:196) is well known and does not need to be reiterated with barrages of quotations. The impressive economic figures of this period are also well known. GNP growth rates of over 10% per year were characteristic, with growth rates for industry even higher, particularly in certain key areas such as automobiles. Tables 4.1 and 4.2 provide a statistical overview of

TABLE 4.1   Sales of U.S. Majority Owned Manufacturing Affiliates in Brazil and Other Selected Markets, 1966-1973 (millions of current $US)

	1966		1973		Growth as a % of 1966 sales
	Amount	%	Amount	%	
Total	47,374	100.0	140,878	100.0	197
Europe	21,738	45.1	75,254	53.4	246
U.K.	8,275	17.4	19,559	13.9	136
France	3,114	6.6	11,774	8.4	278
Germany	4,795	10.1	19,347	13.7	303
Latin America	5,861	12.3	16,220	11.6	185
Argentina	1,302	2.7	2,246	1.6	72
Mexico	1,543	3.3	3,945	2.8	154
BRAZIL	1,283	2.7	5,738	4.1	347

Source: Survey of Current Business, vol. 55, no. 8 (August 1975):22-37.

the growth of investments, sales, and profits, which puts Brazil into perspective as a potential location for investment.

Gross sales statistics of American manufacturers abroad confirm the importance of the Brazilian boom to the expansion of the multinationals. Brazil during this period grew much more rapidly than any other major Latin American market. Even the European markets of American overseas manufacturers, which generally grew faster than their Latin American counterparts, did not match the growth in Brazilian consumption. By 1973 the Brazilian market was the sixth largest in the world for American manufacturing affiliates. Sales in Brazil in 1973 were as large as combined sales to all of the original six members of the European

TABLE 4.2   Growth of U.S. Assets in Brazil and Other Selected
Markets, 1966-1973 (direct investments in manufacturing in millions
of current $US)

| | 1966 | | 1973 | | Growth as a % of 1966 |
	Amount	%	Amount	%	assets
Total	22,058	100.0	44,370	100.0	101
Europe	8,876	40.2	20,777	46.8	134
U.K.	3,716	16.8	6,611	14.9	78
France	1,201	5.4	2,946	6.6	145
Germany	1,839	8.7	4,449	10.0	142
Latin America	3,081	14.0	6,456	14.5	109
Argentina	656	3.0	781	1.8	19
Mexico	802	3.6	1,798	4.1	124
BRAZIL	846	3.8	2,033	4.6	146

Sources: Survey of Current Business, vol. 48, no. 10 (October 1968):19-31; vol.
55, no. 10 (October 1975):43-63.

Economic Community the year before the EEC was formed
(1962).

When comparing the growth of United States manufacturing
affiliates' sales in Brazil to the growth of their sales elsewhere, it
should be kept in mind that the growth of foreign manufacturing
in general was much more rapid than the growth of the domestic
economy during this period. Foreign sales as a proportion of all
sales of American manufactures doubled in the sixties, reaching
13% of the total. The share of foreign expenditures on plant and
equipment rose even faster, reaching 25% of total expenditures
by 1970. Most important, it has been estimated that by the mid-
seventies 30% of all United States profits came from overseas
(Müller, 1975). Overseas manufacturing was a dynamic area of
expansion for American corporations and Brazil was the most
rapidly growing of the major overseas markets of American manufacturers.

Growth in itself is attractive, but new investment must get a satisfactory rate of return. In international terms this means a rate approximating that available in other countries. As Table 4.3 indicates, Brazil has provided good rates of return as well as opportunities for rapid growth.[1] While official rates of return for American manufacturers in Latin America have generally been lower than those available in Europe, Brazil provided, at least during the late sixties and early seventies, among the best such rates available; only Germany provided better.

Gross averages convey the general situation and also are a way of describing the context in which the individual manager is working. Within the Brazilian context, however, it is important to distinguish long-established firms from newcomers. For the latter, the prospect of getting in on a fast-growing market is prob-

TABLE 4.3   Rates of Return for U.S. Manufacturing Affiliates,*
1967-1974 (selected years)

	1967 (%)	1969 (%)	1972 (%)	1973 (%)	1974 (%)
Total	8.5	10.8	13.0	15.0	12.8
Europe	8.7	11.9	15.0	16.8	12.6
U.K.	8.8	9.3	12.4	11.8	6.2
France	5.4	10.0	13.0	17.5	8.9
Germany	11.1	17.7	19.8	22.5	16.0
Latin America	7.4	10.1	11.8	12.0	11.1
Argentina	4.0	11.5	4.4	4.5	loss
Mexico	8.7	9.4	10.9	11.9	12.0
BRAZIL	7.7	11.1	14.5	14.9	11.0

* "Rates of return" are based on figures reported to the U.S. Department of Commerce. They represent the ratio of "earnings" (not "adjusted earnings") to "assets" of "book value."
Sources: Survey of Current Business, vol. 48, no. 10 (October 1968):19-31; vol. 50, no. 10 (October 1970):21-37; vol. 54, no. 8 (August 1974):10-24; vol. 55, no. 10 (October 1975):43-63.

[1] The estimated rates of return are higher in the Senate Subcommittee sample. As mentioned earlier, Connor and Mueller estimate the rate of return on equity for 1972 at 16.1%. The U.S. Department of Commerce figures have been used here in order to provide a broader basis for comparison.

ably the paramount motivation. Newcomers may have to sacrifice short-term profits in order to get started. As Connor and Mueller (1977:50) put it, "Many firms with large start up costs or other transient conditions distort the true profit picture." They corrected for this in their report by eliminating unprofitable firms and came up with an average return on equity of 21.4% for the rest of the sample. This may represent an overcorrection, but it is true that established firms have higher rates of profit than newcomers. McDonough's (1974) analysis of company profitability in 1970 indicates that one of the strongest predictors of the profitability of multinationals in Brazil was the date of their establishment. Long-established multinationals made significantly higher profits than newer ones. The profit rates of longer-established firms are the best gauge of what multinationals can expect to make in Brazil over the long run.

The individual rates of return for large, established companies is a good complement to the aggregate statistics on United States manufacturing affiliates. The rates of return shown in Table 4.4 are based on local accounting procedures and are not equivalent to the U.S. Department of Commerce data, but they do suggest that there is a foundation for the enthusiasm of the multinational managers. Seven of the ten companies received better than 15% on capital and reserves. Even in the early part of the period (1967, 1968) when the economy was still recovering, the average returns for all companies never dropped below 10%. In addition, almost all of the companies experienced these rates of return in conjunction with substantial growth of assets. Finally, it should be noted that these figures underestimate real returns to the parent corporation since they do not include items that appear as costs at the level of the subsidiary but profits at the level of the parent. Official rates of return do not include royalties and fees, or payments for technical assistance, to say nothing of profits on transfer prices (see Vaitsos, 1974).

If ever there was an economic environment in the periphery in

TABLE 4.4 Growth and Return for Ten Selected Multinationals 1967-1973

	1967* Assets	1973 Assets	Growth of Assets 1967-1973 (%)	Rate of Return**							Average Rate of Return 1967-1973 (%)
				1967 (%)	1968 (%)	1969 (%)	1970 (%)	1971 (%)	1972 (%)	1973 (%)	
Volkswagen	107.7	338.3	214	6.5	11.6	7.6	1.6	21.1	18.2	17.7	12.0
Cia. Cigarros Souza Cruz (Brit. Amer. Tob.)	115.2	226.3	96	16.6	19.5	21.9	23.4	31.9	36.7	35.8	26.5
General Motors	83.0	163.5	97	3.3	8.4	12.1	24.7	31.5	22.4	9.5	16.0
Rhodia (Rhone Poulenc)	100.0	160.0	60	4.8	2.3	8.9	7.9	11.2	11.2	18.5	9.3
Pirelli	86.1	139.8	62	3.2	12.5	6.4	7.2	19.0	60.1	28.7	19.6
Shell	54.9	114.7	107	31.3	24.0	16.3	10.9	17.3	3.8	12.2	16.5
Esso	43.5	81.0	86	25.8	3.5	8.5	14.5	13.5	19.2	30.9	16.6
General Electric	62.5	80.4	29	16.2	12.3	11.3	6.8	10.9	44.8	20.4	17.6
Alcan	32.4	71.2	120	3.0	1.7	1.1	1.9	15.2	24.2	25.6	10.4
Nestle	39.9	66.5	68	4.6	5.3	8.4	11.1	26.4	23.5	27.2	15.2
Average Rate of Return by Year:				11.5	10.2	10.3	11.0	19.8	26.4	22.6	16.0 (overall average)

* Assets are in millions of current $US.
** Rate of return is as calculated by *Business Latin America* and refers to ratio of net profit to capital and reserves.
Source: Business Latin America, "Major Brazilian Firms and How They Fared" (yearly feature 1967-1973).

which the multinationals should have been willing to take risks and engage in entrepreneurial behavior, it was Brazil in the late sixties and early seventies. Given the rates of growth and the rates of return available there, the contradictions between global rationality and local accumulation ought to have been minimal or nonexistent. The fact that such contradictions remained, even in Brazil during the boom, suggests that they can never be reduced beyond a certain point.

Multinational Strategy and Local Product Innovation

The behavior of multinationals with respect to local research and development in the pharmaceutical industry can provide only one illustration of the kinds of contradictions that separate global and nationalist rationality, not a proof of their pervasiveness. The development of local capacity for technological innovation is only one of the demands the nationalist perspective would make on multinationals. Investments in forward integration in the case of extractive industry or backwards integration in the case of consumer products, or commitments to local purchase or production of capital goods are others. Nonetheless, research and development in the drug industry provides an excellent illustrative case, one well worth developing in some detail.

As was pointed out in Chapter 3, exclusive new products are the sine qua non of profitable operations for an international pharmaceutical corporation. The question is whether the capacity to develop these new products should be moved to the periphery along with manufacturing operations or kept in the center despite the decentralization of the manufacturing function. This can be put less abstractly: Does it make sense to attempt to develop new drugs in Brazil? Research done in the late sixties indicated that there were two answers, one offered by local capital and one offered by the multinationals.

In 1969 when I began working on this question few multinationals claimed to have developed any products locally. In a sample of 17 American subsidiaries that included all of the largest subsidiaries, only 5 claimed to have developed any products locally within the last five years (Evans, 1971:126). Given the degree of denationalization in the industry, it was impossible to find a sample of local firms whose scale was comparable to that of the subsidiaries, even if only sales within Brazil were taken into account. The majority of the American subsidiaries had annual local sales of over $5 million while only one of the local firms was in this league. Nonetheless, all local firms with sales of over $2.5 million could claim locally developed products. The majority of local firms with sales over $1 million could also make this claim. Only the smallest local firms did not try to develop products of their own.

Data from other investigations generally support these findings. A survey of 183 firms in the state of São Paulo done by the Instituto de Estuodos para o Desenvolvimento Social e Econômico (INED) surveyed 13 pharmaceutical firms, 5 locally owned and 8 foreign-owned.[2] All 5 locally owned were coded as doing research while only 3 of the foreign-owned were credited with having local research activities.[3]

Carlos Bertero, who interviewed 29 pharmaceutical firms, in-

[2] The INED study was done under the auspices of the Instituto Roberto Simonsen and the Federação das Indústrias do Estado de São Paulo in 1967 Some of the results are reported in Chiaverini (1968). The discussion here is based on my own analysis of the data, coded from the original questionnaires. I reanalyzed the data, checking for internal consistency and verifying the information on ownership against other sources. Chiaverini and the original INED report were only able to include two-way tables, but in my own analysis I was able to introduce controls and perform some simple multivariate analysis (see Evans, 1971:145-161).

[3] Obviously there are major methodological problems with using self-report to evaluate a firm's investment in research and development. It might be argued that multinationals have higher standards for what they are willing to label "R & D" and therefore underreport their efforts relative to local firms. It was for this reason that I focused on whether or not firms could point to locally developed products when I did my analysis of the pharmaceutical industry.

cluding both subsidiaries and locally owned drug companies, found that 6 out of 24 subsidiaries claimed to do formulations locally, and one other did toxicological and pharmacological testing (1972:200-201). Bertero's sample of local firms was limited to only 5 of the largest local companies, but among these companies 4 claimed to have engaged in product development (1972:209).

These general results can be supported by some specific examples. Both Bertero (1972:210-211) and myself (1971:136) discovered the local company I called Laboratórios Grande and were impressed by the export business that it had built on the basis of its own locally developed biological products. I also highlighted a company I called Laboratórios Familial, which has succeeded in launching 50 new pharmaceutical and dietetic products based on its own research. Laboratórios Familial's work on barium for radiography of the bronchial tubes even "resulted in a research report of sufficient originality to be published in an American research periodical." Between 1963 and 1968, Laboratórios Familial tested 705 substances and managed to come up with 41 industrial products (Evans, 1971:135, 136). This is, of course, a tiny number by international standards. At the same time, this number of successes also suggests that the substances initially tested were of some known therapeutic value. The fact remains that Laboratórios Familial, like Laboratórios Grande, succeeded until the end of the sixties in maintaining a commerically rewarding research and development operation within Brazil.

To reinforce these Brazilian examples, there is a more spectacular, though admittedly unique, example from Mexico. Syntex S.A., set up in Mexico over twenty-five years ago to exploit locally available raw materials, was extremely successful (see Gereffi, 1978). Until the company was bought out by U.S. capital and its research operations moved to Palo Alto, the productivity of its Mexican research laboratories was impressive. Carl Djerassi, one of the directors of Syntex, wrote: "By 1959 more scientific publications in steroid chemistry had emanated from

Syntex in Mexico than from any other academic or industrial organization in the world. . . . In a matter of ten years Mexico—a country in which no basic chemical research had been performed previously—had become one of the world centers in one specialized branch of chemistry" (1968:24-25).

An even more impressive comparative example is provided by the work of Jorge Katz on Argentina. Argentina is a better place to look at local innovative activity because denationalization has not occurred to the same degree. Local firms represent over 50% of total sales and nine of the top twenty-five firms are locally owned. Katz calculated that it took ten to fifteen thousand dollars to launch a new product on the Argentine market and that the most innovative firms each launched between twelve and fifteen products in the period 1960-1968. Major local firms were quite capable of maintaining a flow of new products by making investments in research and development of about 1% of their sales. It is on the basis of such new products, according to Katz, that local firms were able to increase their share of the market relative to international firms between 1962 and 1970 (Katz, 1974:110-114, 62).

Neither I nor Bertero nor Katz claims that more local product innovation in pharmaceuticals would make important differences to the health of the population. Whether Brazil's most popular cough syrup in the future is locally developed (like BROMIL) or a multinational import (like VICKS) is of little significance to consumers' health. Samuel Pessoa's conclusion (1963:36) that the "fundamental cause of high rates of dissemination of parasite diseases is the pauperism of the Brazilian people" or Edmar Bacha's (1976:16) correlation between rising infant mortality rates and falling minimum wages are more to the point. Insofar as product innovation results mainly in the proliferation of sophisticated and expensive products (cf. Kucinski, 1975), then it can be considered, as Katz (1974:142) says, simply another example of "playing the oligopolistic game of product differentiation." It does not even seem extreme to conclude with Bertero (1972:214) that "most of the country's population is not served by a pharmaceutical industry structured and operated along a capitalist model."

What is being argued is that potentially profitable investments in local facilities for product innovation were avoided by multinationals to the detriment of local accumulation. In short, there would be a greater amount of local technologically innovative work in the Brazilian pharmaceutical industry if more of the larger firms were locally owned. In Bertero's (1972:214) words, "the situation of the pharmaceutical industry in Brazil today, basically controlled by multinational corporations, is one of self-perpetuating dependency, with no prospects for developing technology." While this judgment underestimates the degree to which the behavior of multinationals can be modified, it is certainly true that the tendency of multinationals to neglect or avoid investment in local facilities for product innovation presents an obstacle to the technological evolution of a dependent developing country.

The general lack of multinational investment in local research and development is confirmed by evidence outside the pharmaceutical industry. The strongest correlation in the INED study (see at note 2 above) is that between foreign ownership and lack of research and development. The INED result suggests that even partial local ownership is sufficient to induce interest in R & D. About 60% of all firms with at least 10% local ownership claimed to do research and development locally, the same as the proportion of firms with complete local ownership. Among firms with no local ownership, on the other hand, only a quarter claimed to do any R & D.

The INED study also reveals an interaction between paying royalties, doing research, and the degree of foreign ownership that is interesting. Among firms with some local ownership, paying royalties and doing research locally go together; three out of four of those paying royalties also do research. Among wholly foreign-owned firms, however, there is no such relationship. That is to say, the need for new technology (as expressed by willingness to pay royalties) is associated with attempts at local innovation as long as there is some local ownership, but not if the multinationals are completely in charge.

To look at the periphery and compare the R & D efforts of multinational firms to those of local firms is one way to evaluate the willingness of multinationals to decentralize innovative activities. The situation can also be viewed from the center, as it is in U.S. Tariff Commission's Report on Multinationals (1973:581-604). The commission reported that in 1966 multinationals committed only 6% of their total R & D expenditures outside the U.S., much less than the percentage of their sales accounted for by these markets. At the same time, according to the commission, multinationals "usually finance R & D costs by assessments against all affiliates." Affiliates' payments of royalities and fees alone were equivalent to 7.7% of multinationals' domestic R & D spending, a percentage larger than the share of R & D done overseas. The commission cautiously concludes that "there is a possibility that affiliates (at least in some industries) may contribute more to R & D in the United States than they take from it" (U.S. Tariff Commission, 1973:591, 593).

The research efforts of multinationals in Brazil can be compared with their efforts in the United States itself. Table 4.5 shows the R & D expenditures of U.S. multinational affiliates in Brazil as a percentage of their sales in Brazil in comparison with the R & D expenditures of American multinationals in the U.S. as a percentage of their U.S. sales. Overall, affiliates allocate about one-fifth the expenditures to R & D that their parents do. Industry by industry, with the exception of food, the story is the same. If multinationals allocated to R & D in Brazil the same proportion of local sales as they do in the United States, Brazilian expenditures would have been almost $150 million in 1972 instead of under $30 million.

Whether the comparison is between locally owned firms and foreign-owned or between multinationals' behavior in the center and their behavior in the periphery, whether the comparison is

TABLE 4.5   Research and Development by Multinationals: The U.S. versus Brazil

Industry	Brazil (1972)			U.S. (1970)		
	Sales of U.S. Affiliated Firms in Brazil	R & D Expenditures	R & D as a Percent of Sales	U.S. Multinationals' Domestic Sales	R & D Expenditures	R & D as a Percent of Sales
Food	197	3.7	1.9%	14,300	176	1.2%
Paper	83	0.0	0.	7,500	87	1.2%
Chemicals	672	5.4	0.8%	28,100	1,556	5.5%
Rubber	243	0.0	0.	3,300	169	5.1%
Stone, Clay & Glass	70	0.6	0.8%	4,700	150	3.2%
Metals	85	0.3	0.4%	22,700	363	1.6%
Machinery	392	0.7	0.2%	20,600	984	4.8%
Electrical Machinery	347	3.7	1.1%	27,900	2,172	7.8%
Transportation Equipment	867	12.3	1.4%	55,200	2,790	5.1%
Instruments	25	0.0	0.	7,600	590	7.7%
All Manufacturing	3,056	27.0	0.9%	207,800	9,200	4.4%

Note: Individual industries will not add up to all manufacturing because "other" has been excluded. U.S. sales are rounded to nearest $100 million, Brazilian sales to nearest $1 million; U.S. R & D to nearest $1 million except total, which is to nearest $100 million, Brazilian R & D to nearest $100 thousand. All figures are in millions of dollars.
Sources: Newfarmer and Mueller, 1975:178; U.S. Tariff Commission, 1973:556, 733.

made within an industry or across the industrial spectrum, the conclusion is the same. Multinationals are reluctant to engage in technologically innovative activities in the periphery, even in the favorable investment climate of Brazil in the late sixties. With the transition to dependent development the multinationals were induced to decentralize the process of production, but the generation of knowledge is still kept at home.

Global Rationality and the Allocation of Innovative Activities

The multinational managers are aware of the geographic distribution of their R & D. While they may disparage the efforts of local firms to create new products, they know that product innovation takes place locally. But they consider the current geographic allocation of innovative activities to be the result of a neutral economic logic that no one but a romantic ideologue could quarrel with. To allocate them in any other way would simply waste valuable resources, rather than advance the pace of local accumulation. If pressed, their arguments tend to take two forms. One concerns the unsuitability of the Brazilian environment for research operations. The other is based on the idea that there are very important economies of scale in research, such that any decentralization, even to an appropriate location, would result in diminished research efficiency.

Raymond Vernon characterized the strength of the economies of scale argument nicely when he said (1970:57), "The existence of important economics in large scale research is so thoroughly taken for granted that it is difficult to find an explicit rationalization for their assumption." The statements of the pharmaceutical executives I spoke with in 1969 provided some good examples of the economics of scale argument (Evans, 1971:171). One said, "We spend $25 million a year on R & D. Their [the subsidiary's] sales in Brazil are less than half that. Do you want them to go bankrupt?" Questions regarding the possibility of spending part of the $25 million in one place and part in another were answered in terms of particular pieces of expensive equipment and the general impossibility of separating parts of a research operation.

The interesting thing about these arguments is that they are advanced almost entirely without systematic evidence to back them up. There are, of course, studies of pharmaceutical research that emphasize the tremendous costs of the overall effort and the large risks involved (e.g., M. Cooper, 1966; J. Cooper, 1970). But even these studies do not present arguments as to the necessity of performing research at a single location. The classic general studies of invention like Jewkes, Sawyers, and Stillerman (1958) or Schmookler (1957) provide no evidence that large laboratories are more productive than small ones, relative to the resources that are put into them. Nor do the standard sociological studies of research organizations (e.g., Pelz and Andrews, 1963; Kornhauser, 1963) offer any substantial evidence that would support the idea that big research labs should be more efficient than small ones.

Such sociological evidence as might be tangentially applied to the question of economies of scale in research suggests that smaller organizations, or large organizations in which effort is dispersed to several different locations, may have an advantage over large centralized groups. Burton Klein (1958) and Richard R. Nelson (1961) have argued that several smaller groups working on a problem independently and in parallel may have a better chance of coming up with solutions than a single larger group working according to a single plan. Burns and Stalker (1961) argue that "organic" structures, such as one might find in smaller groups, are the appropriate organizational form for situations where innovation is the aim.

In the pharmaceutical industry it is true that certain pieces of equipment are expensive and that a small laboratory might suffer from their absence, but such equipment is relatively rare and most of the cost of maintaining a laboratory goes into salaries. The central question is whether interaction among large numbers of researchers enhances the efficiency of each of them. Pharmaceutical research involves testing a great many compounds, but the testing of each set is carried out by relatively small groups of researchers. Each group is concerned mainly with its own compounds and, while there may be some cross-fertilization, each works independently for the most part. One scientist, director of a laboratory employing 1,600 people, suggested that 40 scientists were the "critical mass" necessary to undertake basic research. Another agreed and pointed out that most university chemistry departments were no larger. If these estimates are valid for basic research, then the optimum number required for the kind of applied research and product development likely to take place in Brazil should be very small indeed.

The most systematic and credible quantitative pharmaceutical research probably does not embody important economies of scale. After examining the output of the research establishments of small and large firms, Comanor (1963) concluded that "there is likely to be decreasing returns to scale when the firm becomes large" and that "there appears to be some validity to the position that small firms have more efficient research establishments than their larger counterparts" (1963:140, 141). He also (1963:142) found that the elasticity of sales of new chemical entities with respect to the number of R & D personnel was twice as high in smaller firms (less than $1 million annual sales) than in larger ($5 to $15 million annual sales). On the basis of Comanor's data one would have to decide that any increases in R & D expenditure might be more fruitfully allocated to firms on the scale of Brazilian subsidiaries than to larger-scale domestic operations.

The "inappropriate environment" argument is harder to refute. It is probably in fact more difficult to conduct research in Brazil than in the United States. One might easily say, as some of the managers I talked to did, that "there are no well-known Brazilian chemistry journals" or that "Brazil lacks a scientific tradition."

There are, however, several reasons to be suspicious of the "inappropriateness" argument. There is a tendency for multinationals to find any environment outside their home environment "inappropriate," as the findings of the Tariff Commission indicate. The literature on foreign investment that came out of the sixties, reveals the absence of R & D efforts not only in India (cf. Kidron, 1965, and Copen, 1967) but also in Australia (cf. Fitzpatrick and Wheelwright, 1965, and Brash, 1965), not only in Brazil but also in Europe (cf. Johnstone, 1965; Layton, 1966).

Another reason for questioning the difficulty of doing research in Brazil is the history of efforts by local firms. Katz's results for

Argentina offer evidence in this regard. He estimates that the marginal return from local investments in research and development in the Argentine pharmaceutical industry is about 35%, and points out that this figure is about the same as that estimated for other countries. He also found that firms with greater local expenditures on research and development had faster rates of growth and more rapid increases in productivity than firms with smaller levels of local R & D expenditures (Katz, 1974:116, 113).

If Brazilian and Argentine firms can turn out new products by dint of their own efforts, then it seems unlikely that the efforts of multinationals would go unrewarded. The behavior of the multinationals themselves in the early seventies provides an additional reason for believing that pharmaceutical research is possible in Brazil. But before looking at changes in the mid-seventies, it is worth developing a more plausible alternative explanation for the behavior of the sixties.

It must be recognized that the returns on innovative activity are essentially unpredictable. Major drug companies with annual research budgets in the millions, and hundreds of R & D personnel, may go for years without an important discovery. Even without "dry spells" the productivity of an R & D operation is very difficult to predict. If, for example, one compares the new drug sales of major companies in the early seventies with the number of research personnel they employed in the late sixties, the variation in results is large. New sales per research employee range from just over twenty thousand to just under two hundred thousand. To decide on the appropriate gross levels of investment in research is obviously difficult; to decide on how best to allocate or organize research efforts even more so.

Those who direct R & D activities are likely to believe that "the surest way to get bad work is to start telling people what to do." In the drug industry at least, the enthusiasm of a scientist for a particular project may gain it priority over another project with twice the market potential, simply because enthusiasm increases the expected likelihood of results. At the same time, there is a certain distrust of the research scientist as lacking in profit orientation. Wortzel (1971:11) reports that management sometimes fears that scientists "may undertake research projects because of their general intellectual interest rather than their interest to the firm." Unfortunately for management, it is very difficult to tell whether researchers are behaving "inefficiently" or not.

Given the difficulties of prediction or control, the relation between top management and the research staff must be based on "confidence" or even "faith." Employing research personnel who have been trained at well-known elite universities may help provide reassurance. Personal contact with research personnel is also likely to be reassuring. Consequently, management is likely to prefer a situation in which "the research group is located in close physical proximity to the management group" (Wortzel, 1971:11). If control over research and development is approached this way, a research operation in a less-developed foreign country 7,000 miles away is obviously an anathema to any risk-avoider.

Another possibility that cannot be dismissed is that, if the distant foreign research facility is successful, difficulties of control may become difficulties of appropriation. Drug companies will not forget quickly the American scientists who "deserted" their parent companies and enabled the Italian "patent robbers" to produce tetracyclines (Pearson, 1969). Any multinational might be skeptical about the chances of a Brazilian court being willing to punish a Brazilian researcher for having sold something he discovered while working for an international firm to a local company.

The economies of scale and inappropriate environment arguments are almost irrelevant from the point of view of the multinational manager. No good "satisficing" manager decides to go for a Brazilian research facility, regardless of whether these two arguments have any truth to them. What is there to gain? He acquires responsibility for an operation he cannot control. He makes the unpredictability of research more obvious by strengthening the possibility of independent evaluation of subunits. Even if risks aren't increased, the appearance of risk is increased and there is no compensating prospect of increased returns. From the point of view of the multinational manager, dispersion of research is "irrational" regardless of the caliber of the Brazilian facility that would be created.

It was not a neutral economic calculus that led multinationals to centralize the production of new knowledge. It was instead the specific "bounded rationality" of the multinational corporation. The "boundaries" on this rationality were not simply, or even primarily, cognitive. Cognitive problems made evaluation in terms of the profitability of dispersed R & D ambiguous, but the resolution of this ambiguity was straightforward because centralized R & D was clearly superior in terms of the organizational needs of the multinational. As Herbert Simon has pointed out (1965:199), there are different kinds of "correctness" and a decision is "correct" in one sense as long as it is "consistent with the frame of reference that has been organizationally assigned to the decider."

Because the neutral economic evidence is unclear, the definition of "correctness" produced by the organizational needs of the multinationals holds sway. But from the point of view of a nationalist interested in local accumulation, the ambiguity of the evidence bearing on the profitability of investment in local research and development would argue in exactly the opposite direction. Since companies cannot show that they would lose by investing in local facilities, and since the effects for Brazil would be positive, the nationalist feels they should take the risk. The conflict is clear and the argument becomes political.

Nationalist Pressure and the Multinational Response

If there are differences between "correctness" born of the organizational frame of reference of the multinationals and "correctness" in terms of local accumulation, then shaping the behavior of the multinationals through political pressure becomes a central element of successful dependent development. To the degree that "correctness" in local terms can be imposed without jeopardizing the commitment of the multinationals, prospects for local accumulation will be enhanced. The pharmaceutical industry in the seventies saw some interesting attempts at such shaping.

The foreign sector of the pharmaceutical industry was in a rather precarious political position in the 1960's. Before the military coup, some had advocated nationalization of the industry. In the series "Notebooks of the People," one of the volumes was entitled "Shall We Nationalize the Pharmaceutical Industry?" (Miranda, 1963). The pharmaceutical industry experienced price controls before they were generalized. In the early part of the decade President Goulart formed a commission of inquiry to look into the situation of the industry. Many of the accusations against the foreign sector arose over the issue of denationalization. Critics like Colonel Mario Victor de Assis Pacheco (1962:28) inveighed against the misguided government policies that aided foreign capital while the local entrepreneur lived "without any privilege whatsoever." A favorite target of critics of the industry was the lack of local research. Pacheco wrote (1962:15): "If our technicians weren't pulled away, attracted by better salaries, better working conditions and other advantages they would stay in our own laboratories, private or state owned, doing research, improving the quality of our production and discovering new products, but this is exactly what the foreign trusts want to avoid and have succeeded in avoiding." Displeasure over the absence of local research and concern over the cost of importing basic pharmaceutical inputs combined to produce the elimination of patent protection in pharmaceuticals in 1969.

Those in the industry on the local level were well aware of their weak position. They responded with publications demonstrating the technological progressiveness of the industry and the extent to which it was harassed by government policies. Privately at least, some of the local managers were more candid. One of them, a Brazilian with long experience in the foreign-owned sector, related a conversation he had had with a military man in the government over the issue of abolishing patents. The manager reported that although the Colonel was "someone with whom it was possible to dialog" it had not been possible to change his mind on the issue of patents because "logic was on his side." The manager tried to argue that no country without patent laws ever produced any new discoveries. The Colonel replied, "Do you think that anyone will discover anything even if we keep the patent laws?" The manager felt he couldn't refute the point.

At the same time as the Brazilian government made it harder for international drug companies to appropriate returns from discoveries made elsewhere, it undertook measures to stimulate research. It set up the National Fund for Scientific and Technical Development that would provide financing and technical assistance to enterprises establishing or expanding local R & D facilities and made local R & D expenditures tax deductible (*Business Latin America*, 1970:264). The attempt to combine sanctions and incentives was obvious. *Business Latin America* (1971:374) reported: "In not allowing royalty payment or patent protection the government has given for a reason the fact that companies actually perform little or no research in Brazil and are not discovering anything patentable. At the same time, the government has hinted that it might take a more lenient attitude if companies were to engage in R & D in Brazil."

Continued local discontent with the operations of the pharmaceutical industry manifested itself again in 1971 with the creation of the Central de Medicamentos (CEME, 1974; Bertero, 1972:243). The initial rationale for it was simply that it would complement the existing health insurance system and provide medicines for those too poor to buy them. Its functions soon expanded. By 1973, CEME was supporting research on basic pharmaceutical inputs and the government had published a decree amplifying the "Directive Plan for Medications" to include "studies for the implantation of a system which would oblige large pharmaceutical companies to apply a certain percentage of gross sales to local research projects" (Decreto No. 72.522, Art. 2, IV.d).

At the end of 1974, the head of the powerful Council on Industrial Development (which must approve any investment that is to benefit from fiscal incentives) made a speech that *Business Latin America* considered to contain "warning signals" for the drug industry. He spoke of past denationalization as "disquieting" and held it responsible for "making difficult local research and the adoption of new technological processes within the country." *Business Latin America* commented that it was "the first time that an official has linked foreign domination—particularly through acquisitions—with the frustration of Brazil in moving ahead with its prime goal of greater local R & D" (1975:26).

None of these pressures or accusations were particularly disturbing in themselves. But, as managers discovered in the seventies, the military government's support of "private enterprise" did not preclude the possibility of increased participation by the state in industry. In the pharmaceutical industry they spoke in 1974 of the possibility of CEME becoming a "Medíbrás" on the order of Petrobrás. They did not consider this likely, but it was worrisome nonetheless.

Confronted with persistent nationalist pressures even after ten years of military government, multinational managers had to respond. No manager would want to risk being cut out of the Brazilian market; returns on equity among U.S. subsidiaries were running over 20% (Connor and Mueller, 1977:50). The need to reduce political risks, to strengthen the security of the whole Brazilian operation, became the justification for investing in local research facilities regardless of expected rates of return from those facilities. Managers found themselves exchanging one kind of uncertainty for another. Neither political factors nor research and development are easily controlled at a distance. Both are somewhat unpredictable; but between the two kinds of risk, local research and development is the less dangerous.

The Brazilian pharmaceutical industry in the early seventies provides a good illustration of the central role played by political pressure in pushing multinationals toward investment in local research facilities. The U.S. Tariff Commission's (1973:587) observation that "pressures and encouragement by host governments are often a deciding factor" in the decision to disperse research, and Wortzel's conclusion that in the pharmaceutical industry "by far the strongest motivation for setting up research facilities outside the U.S. comes from governments" (1971:10) could both serve as summaries of the Brazilian case.[4]

Given the generality of the pressure, the differential response among different firms was striking. A few responded strongly. Johnson and Johnson is the most often cited example. It started the Johnson and Johnson Research Institute in Brazil in 1970 (*Business Latin America*, 1971:374) and is reputed to have invested over 2 million dollars in the institute in the first two years of its operation (Kucinski, 1975:70). Johnson and Johnson was testing about 500 substances a month by 1974, not a large number by international standards, but far larger than any previous Brazilian operation. American Cyanamid, which has done work on veterinary products in Brazil for quite some time, may extend its work to products for human use. The Beecham group, a new entry into the Brazilian market, has reputedly undertaken to make Brazil one of the four countries in its worldwide operations in which research would be carried on.

[4] One of the ironic aspects of the development of the pharmaceutical industry is that because political pressure fell more heavily on foreign than on locally owned firms and because of the effects of denationalization discussed in Chapter 3, local firms became less involved in research at the same time that foreign firms were becoming more involved.

Companies that engaged in research and development had reason to perceive the attendant risks differently from other firms. Their decisions were incremental, built on the previous existence of a certain level of R & D. Johnson and Johnson could cite products developed in Brazil as early as the fifties (*Business Latin America*, 1971:374). Beecham bought out a local company, Maurício Villela, one of the most respected research and development operations in Brazil. Having acquired it, Beecham would have had to make a decision to stop doing research in Brazil rather than take steps to *start* doing research. Given their delicate position in having just "denationalized" one of the largest, most prestigious locally owned drug companies, a commitment to local research obviously made sense.

The tendency toward incrementalism, or working on the basis of what exists, was evident in my discussions with drug company managers in the late sixties (Evans, 1971:183-189). One company had started a research lab in Europe as a result of host government pressure and it had "just snowballed." Another had acquired a European firm with an ongoing research operation. "There was never a conscious decision to create a development unit there," the manager explained. "They just had the men so we had to give them something to do." Once established the European development unit "grew like Topsy."

Incrementalism is exactly what would be expected of a satisficing, risk-avoiding, information-short manager, and the importance of incrementalism in determining the differential response among firms is indicative of the way in which uncertainty magnifies interest-based resistance to decentralization. The ease with which some firms were able to overlook the economies of scale and inappropriate environment arguments also supports the idea that these arguments represent rationales rather than reasons for the centralization of R & D facilities. Predictably, those companies which already had some dispersed research units were unlikely to raise questions of the inappropriateness of the environment or economies of scale. They were more likely to praise the low costs or productivity of their overseas operations. Likewise, there were few complaints from Johnson and Johnson about the difficulties of engaging in research in Brazil.

It is not surprising that some firms responded to nationalist pressure to invest in local R & D nor that those who responded were firms which could do so on an incremental basis. What is surprising is that the response was not greater. Given the favorable economic climate for expanding operations in Brazil and the extreme political vulnerability of the industry, what is strange is that subsidiaries were not falling over each other in a rush to set up local R & D facilities. But they were not. Johnson and Johnson remained the exception rather than the rule. Furthermore, when ABIF, the local equivalent of the Pharmaceutical Manufacturers Association, made an attempt to improve the industry's image with respect to local research, the response was grudging at best.

At the end of 1970, ABIF created the Fundação ABIF, a general fund based on contributions from individual companies. Its purpose was to provide support for students and researchers in organic chemistry, pharmacology, and other areas related to parmaceuticals. The connection between external political pressue and the organization of the Fundação ABIF was undisguised. In its fund-raising letter for 1974, the Fundação ABIF pointed out to its member companies that the investment of an obligatory percentage of sales in research was envisaged in Decree No. 72.552 and suggested the Fundação ABIF as a potential way of investing those funds.

To one Brazilian, managing an American firm, it was incredible that some multinationals were apparently so obtuse as to miss the political connection. He claimed that it had been a terrible struggle to get the Fundação ABIF started. In his eyes the free advertising alone made it more than worthwhile and he could not understand why some multinationals were unwilling to contribute the few thousand dollars a year that the Fundação ABIF was asking for. It represented after all only a few tenths of 1% of their sales, much less than the obligatory contribution seemed likely to be. Most of the large firms did decide to contribute. By 1972 the Fundação was able to disburse almost $70,000 based on contributions from eighty-one companies (Fundação ABIF, 1973:43, 67-68) with the largest contributions running between $5,000 and $10,000. But by 1974, there were rumors that several of the largest contributors wanted to withdraw.

The history of nationalist pressure and multinational response in the area of research and development suggests three conclusions. First, it is clear that a surprisingly large amount of political pressure may be required to produce modest changes in the behavior of multinationals, even in the most favorable context. At the same time, it would appear that even modest successes are useful from the nationalist point of view in that they provide a base upon which future changes can be built incrementally. Finally, given the importance of incrementalism, it is clear that the success of nationalist pressure will vary not only by industry but also issue by issue and firm by firm. This last conclusion can be reinforced by a quick examination of another aspect of the pharmaceutical industry, the issue of backwards integration.

Pharmaceutical raw materials are an expensive item in Brazil's balance of payments. The government was willing to provide attractive fiscal benefits to those who would produce them locally, including "duty-free importation of manufacturing equipment, exemption of such equipment from the IPI and ICM indirect taxes, accelerated depreciation, and preferential treatment by government agencies in handling requests for import licenses and other formalities" (*Business Latin America*, 1975:26). Moreover, if no one is willing to produce a raw material locally, then there is the potential threat of duty-free, government-sponsored importation at the competitive international price rather than the parent-subsidiary price, which would wipe out the private, duty-paying competition.

If my 1974 interviews with multinational managers in pharmaceuticals are any indication, the campaign for local production of raw materials has been received enthusiastically. Since every project must be approved by the CDI (Council on Industrial Development) and the CDI is not likely to approve overcapacity, the chances of getting something close to a local monopoly are great. The fiscal incentives are sufficient to give the promise of good profits, and in addition to the threat of government importation there is always the threat that some competitor will take advantage of the incentives. The multinationals I spoke to were almost uniformly contemplating getting into the production of raw materials.[5]

Any firm that does not go along runs the risk of finding itself at a severe disadvantage. There are already some firms in Brazil that have been forced to buy their own patented exclusive active ingredients from third parties because a competitor set up local production and received tariff protection from the government. The situation parallels closely that which allowed the implanta-

---

[5] An interesting sidelight on raw material production is that it may in fact have as great an effect on local technological innovation as the direct implantation of facilities for product innovation. One of the things that struck me in my 1969 interviews in the pharmaceutical industry was that companies which produced raw materials needed to engage in technologically innovative activity even if they didn't explicitly acknowledge it. The available examples were connected with the production of antibiotics. One of these companies (Evans, 1971:130) was engaged in irradiating its antibiotic-producing micro-organisms in order to obtain more productive mutants. The same company was developing diets for its organisms based on locally available foods. Another foreign company had worked out a way to save on raw materials (which were more costly in Brazil) by extending the length of the fermentation cycle used to produce penicillin.

Moving backwards to the production of raw materials meant becoming interested in local technological innovation. The kind of research entailed in backwards integration is process-oriented rather than product-oriented as official R & D facilities would be, but the positive externalities are much the same. Both develop local skills and offer the possibility of making the industry more responsive to the local environment.

tion of facilities for mixing and packaging in the early fifties. When Getúlio Vargas "virtually banned imports of finished packaged drugs by raising the duties and applying exchange restrictions" (U.S. Dept. of Commerce, 1967a:26), most multinationals realized that if they did not go into fabrication their competitors would.

Pressuring the multinationals into backward integration was easier than pressuring them into research and development because the latter put their profits more clearly in jeopardy. There were fewer uncertainties as to the consequences of the actions advocated. Research and development offered potential long-run gain, but a reduction in the bill for imported pharmaceutical inputs was clear-cut immediate gain. Moreover, the pressures of oligopolistic competition could more easily be brought into play. The gains of competitors could be linked explicitly to the failure to integrate backward in a particular product; and the loss of the market in that product could be attributed directly to a competitor. Refusal to grant fiscal incentives could, of course, have been used as a punishment for failure to make investments in R & D. But failure to engage in R & D does not open up any direct opportunities for competitors in the same way that failure to integrate backward does.

The contrast between research and development and the local production of raw materials suggests that nationalist pressure will be more effective insofar as the effects on local accumulation are concrete and unambiguous, and even more crucially, insofar as failure to comply can result directly in advantages to competitors. Nationalist pressure will succeed more often if it parallels the forces of oligopolistic competition. The implication of this last point is, of course, that nationalist pressure will be successful only if it refrains from trying to shape the process of accumulation in ways that deviate too much from the logic of profitability.

If it is difficult to push multinationals in the direction of investing in local product innovation, the difficulty of shaping the content of that innovation in directions other than those indicated by profitability is greater. Nationalist victories result in the expansion and diversification of the productive resources located in the periphery. The appropriateness of those productive resources to the satisfaction of needs is another question altogether. Illich's warning that the "ploughs of the rich may do more harm than their swords" remains completely outside the purview of bargaining between nationalists and multinationals. There is only one consolation for those taking Illich's point of view. If the nationalists win and innovative facilities are located in the periphery, then the population of the periphery may someday be able to shape the ends toward which those facilities are used. Without the prior nationalist victory there would be nothing to fight over.

The pharmaceutical industry illustrates the necessity of nationalist pressure, the possible gains that may result, and the limits of those gains. But, while pharmaceuticals shows neatly the divergence of "nationalist" and global rationalities, it provides only limited information on the strategies that may be used to bring the behavior of the multinationals more in line with the requirements of local accumulation. Denationalization has left the local bourgeoisie in pharmaceuticals marginalized. Consequently, there is no real question of alliance within the industry itself. Pharmaceuticals illustrate how the behavior of the multinationals can be modified even in an industry in which their control is essentially uncontested. But relative to other sectors, pharmaceuticals are a multinationals' preserve. As Chapter 3 made clear, there are other sectors in which the question of joint control is meaningful and the alliances are more concrete.

The Multinationals and the Question of Control

How rapidly local accumulation takes place depends in great measure on how much of the surplus generated by the multinationals is directed toward further capital accumulation on the

local level. Profit remittances, transfer prices, royalties, rein-
vestment in diversification, backwards integration, and even the
division of export markets, are all issues that involve dividing the
surplus between the periphery and the center. From the multinational's point of view, it is an advantage to be able to remove
the surplus if it can be used more profitably elsewhere. From a
nationalist point of view, projects that lower the costs for other
producers are worthwhile even if their rate of return to the company in the short run is less than satisfactory. High cost polyvinyl
chloride production may mean more profitable plastic manufactures. A project that loses money for five years, but creates the
base for subsequent projects may be good from a nationalist perspective but absurd from the multinational perspective, especially if the profits from the subsequent projects will be appropri-
ated by other firms.

For the nationalists to prevail, there must be a way of exercis-
ing control over the multinationals, of changing certain of their
decisions to make them conform to the requirements of local accumulation. But, for the multinational to maximize its own expansion it needs thorough control; sharing control with fifty different nationalist groups would largely negate the advantages of
being multinational. The fight over control is a fight over the
right to direct future expansion. As such, it is perhaps the most
interesting area of struggle between multinational and nationalist
interests. Conflict over control should not, however, obscure the
broad areas of consensus. Neither local entrepreneurs nor the
state begrudge the multinationals the right to earn profits. High
profits are fine as long as they are reinvested in local accumulation. Likewise the multinationals are firm supporters of local accumulation at as high a rate as possible, as long as their global
profits are not prejudiced.

Shared interest in profits and accumulation mitigates the conflict over control. So does mutual recognition of the importance
of the economic context in determining the actions of both multi-

nationals and locals. If the local environment is sufficiently favorable, as it was in Brazil in the early seventies, conflict over allocating the surplus almost disappears. As one multinational manager told me, "If you are going to have to double capacity every five years then it is no problem having partners, because you will want to reinvest the money anyway." For American firms in Brazil in 1973 and 1974 ratios of reinvested earnings to total earnings were over 85% (*Survey of Current Business*, 1975, 10:43).

Despite the broad general consensus on the desirability of profit-oriented accumulation, despite general recognition that all corporate decisions are constrained by the external economic environment, and despite the temporary mitigation of conflict by favorable economic circumstances in the early seventies, the struggle over control will continue. It is a long-run fight, fought on both sides with a variety of strategies.

Some ways of controlling multinationals do not involve local participation in internal corporate decisions. Legal restrictions, fiscal incentives, and bureaucratic regulations are all external. When these are employed, bargaining will be over the content of the controls more than over the issue of control itself. When the issue is whether a local partner will have a say in strategic decisions, the problem is more subtle. The multinationals have to guess at how serious future differences will be and therefore how risky it is to share equity. Sharing equity is a more interesting indication of the multinationals' willingness to share control, even though local partners may not always adopt a "nationalist" perspective.

The question of control is also played out in a minor way within the organization of the multinational itself. Conflicts between local managers and headquarters sometimes parallel conflicts between nationalist and multinational perspectives. Artificially high transfer prices, for example, make the local manager look as though he is running an unprofitable operation. One manager told me that in the various divisions of his company in Brazil, "the people who run the local plants fight like hell over these issues, and the guy who fights the hardest is an American who doesn't like to lose money."

Debates between local managers and headquarters may also parallel the nationalist/multinationalist debate on the issue of expansion. The manager of a major chemical subsidiary explained to me that the subsidiary's projected diversification in Brazil was "our own idea." Their diversification plans involved getting into areas that the parent was abandoning in the United States because it considered them unprofitable. The parent had to be convinced that "Brazil is different." The subsidiary won, primarily because legal restrictions made it difficult to get existing profits out of Brazil, and so, rather than simply let them pile up, it made sense to invest them. Otherwise, the parent, whose major activities were in the petroleum industry, would have much preferred to use the profits generated in Brazil to explore for oil elsewhere. As this case illustrates, managers taking a "local perspective" are more likely to prevail when their position is reinforced by legal or political sanctions.

There is, however, an essential limitation on the extent to which a manager can be the advocate of a nationalist perspective on accumulation. The manager must accept in principle the primacy of global maximization of profits. Differences of opinion must be argued in terms of the parent not appreciating the true profit potential of the local environment, underestimating the extent to which local accumulation will contribute to global maximization. No manager can afford to be viewed as putting his parochial interests ahead of the interest of his corporation; his arguments with the center must be in terms of misunderstandings rather than conflicts of interest.

Sometimes conflicts of interest are conveniently described as misunderstandings. One manager, a Brazilian, but unquestionably a loyal company man, berated the multinationals in general for being "stupid." "They just don't seem to realize," he said, "that a country has to defend its own interests. You can exploit (to use communist terminology) little countries, but Brazil is no longer one of those." On the grounds of adapting to the political realities, he went on to advocate a series of policies that would bring the multinationals more in line with nationalist perspectives. For him, of course, the risk of misestimating the future political climate is not loss of a small percentage of global profits; it is a risk of his job and his way of life. As he said, "I am a Brazilian and I have to go on living in Brazil."

Brazilian managers may be more prone than foreign ones to see virtue in nationalist perspectives. But the national origins of managers are less important than the demands of their role. As the number of top managers who are Brazilian by birth increases from the current handful, the main result is not likely to be greater nationalism, but an increase in the number of Brazilians with a global perspective. Within the drug industry in Brazil there already exists a group of Latin American managers, who may be Argentine, Chilean, Venezuelan, or even Cuban, but who are essentially international managers. Eventually Brazilians may join this pool, seeing their futures as not necessarily tied to the evolution of the Brazilian economy but rather to the global evolution of their company.

Even if the likelihood of conflict within the multinationals along nationalist versus globalist lines were greater, such conflict would be unlikely to have any substantial effect on policy. While leeway on operational matters may be broad, the subsidiary's long-run agenda is embodied in a five-year plan and the annual budget, both of which must be approved by headquarters. Monthly reports and regular meetings make it hard to disguise deviations, but even if the manager succeeds in deviating, his job depends on producing a profit for the parent. If he does not produce, he will not be a manager. Managers' opinions are effective only as long as they are consistent with profits.

Even in joint ventures, the tightly organized relation between subsidiary and parent also limits the influence of local partners, but the potential autonomy of a local partner is immeasurably greater than that of a local manager, particularly if the local partner is attached to a powerful local economic group or to the state. Local partners are sometimes without influence and always primarily interested in seeing the partnership turn a profit, but joint ventures are still the best indication of shared control. The propensity of multinationals worldwide to enter joint ventures has been analyzed in some detail (e.g., Franko, 1969; Friedman and Béguin, 1971; Stopford and Wells, 1972). The discussion in Chapter 3 of ties between multinationals and local economic groups provided a number of illustrations of the conditions under which multinationals have been induced to share control in Brazil. Building on these illustrations and some quantitative data from the sixties, it is possible to arrive at a more general analysis.

To judge from the behavior of the multinationals in Brazil over the past three decades, it is the general economic and political context that weighs most heavily in determining the rate of joint ventures. Within this general context, industry characteristics and the resources of local partners make a difference. Strong, established local organizations offer the multinational help in overcoming handicaps in its competition with other multinationals, particularly if it is entering the market for the first time. We have already seen some examples in the textile industry where foreign firms with synthetic fiber expertise but not much experience in Brazil were willing to set up joint ventures with large established local groups who could offer well-developed marketing organizations.

The existence of economically motivated partnerships in textiles was contrasted in Chapter 3 with the absence of joint ventures in pharmaceuticals. The multinationals' desire for control in pharmaceuticals is reflected in internal organizational structures as well as in the reluctance to enter joint ventures. Bertero concludes his analysis of the organization of the pharmaceutical sub-sidiaries by reporting (1972:149), "In surveying the several func-tional areas essential to the conduct of the business, it was found that all strategic decisions are made at the center, e.g., at the International Division in corporate headquarters."

The desire of drug companies to retain maximum control makes good sense in view of the nature of the industry. As long as the most important resource of an international drug company, its ability to produce new products, remains centralized, and as long as a large portion of the profits at the subsidiary level are attributable to this centralized activity, the problem of allocating returns will be severe. Drug companies will want to reinvest substantial portions of their profits back in the center where the activities crucial to their expansion are going on. If they cannot remit profits they will try to reallocate by means of transfer prices. Conflict with local partners is an obvious result. In the careful understatement of Stopford and Wells (1972:120), the multinationals "cannot easily arrive at what they consider to be a fair return for the technology that they contribute."

The issue of research and development has come full circle. In the earlier discussion, the connection was drawn between the desire for control and reluctance to disperse R & D. Now the re-verse connection has been added. As long as profits depend sub-stantially on new knowledge produced at a centralized location, resistance to shared control will be stiff. This relation can also be seen in terms of bargaining power, as Moran (1975) has pointed out. The source of the multinationals' profits is safe from any local threat. Even threats by the state to follow policies favoring com-petitors can be applied only after a new product has been copied by others elsewhere. The position of the multinational is never stronger than when it is based on monopolistic control over new knowledge.

The effect of centrally produced knowledge is not limited to new products and processes. When the commercialization of a product depends primarily on advertising, control is also unlikely to be shared. Thus, multinationals with high promotion expenditures are highly unlikely to enter joint ventures. They can also control the activities of their local managers in detail. The prepackaged advertising of the giant soft drink companies is perhaps the best example (cf. Stopford and Wells, 109-110). In Brazil, the tobacco industry, whose domination by foreign capital was noted in Chapter 3, is a good example of the connection between reliance on advertising and foreign control. In advertising as in R & D, the source of profits is generated at the center, and the multinationals' bargaining power is correspondingly increased.

Recognition of the relation between knowledge-based profits and resistance to shared control reinforces the arguments in favor of local innovative facilities that were made earlier. In addition to its other disadvantages from the point of view of the periphery, centralization of innovation stands in the way of the peripheral country's gaining a larger share of control over the local operations of the multinationals. Centralized innovative facilities and centralized control reinforce each other, just as dispersion of control and dispersion of innovative facilities reinforce each other.

In contrast to R & D and advertising, natural resources provide good leverage for local interests trying to gain a share in control (cf. Moran, 1975). The empire of Azevedo Antunes, discussed in the last chapter, is a good example. When the Dutra government gave Antunes the rights to the Amapa manganese deposits in 1947, he became an attractive partner for Bethlehem Steel. Two decades later, his ability to open up rights to the Aguas Claras made it worthwhile for Hanna mining to enter a joint venture with him.

What the local partner offers in these cases is, of course, an essentially political contribution. While the 1967 Brazilian constitution eliminated some of the earlier legal restrictions on foreign participation in mineral ventures, it is still a sensitive area. The government has generally been unwilling to grant concessions to foreigners without local partners. A rich mineral deposit offers potential for monopoly returns just as a new drug does, but to realize this the multinational must have the acquiescence of local political forces. The multinational may offer access to international marketing channels (cf. Moran, 1974) but the leverage is on the side of the locals if they choose to take advantage of their political bargaining power.

Politically based disadvantages are at the core of most situations in which multinationals are likely to share control. In some cases, legal regulations make a local partner a necessity. While there is no set of laws in Brazil equivalent to "Mexicanization," there are a number of restrictions on the participation of foreigners. Petrochemicals, which will be discussed in the next chapter, are a prime example. In other cases, having a local partner opens up the possibility of certain legal advantages, such as low-cost loans from the National Development Bank (cf. *Business Latin America*, 1975:388).

In the last chapter it was argued that the local bourgeoisie, because of its embeddedness in the local social structure, could perform certain integrative tasks better than the multinational managers. One component of the political advantage of the local bourgeoisie has to do with the existence of personal ties to the state apparatus, and is therefore similar. But the political disadvantage of the multinationals is not due just to differential connectedness. Local capital has a legitimacy that the multinationals cannot match; it is for this reason more than any other that the multinationals are compelled to share control of their enterprises. Sometimes the multinationals find sharing control justified, not so much by any immediate political threat as by their experience in other countries. One manager in discussing his impending joint ventures said, "We don't like joint ventures. We are used to running our own show and we don't need the money or the skills. But they (the Brazilians) have a point. It is better to share a project with national capital and let the state harmonize than to have it taken away." The experience of Anaconda and Kennecott in Chile was this manager's model for the disadvantages of attempting to retain exclusive control. "If Kennecott and Anaconda had had local partners then maybe they would still be there," he said, and then added, "We lost one in Chile too."

Lessons from the international context force multinational managers to take local political concerns like "denationalization" more seriously than they might on the basis of their experience in Brazil alone. They are aware that even in Brazil, acquisitions of local firms are uncomfortable events for the local elite. One way of making them less uncomfortable is to allow a former owner to remain as a local partner. Even in new ventures, local partners may provide important informal political resources of a more positive kind. The skills and contacts of a local partner can be extremely valuable in dealing with the complexities of the state bureaucracy, ferreting out favorable regulations, or escaping the effects of unfavorable ones.

To put the argument in its most simplistic form, the best cards on the side of the locals are political. The multinationals' best cards are technological. In order to retain an upper hand in the bargaining, the multinationals must have knowledge that is applicable to the periphery and that the periphery cannot buy on an open market. It is for this reason that the multinationals have an interest in preventing the dispersion of R & D operations. It is also for this reason that they have an interest in standardizing consumption patterns across as many markets as possible. Since consumption patterns (especially among consumers with enough income to make a difference) are becoming more homogeneous at a rapid rate while the multinationals' control over new knowledge is eroding only slowly, technology continues to be a strong card in most industries.

There is an additional factor that makes the bargaining difficult from a nationalist point of view. Arguments over control presuppose that the expansion of the system at an acceptable rate is ensured. The discussion here has been premised on the existence of a particular economic context, the immensely attractive Brazilian economy of the late sixties and early seventies. Arguments over control take on a different quality when expansion itself is in question. When the multinationals are not confident about future profits then they will be likely to respond to demands for local control by refraining from increased investment, thereby threatening overall economic expansion.

In order for their bargaining efforts to succeed, the nationalists require a favorable economic environment as well as political pressure. The inability of Brazil to increase the rate of joint ventures during the more nationalist period of the early sixties illustrates this point well. The best available systematic quantitative evidence on joint ventures, the data of the Harvard Business School's multinational enterprise project (Vaupel and Curhan, 1969, 1973) shows that relative to its earlier experience and relative to the experience of other Latin American countries, Brazil did very badly on joint ventures from 1960 until the beginning of the "economic miracle."

Changes in the proportions of Brazilian joint ventures over time make the connection between the economic context and multinational willingness to share control blatantly clear. During the rapid growth of the fifties, as Table 4.6 shows, the majority of multinationals starting manufacturing operations in Brazil were willing to share control.[6] As soon as the lean times of the early

[6] In interpreting the Harvard multinational enterprise project data on joint ventures presented in Table 4.6, two things should be kept in mind. First, the multinational enterprise data counts associations among multinationals as joint ventures. A good proportion of the joint ventures in the table do not represent any sharing of control with local interests. Second, looking only at the proportion of subsidiaries that are joint ventures at the time they begin their operations overestimates the number of joint ventures, since there is a tendency for joint ventures to degenerate into wholly owned subsidiaries. Once the data are corrected for changes in ownership after manufacturing has begun, the proportion of joint ventures drops substantially (almost a third of the subsidiaries that started out as joint ventures ended up as wholly owned). If only joint ventures with local

TABLE 4.6   Patterns of Ownership for U.S. Manufacturing Subsidiaries
(subsidiaries of 187 U.S. multinationals)

	Total	Date Began Manufacture		
		pre-1946	1946-1959	1960-1967
Joint Ventures as a % of total number of subsidiaries (at date of beginning operations):				
All Subsidiaries	38%	25%	34%	46%
Latin America	46%	33%	39%	53%
BRAZIL	39%	24%	53%	34%
Joint Ventures as a % of total corrected for J.V.'s that became wholly owned:				
All Subsidiaries	28%	19%	27%	33%
Latin America	33%	28%	34%	35%
BRAZIL	25%	21%	35%	5%

	Total	pre-1946	1946-1959	1960-1967	(date unknown)
Gross numbers of manufacturing subsidiaries:					
All Subsidiaries	5209	1031	1444	2610	124
Latin America	1325	206	474	616	29
BRAZIL	200	34	101	63	2

Source: Vaupel and Curhan, 1969:124, 242, 243, 249.

sixties began, the proportion of new joint ventures dropped and the tendency to turn old joint ventures into wholly owned subsidiaries was accelerated. The number of joint ventures that became wholly owned was almost as large as the number of new joint ventures formed. The net increase in the number of joint ventures amounted to only 5% of the increase in the total number of manufacturing subsidiaries. The difference was not, of course, solely due to changes in the policies of the multinationals. A less bouyant economic climate also worsened the bargaining position of local partners. The proportion of subsidiaries formed by acquisition of local companies rose at the same time as the proportion of joint ventures was falling (Vaupel and Curhan,

---

Brazilian partners were considered, the proportion would be smaller still. Of the total number of Brazilian subsidiaries that were not wholly owned as of 1967, only 40% had local partners. The rest either had foreign partners or simply sold stock to a diverse set of investors. Thus, the proportion of cases in which there was real shared control was more like 10% of the total number of subsidiaries than the 25% shown in Table 4.6.

1969:256). Finally, of course, Brazil's share in the total number of subsidiaries formed fell dramatically.

There was no trade-off between expansion and control. Fewer multinationals were willing to enter and those that entered were less willing to give up control. Since the rate of acquisitions was increasing, "denationalization" was exacerbated. Brazil in the early sixties illustrates perfectly the extent to which an attractive "investment climate" is the sine qua non of bargaining over control. Without the promise of profits, political pressure will undermine expansion without increasing local control.

No systematic data comparable to the multinational enterprise project data has been collected for the years since 1967. Impressionistic evidence points, however, toward an increase in the propensity of multinationals to share control. Certainly that is the perception of the local multinational managers. One of them explained to me in 1974, "Ten years ago you could come in on a 100% basis, a few years ago you could come in with 51%, now you have to come in on a minority basis." As a statement of fact, this is an exaggeration of the change; as the perception of the manager of one of the largest European subsidiaries in Brazil it is significant in itself.

In the last chapter the establishment of concrete ties in the form of joint ventures during the late sixties and early seventies was viewed from the point of view of local economic groups. It is worth reviewing the process from the point of view of the multinationals. One of the best illustrations is provided by E. I. Dupont de Nemours. Dupont's history in Brazil is a long one, but until 1953 it was always in association with Imperial Chemical Industries Ltd. When the ICI/Dupont link was declared in violation of American antitrust laws, Dupont remained in Brazil on its own, but with a limited range of activities. Its most important manufacturing operations were in its most traditional product line, gunpowder and dynamite. Its major subsidiary was a wholly owned operation and had no Brazilian partners.

Dupont did not become seriously interested in overseas manufacturing investment until the late fifties, but within ten years foreign sales had become a major source of growth. Its foreign sales grew twice as fast as its domestic sales between 1965 and 1974 (see Dupont *Annual Reports*, 1966-1974), until they were over 35% of total sales and represented a market of over $2 billion. Most of the goods sold abroad were also manufactured there. Latin American sales quadrupled in this period, amounting to almost half a billion dollars by 1974.

Dupont's position at the end of the sixties in Brazil was not consistent with its position as one of the top three chemical companies in the world, nor with the tremendous growth of its overseas sales, nor with the apparent potential of the Brazilian market. It was still primarily an explosives manufacturer with some local production of freon, fungicides, and chemical specialties (*Annual Report*, 1968). Over the next five years the profile of its involvement in Brazil changed dramatically. Part of the strategy of expansion involved sharing equity with a variety of local partners.

The first step was to get involved in a massive caustic soda/chlorine project, Salgema (*Annual Report*, 1971:15). This was hardly a Dupont specialty; it was not even something that Dupont produced elsewhere. It was not a high technology project and the most important resources were the salt deposits controlled by a local entrepreneur, Euvaldo Luz. But the project was an attractive one from the point of view of the Brazilian government, since half of the country's caustic soda was being imported. Dupont got 45% of the equity in the project, Luz got 45% and the balance remained with the national development bank.

The Salgema project is a textbook example of a situation in which a multinational is likely to relinquish control. Initiated at the beginning of the "economic miracle" by a company anxious to get into the Brazilian market, it involved no exclusive knowledge, either in the process or the products, nor any special marketing techniques that might be generated by the multinational at the center. It did involve natural resources, which increased the leverage on the local side.

Given the weak bargaining position on the multinational side inherent in the Salgema project, it is not surprising that other multinationals, better established in Brazil, were reluctant to come in. With this project, however, Dupont had demonstrated its commitment to expansion in Brazil and was in a good position to get approval for other projects. One of these was a toluene diisocyanate plant in the new northeast petrochemical capitalization, Isocianatos S.A. In this case, the product was a Dupont specialty and the technology less widely available. Reportedly Dupont's bid for the TDI plant was approved by the CDI over projects by Bayer and Dow Chemical. Because it was "sensitive to the government's desire for Brazilian control" (*Business Latin America*, 1972:132), Dupont took a minority position in the equity.

Dupont's willingness to accept partners may have also been based on the political assets such partners could provide. Petroquisa, which holds 40%, is an invaluable partner, as will become evident in the next chapter. The local private group holding 20% has no particular industrial skills to offer but is headed by Clemente Mariana, notable in Brazilian politics as well as being an important financier.

While Dupont was establishing its joint venture in petrochemicals, it was also involved in buying out one of the most important locally owned paint companies (*Annual Report*, 1972). Retaining the local management and allowing them to keep a minority share of the stock diminished the possibility of negative political reactions. The project was also attractive from the point of view of the government because Dupont could increase plant capacity substantially, something that the local owners were not able to do. For Dupont the move was obvious. As one of the two or three largest paint manufacturers in the United States it made sense to enter the market in Brazil. What could be more sensible than putting one of the firm's most well-developed products and marketing technologies to use in yet another area of the globe?

By 1973 Dupont in Brazil was a diversified company with major new affiliates coming into production. Eighty-three million dollars had been put into Brazil at this point (*Annual Report*, 1973:14). Not all of the new investment was in joint ventures. The original wholly owned subsidiary was also engaged in a major new project, the construction of the first lycra spandex plant in Latin America. In this venture Dupont was in an excellent bargaining position. Most of the world's lycra spandex is produced by Dupont; the technology is new and not likely to be available from anyone else; and, as an extra attraction, the product, which is used in bathing suits, gave every promise of providing multimillion dollar exports to the European market. There was no need to share control with a local partner. New investments in photographic supplies and teflon processing were also done without partners.

This example, seen from the perspective of a multinational, helps to clarify the nature of the alliances that bind together multinationals and local economic groups. In the discussion in the last chapter it was noted that most local economic groups do not allow multinationals to gain equity positions in their central firm. The same is true for the multinationals. Dupont never considered sharing control by allowing a local partner a piece of the equity in its principal subsidiary. Locals were given (or allowed to keep) a share of certain strategically chosen new ventures. When Dupont's bargaining position was sufficiently strong, it retained control for itself.

Joint ventures with the large local economic groups do not threaten the multinationals' control over their most important enterprises. Among the very largest foreign companies there are very few joint ventures. Among the fifty-one "major Brazilian firms" listed by *Business Latin America* in 1975 there were only four joint ventures between Brazilian and foreign firms (*Business*

Latin America, 1975:389). Aside from the minority local equity participation in Volkswagen and one partnership with the federal government, the companies of Azevedo Antunes were the only joint ventures among these top fifty firms. Many of the other companies participated in smaller ventures involving local partners, but the subsidiary remained under the parent's exclusive control. A comparison of this list with *Business Latin America*'s list for 1967 shows that the role of joint ventures among the very largest subsidiaries was virtually the same before the "economic miracle" as after. In 1967 there were six joint ventures among the top fifty firms instead of four (*Business Latin America*, 1967:310). Multinationals in the late sixties and early seventies never opened their existing principal subsidiaries to Brazilian participation. When multinationals shared, it was in the interest of expanding their sphere of operations.

The consequence of shared control was the creation of a "buffer zone" of mixed enterprises, located in areas of the economy that were of interest to the multinationals but where their bargaining power was weak. The creation of joint ventures has strong implications for the integration of the strongest local economic groups into networks of international capital. The implications are much weaker when it comes to any erosion of the autonomy of the multinationals. Only in the buffer areas do multinationals have to contend with the interests of local partners. Since these are the areas in which they would have had a harder time entering or been more strictly subjected to external controls had they not had local partners, the extent to which they were forced to compromise their "drive for unambiguous control" (Stopford and Wells, 1972:107) was marginal.

As Brazil's rate of growth slows and economic conditions become less favorable, persuading multinationals to share control becomes more difficult. If expansion, the multinationals' primary goal, is uncertain, Brazil is in a weak position to demand shared control. In the chemical sector for example, there are two major American chemical firms that got into the industry behind Dupont: Dow Chemical and Monsanto. Despite its late entry, Dow set up a "salgema" project in the northeast very similar to Dupont's, but on a wholly owned basis (*Business Latin America*, 1975:299). If its $500 million northeast ethylene project is approved, it will have succeeded in carving out a second substantial project without a local partner (*Business Latin America*, 1975:196). Likewise, Monsanto has not had to bring in a local partner in rubber chemicals and phosphates projects (*Business Latin America*, 1976:122). Both of these companies have local partners in other ventures, but they were able to enter, on a wholly owned basis, areas that seemed to be part of the "buffer zone" at the time Dupont was making its plans.

The immediate future is unlikely to produce any substantial changes in the direction of greater sharing of control with locals. The creation of joint ventures will proceed at a slower rather than a faster pace. The rate of change should not, however, obscure the direction of change. Even if Brazil experiences an economic downturn and a decrease in the rate of expansion of areas amenable to local control, consequences of past joint ventures will remain. We have already seen how past joint ventures have helped strengthen and diversify major local groups. These groups will not be dislodged in the future. More important for the long run has been the creation of joint ventures between the multinationals and the state, and a closer examination of these ventures is the subject of the next chapter. Even if the multinationals have managed to retain control over existing ventures, they have also been forced to allow the creation of a buffer zone that will play a central role in Brazil's future industrialization.

The multinationals have succeeded in preventing an erosion of their control over previously established enterprises, but control over the process of accumulation in Brazil is a different matter. Their behavior has been constrained even in sectors (such as pharmaceuticals) where their proprietary control remains unquestioned. Expansion into new areas has been conditional on sharing control in a number of important instances. The process of accumulation is increasingly shaped by the joint decisions of the triple alliance, and the multinationals can no longer hope to avoid participation in this alliance.

In the new joint ventures, in the old redoubts of the multinationals, and in the areas that the multinationals have been allowed to develop without sharing control, the struggle between nationalist versus multinational versions of correct accumulation must continue. Nothing happened during the miracle to change that; the temporary economic euphoria may have mitigated the conflict, but the differences remained. The conflict will get worse if the economic situation worsens.

The most important scene of battle between nationalist and multinational strategies of accumulation is and will be in the area of relations between the multinationals and the various segments of the state apparatus. On the one hand, the state is responsible for providing the external controls that become more necessary as times grow more difficult. On the other hand, state-owned corporations play a central role in the buffer zone of shared control. They have become an integral part of the international capitalist network. At the same time they have special leverage vis-à-vis the multinationals. The most important resource that local partners may possess is political power, and the local partners with the most direct political leverage are state-owned firms.

The external controls enforced by the state combined with the internal leverage exercised by state corporations provide the most convincing reason to believe that a nationalist logic may prevail over the multinational logic of accumulation in the future. Nationalist logic is, of course, no guarantee of continued expansion, nor of the welfare of the population. At this stage, substantial differences between the logic of local accumulation and the logic of global profit maximization continue to exist, and the most powerful forces on the side of the former are state-owned enterprises and other parts of the state apparatus.

5.

The State and the Multinationals*

DURING the Brazilian "boom" the upper floors of the metallic Edifício Horsa on São Paulo's prestigious Avenida Paulista included two of Brazil's major petrochemical companies among their tenants: Union Carbide and Petroquímica União. Harold Walker, the man in charge of Union Carbide's operations at the beginning of the boom, had the confident expectation in 1969 that his company would soon be one of the major ethylene producers in Brazil. By 1974, he was no longer in Brazil and the Wulff cracker that he had based his hopes on had proved a technological misadventure.

Petroquímica União had also gone through some difficult times. By 1974, financial difficulties had forced its former owners to take a minority position. The dominant shareholder was now Petrobrás's subsidiary, Petroquisa. Orfila Lima dos Santos, who arrived to take over the company's affairs for its new owners, did not have quite the cosmopolitan air of Walker, but he did have what Walker had hoped for, a naphtha cracker that worked. He was an engineer by training and had worked for years in Petrobrás before becoming the head of Petroquímica União.

Walker's departure was almost fortuitous, the result of a technological fluke. The arrival of Orfila Lima dos Santos was not. It was part of the general expansion of state enterprise in var-

---

* The analysis of the petrochemical industry presented in this chapter draws on the ideas I developed in "Multinationals, State-Owned Corporations, and the Transformation of Imperialism," which appeared in *Economic Development and Cultural Change* in 1977, 26(1):43-64.

ious branches of the petrochemical industry. Orfila Lima dos Santos may be considered a member of the "state bourgeoisie" or simply a "public sector technocrat." Whatever they are called, he and his confreres have become part of the corporate power structure in several key industries. Their rise to power, and the general expansion of state enterprise behind it, has given the Brazilian state an increasingly central role in bringing about basic industrialization.

Because of its ties with international capital the Brazilian state may be seen as an "entreguista" state, one that is "selling out" Brazil. Its powerful role in generating basic industry and its proven capacity to expand into areas previously controlled by foreign capital, enable it to be seen as a nationalist state, the last hope and defender of the local bourgeoisie. The power and autonomy of state enterprises make them plausible instruments of "estatização" (literally "statization"), representing their own interests, the interests of a state apparatus "out for itself."

The images of the "entreguista" state, the nationalist state, and the "state for itself" are not so contradictory as they appear. They are three roles played by one complex actor. To put them together to form a more complete picture of the way in which the Brazilian state has inserted itself into the process of industrialization is the aim of this chapter. The principal focus will be on those parts of the state apparatus most directly involved in the process of industrialization, state-owned industrial enterprises. The background for the analysis has already been set out in Chapters 3 and 4. Given the relations between local and multinational capital that were described in Chapter 3, it is clear that the state cannot take a purely "nationalist" stance. Not only would this put it in conflict with the foreign capital that controls a growing share of the most dynamic sectors of the economy, it would also put the state in conflict with the best organized, most powerful local industrial groups who have themselves formed alliances with the multinationals.

Chapter 3 shows why the state cannot be nationalist in the sense of simply being against multinational capital. Chapter 4 shows why the state must be nationalist in another sense if it is to serve as a promoter of accumulation at the local level. The pursuit of a "nationalist logic" of accumulation is necessary in order to maximize long-run local expansion. Multinationals are likely to conform to this logic only under pressure from the state. Another reason for the state not being purely "entreguista" was presented in Chapter 4 in the discussion of control. It was argued there that nationalism and political pressure were the most effective levers for inducing multinationals to share control. Even those local economic groups most closely allied to the multinationals have an interest in ideological nationalism, up to a point, since it improves their bargaining position vis-à-vis their foreign partners.

Implicit in Chapters 3 and 4 is an argument as to why the state could not be simply "for itself." The idea of a state being "for itself" implies that there is no class or other social grouping with sufficient power to push forward its own "project" for the future or to control the state apparatus. The ties between important local groups and the multinationals, the strong common interest of these allies in profitable expansion of industrial production, and the importance of their support in maintaining expansion, all make it unlikely that the state could ignore or easily dominate them. The state does have an external constituency interested in development and it must be responsive to this constituency if it is to foster rapid accumulation.

Playing three roles at the same time, yet none of them exclusively, means that the state must juggle a complex set of aims and strategies. But the aims and strategies are not, of course, juggled by a single monolithic entity. "The state" exists as an actor only in the form of a diverse collection of organizations and individuals. While the various organizations that make up the state apparatus are linked by legal obligations and bureaucratic ties to the executive, the degree of their autonomy is often substantial. Different aims and even contradictory aims may be pursued by different parts of the state apparatus.

State enterprises, which are the focus here, may have interests that conflict with the regulatory apparatus of the state or with the executive. For that matter, different state enterprises may vary in their strategies. The potential for diversity is not simply a complicating factor in the analysis but is theoretically important in itself. Nonetheless, the existence of diversity should not be allowed to obscure the fact that the various parts of the state apparatus together occupy a distinctive position that sets them apart from both the national bourgeoisie and the multinationals and gives the state its central role in the process of accumulation.

The state did not, of course, suddenly spring into action as a central economic actor with the advent of military rule in 1964. As the discussion in Chapter 2 indicated, the state played a central role in the transition from classic dependence to dependent development. By the time the military took over in 1964 the foundations of state entrepreneurship had been well laid. Curiously however, the initial impulse of the new military rulers was to refrain from taking advantage of these foundations.

State Enterprise and Military Rule

General Humberto Castello Branco was more in the mold of General Eurico Gaspar Dutra than in the mold of Getúlio Vargas. As the first post-1964 military president, Castelo Branco hoped, like Dutra, to base Brazil's economic development on internationalism and economic liberalism. Roberto Campos, his principal advisor in economic matters, was a devout economic liberal who believed that a return to competition was the only way out of Brazil's stagnation. If international firms were the strongest in the competition, so be it as far as Campos was concerned (cf. Galeano, 1969; Fishlow, 1974). The first military regime did make some attempts to reverse the trend toward increased state presence in the economy. The Fábrica Nacional de Motores was sold to Alfa Romeo. Thyssen Steel was allowed to purchase some equity in Cosigua, the steel company owned by the state of Guanabara. These gestures were considered "precedent setting" in the international business press (*Business Latin America*, 1968:232), but the major trends of the period were in quite the opposite direction. The disastrous performance of the Brazilian economy from 1964 to 1967 discredited economic liberalism even more thoroughly than the Dutra period had. The state-owned enterprises created in the forties had reached maturity by the late sixties and had thoroughly consolidated their positions in several basic industries.

Petrobrás had become one of the hundred largest corporations in the world and the largest corporation in Latin America. Its refining capacity was a far cry from the 20,000 barrels per day that the Conselho Nacional de Petróleo had been able to solicit from the private sector in 1946. By 1967 Petrobrás had a total refining capacity of over 500,000 barrels a day, sufficient to supply over 90% of the demand for petroleum derivatives (Banas, 1969:48). Despite poor luck in its explorations, Petrobrás was supplying about a third of the country's crude oil by the end of the sixties (IBGE, 1972).

The Companhia Siderúrgica Nacional also had an impressive record. Baer (1969:125) estimated that the CSN's Volta Redonda plant returned in 1965 between 22% and 29% of the value of equipment and installations. Judged on the same basis, U.S. Steel would return about 10%. On rail plates and hot rolled sheets, the selling price per ton of steel produced at the Volta Redonda plant in the mid-sixties was less than the price per ton produced by American companies in the United States. In addition to simultaneously supplying steel at internationally competitive prices and making a good return, the CSN in the mid-sixties was providing 80,000 jobs and saving Brazil over $250 million on its balance of payments (Baer, 1969:128, 146).

Tendler's (1968) analysis of the state-owned generating companies shows them to be equally successful. They constructed the dams and hydroelectric facilities necessary to break the industrial bottleneck caused by insufficient electricity, and so with a technological entrepreneurship that caused foreign consultants to "marvel at the Brazilian engineers' ability to resolve quickly and imaginatively a problem never before encountered." According to Tendler, at least one of the companies, CEMIG in Minas Gerais, was reputed to be "one of the best run companies in Latin America" (Tendler, 1968:21, 155).

Given the central place in the process of accumulation that state enterprises had carved out for themselves, it would have been extremely disruptive to try to dislodge them, but the military also had positive reasons for supporting state enterprises. To abolish them would have meant diminished central control over the economy, which would have run directly counter to the government's strategy. Despite the pro-laissez-faire convictions of many of the military's early supporters (cf. Blume, 1968; Hall, 1964; Seikman, 1964), the major impact of the military's takeover was a centralization of economic power (Schmitter, 1973; Evans, 1974). Price controls and regulations became harder to avoid. An ever growing share of public revenues went to the federal government. Even the military's responses to problems like housing and social security had the result of centralizing financial resources in government hands. The National Bank for Habitation (BNH), the Fund for the Guarantee of Time in Service (FGTS), and the Social Integration Program (PIS) provided the central government with vast resources for investment and lending.

A greater role for state enterprises was quite consistent with the military's general strategy of increasing political and economic centralization. Instead of diminishing under the military, the number of state enterprises increased more rapidly than in any previous era. According to a survey done by *Visão* in the mid-seventies (1975:51), most were not inherited by the military regime; they were created by it. Some of these were established for the same reasons that the military had supported the CSN and Petrobrás. No private firm would have considered producing indigenously designed light aircraft in Brazil. The potential profits were not commensurate with the risks. But the logic of the military went beyond profit and loss. They felt that national security required a national capacity to produce planes, so Embraer, a state enterprise, was created to enable Brazil to produce planes. Other state enterprises were created for reasons similar to those which had drawn the state into electrical generation. Allowing private companies to make what they considered adequate profits would have required lifting price controls on telephone communications. Without higher profits private firms were not willing to invest. The results were Embratel and Telebrás, two state-owned holding companies in telecommunications. These companies were an answer to the difficulties of getting the private sector to invest in areas where prices and returns are held low in order to stimulate other investors. They also reflect the desire of the military to centralize control over the burgeoning number of state enterprises by creating holding companies. Siderbrás in the steel industry is another example of this same tendency (Bacha, 1976:31).

Liberal economics were incompatible with the military's desire to develop Brazil's industrial potential—especially given the persistent element of nationalism within the military's ideology. Private firms would have been happy to take over the CVRD's export operations, but they would have been foreign or joint ventures at best. Foreign firms could also have been found to take over the Pignatari copper interests. Foreign domination in either sector would have been unacceptable to the military.

So far the expansion of state enterprise has not been the result of an explicitly statist ideology, although it is hardly fortuitous. Even Carlos Langoni, an ex-student of Milton Friedman (*Visão*, 1975:46), found the expansion of state enterprise a "response to the inherent characteristics of our process of economic development" rather than the result of the victory of statist ideology. The apparently "inexorable" growth of state enterprise has produced a situation in which the state accounted for, according to one estimate, the majority (60%) of fixed investment in Brazil in 1969 (Baer et al., 1973:30). It has also produced a pattern of differentiation of public and private capital that complements the pattern of differentiation of foreign and local capital that was described in Chapter 3.

Despite the expansion of state enterprise, the state was still absent from most industrial areas at the close of the "boom." Its strongest presence is in traditional infrastructure investments. It also dominates in raw materials—mining and petroleum refining. As Table 5.1 shows, the state's involvement within manufacturing is in intermediate products. The steel and basic petrochemical products produced by state enterprises are inputs for other manufacturers. Finally, the heavy involvement of the state in the financial sector gives it a role in providing another "input" or service for the manufacturing sector. The division of labor between the state and private capital is more clear-cut than the division between foreign and local capital that was discussed in Chapter 3. The areas of overlap, and therefore of potential competition are fewer.

Some have looked at the complementarity of state and multinational capital and drawn the conclusion that the state is serving as the "handmaiden" of multinational expansion. Tavares and Serra (1973:78) argue that the current pattern of differentiation implies "a division of labor where the state took up the heavier responsibility of supplying the domestic market at low costs with basic inputs and external economies which were used by MNC's for their own expansion, both domestically and in export markets." Insofar as the state has gone into some sectors, such as hydroelectric power and telecommunications, specifically because foreign firms could not be induced to expand their investments in

TABLE 5.1   Participation of State Enterprises in the Brazilian
Economy, 1973 (share of assets of the 269 state-owned firms included
on the *Visão* list of the largest 4,160 firms in 1973)

Sector	Proportion of Assets in State-owned Firms (%)	
Mining	63	
Industry	19	
Nonmetallic minerals		2
Metal fabrication		37
Machinery		0
Electrical machinery		0
Transport equipment		2
Wood products and furniture		0
Rubber		6
Chemicals*		50
Textiles		0
Food and beverages		1
Tobacco		0
Printing and publishing		0
Leather products		0
Agriculture and Forestry	4	
Construction and Engineering	8	
Public Utilities	84	
Railways		100
Road transport and passengers		6
Water transport		45
Air transport		22
Telegraph and telephone		97
Radio and television		0
Electricity		79
Water, gas and sewers		99
Port services		100
Developmental services		51
Other		76
Commerce	0	
Services	36	
Banking and Finance	38	
Total	39	

* Includes petroleum refining.
Source: *Visão*, 1975:67.

those areas, to view the state as working "in the service" of the multinationals is sensible. Indeed, it would be difficult for the state to work in the service of accumulation without also working in the service of the multinationals. Before trying to assess the extent to which the role of the state should be seen as primarily supportive, it is worth looking at the dynamics of the division of labor between the state and the multinationals.

Even during the years of the "miracle" when the multinationals were expanding their investments in Brazil most rapidly, the influx of foreign capital was more than matched by the growth of state enterprises. The data in Table 5.2 are from the same source that was used to compare multinational and local capital in Chapter 3. It is not the rise of the multinationals that stands out as the most important trend in manufacturing during the period of the boom, it is the rise of state enterprises. Table 5.3 shows data for five of the largest state enterprises between 1967 and 1973. In the seven-year period in question the five state-run organizations considered here increased their capital and reserves by a total of over $2.2 billion. This figure is not only three times the total increase for the ten selected multinationals considered in the last chapter, it is also almost double the total growth in U.S. man-

TABLE 5.2   Growth of State Enterprises Among the Largest 300 Manufacturing Firms, 1966-1972 (percentage of assets)

	1966			1972		
	Multi-	Local		Multi-	Local	
Selected Sectors	national	Private	State	national	Private	State
Iron and Steel	4	34	62	15	16	70
Chemicals	69	24	7	69	19	12
Petroleum refining						
and distribution	25	11	64	12	6	82
Total for all manufacturing						
(excluding petroleum)	51	41	8	50	35	15
Total share including petroleum	47	36	17	42	28	30

Source: Newfarmer and Mueller, 1975:108-110. Based on Visão lists supplemented by other sources to determine ownership.

TABLE 5.3 Performance of the Largest State-owned Industrial Firms, 1967-1973

| Firm | Assets[1] 1967 | Assets 1973 | Growth in Assets (%) | Rate of Return[2] | | | | | | | Average Return (%) |
				1967 (%)	1968 (%)	1969 (%)	1970 (%)	1971 (%)	1972 (%)	1973 (%)	
Petrobrás	853.0	2,141.9	151	10.8	10.7	9.7	14.4	17.9	17.8	16.3	13.9
CVRD (Cia. Vale do Rio Doce)	133.8	637.4	376	21.7	16.3	26.2	27.9	24.1	15.5	21.1	21.8
CSN (Cia. Siderúrgica Nacional)	356.0	352.7	−1	0	4.5	7.8	12.8	11.8	17.4	12.9	9.6
Cosipa (Cia. Siderúrgica Paulista)	126.5	399.9	216	−21.6	−5.1	−0.3	1.1	0.6	24.3	4.1	0.4
Usiminas[3] (Usinas Siderúrgicas de Minas Gerais)	168.4	271.4	61	−5.8	2.3	4.7	11.4	13.8	20.4	10.7	8.2
Averages	327.5	760.7	161	1.0	5.7	9.6	13.5	13.6	19.1	13.0	10.8
Comparative Multinational Averages[4]	72.5	144.2	94	11.5	10.2	10.3	11.0	19.8	26.4	22.6	16.0

[1] Capital plus reserves in millions of current $US. Averages are unweighted.
[2] Ratio of net profits to capital plus reserves, calculated by *Business Latin America*.
[3] Nippon Steel is a minority shareholder in Usiminas.
[4] Table 4.4 above, figures are for ten selected multinationals.
Source: Business Latin America, "Major Brazilian Firms and How They Fared," various issues, 1967-1973.

ufacturing assets in Brazil during the same period (cf. Chapter 4, Table 4.2). These data are confirmed by broader-based comparisons. Examining Visão's largest hundred corporations (which include public utilities), Bacha (1976:32) found that the share of state enterprises in total assets increased from 67% in 1970 to 74% in 1974. The central and growing role of state-owned operations in the buildup of industrial capital is undeniable.

Taking state sector expansion into account changes the picture as far as "denationalization" is concerned. Chapter 3's comparison of foreign and local shares within the private sector produced the conclusion that the multinationals were gaining ground, but that they were gaining it more slowly than had been imagined. For manufacturing overall there was a growth in the multinational share in the late sixties and early seventies, but trends for individual sectors were ambiguous. Once the state sector is included, however, there has been no denationalization. The share of Brazilian capital among the top three hundred manufacturing firms has grown, not fallen. The relative decline of the multinationals is accentuated because of the dramatic growth of the petroleum sector during the period. But even discounting the effects of the state monopoly in petroleum refining, there is still a slight increase in the Brazilian share of assets among the top three hundred manufacturing firms. Queiroz (1972:155-159) arrives at essentially the same conclusion by comparing the thirty largest firms in 1962 with the thirty largest in 1972.

Including the state does not erase the relative decline of local private enterprise. Table 5.2 provides no evidence that local private capital was able to "ride the coattails" of the expanding state sector. In steel and chemicals, the growth of the state share was accompanied by a worsening of the position of local capital relative to the multinationals. The percentage distributions in these sectors might suggest that the increased state share was taken not from the multinationals but from local capital. The growth of state enterprise has protected the overall Brazilian share of manufacturing, but it has hardly protected the share of the local private entrepreneurs.

When judged by growth, the performance of the state sector is unambiguous. If returns are the focus, state enterprises do not have as good a record as the multinationals. The overall averages shown in Table 5.3 indicate that the state enterprises considered here are making significantly lower profits than the multinationals considered in the last chapter. While the ten selected multinationals averaged 16% return on investment, the five state companies averaged under 11%. The same discrepancy is found in broader-based comparisons. Bacha (1976:32), basing his estimates on Visão's full listing of over 5,000 companies, reports profit rates for state-owned firms at 9% in the period from 1968-1974. According to these same estimates, the multinationals enjoyed an average rate of profit of 15.8% during the same period.

Low rates of return can be interpreted in several ways. Supporters of an "anti-statist" position argue that it indicates inefficiency and is a sign that the growth of the state sector is artificial, excessive in relation to the real contribution of state enterprises. Comparisons of foreign and state-owned steel companies might be taken to support this critical interpretation. The two largest foreign steel companies, Belgo Mineira and Mannesmann, averaged double the rate of return that was achieved by the three state-owned steel companies listed in Table 5.3. Recent critiques of the state-owned steel companies by the World Bank (see *Business Latin America*, 1977:173) lend support to this view, but a very different interpretation would flow from the Serra/Tavares analysis (see above) of the role of state enterprises.

If, as Serra and Tavares suggest, the state has really taken on the role of supplying basic inputs at low cost, then it is not surprising that state enterprises are making low returns on their investments. This interpretation suggests that the outputs of state firms are deliberately priced low, raising the profits of the multinationals that buy them and lowering the profits of the state enterprises that sell them. It does not explain differences within the steel industry, but it is consistent with the relatively higher profits of the CVRD. The CVRD is the only state enterprise whose output is primarily exported rather than used as an input for local industry and it is the only state enterprise that has consistently made profits greater than those achieved by the multinationals. A definitive explanation for the rates of return of state firms must await more evidence. For the present, one thing is clear. The state has not so far used the leverage inherent in its position to boost the profit rates of its enterprises above those of the multinationals.

The current discrepancy between multinational profits and state profits should not obscure the potential power of the state to shift returns by shifting state-controlled prices. The state could, for example, make life very uncomfortable for Ford, Chrysler, and GM by increasing their costs through higher steel prices while simultaneously cutting demand by raising the price of gasoline. Both these policies could be profitable for state enterprises at the expense of the foreign auto-makers, but such tactics are unlikely to be used since to do so would undermine expansion by demoralizing the multinationals. The managers of state enterprises can afford to accept lower rates of returns as long as their expansion is not dependent on internally generated funds. Policies that lower rates of return in the foreign sector would directly threaten multinational managers.

The expansion of state enterprise over the last three decades has created an implicit partnership between state enterprises and the multinationals built around their complementary roles and their common interest in accumulation. The basic division of labor between them grew out of the "infrastructure versus direct production" tradition and retains some of the characteristics of that complementarity even though the state has gradually shifted the boundaries of its sphere. More important, however, than the gradual shift in what are defined as appropriate areas for state entrepreneurship has been the creation of newer, more explicit partnerships—joint ventures in which the state and foreign capital share ownership of the same enterprise.

State enterprise has been incorporated into the network of international capital just as the largest local private economic groups have been. Joint ventures that combine state and foreign capital are fundamental to the current phase of the expansion of state enterprise. They are a new way of drawing the multinationals into a "nationalist" schema of accumulation. They also allow the state to participate in operations where it would have had difficulty working on its own. Through concrete alliances the state can enter areas that lie outside the production of basic services and inputs without actually displacing the multinationals. By bringing the multinationals into ventures that provide basic inputs, the state can retain control over these strategic goods while forcing the multinationals to share in underwriting their production.

The new partnerships between the state and the multinationals also have implications for the future position of local capital. The setting up of a joint venture provides a context for bringing in the "national bourgeoisie" as a third partner. The creation of "tri-pé" or "tripod" ventures reinforces the tendency toward alliances between the local elite groups and the multinationals. It also gives local capital another way of expanding the sphere in which it can operate. The creation of partnerships does not abolish the previous division of labor, either between local and foreign or between state and private capital. In fact, joint ventures tend to take place in sectors that lie on the "buffer zones" between the territories of different kinds of capital. Alliances blur the boundaries, while at the same time fostering a new, more tightly knit kind of integration among the different kinds of capital.

Building Alliances: The Discovery of the Tri-pé

When Ford, Chrysler, and General Motors were persuaded to build assembly plants in Brazil in the 1950's, not even the most nationalist/statist Brazilians would seriously have suggested that they form partnerships with the state. Had it been put forward, Ford, Chrysler, and General Motors would probably have considered the suggestion absurd. When Fiat decided to build an assembly plant in Brazil in the early seventies, it was considered natural by both sides that Fiat should enter as a partner of the government of the state of Minas Gerais. The change seems dramatic in the context of the auto industry because the auto industry did not go through the intervening evolution. The development of relations between the state and multinational capital took place in other industries, most notably in petrochemicals.

The history of the petrochemical industry in the sixties and early seventies is an archetypal example of alliance-building on a foundation of differentiation. The initial structure of the industry featured a clear differentiation of different kinds of capital. The refining of imported and domestic crude was the prerogative of Petrobrás and a few small nationally owned refineries that had been granted concessions before the Petrobrás monopoly was declared. On the other side of the industry, the production of plastics and other petrochemical products was dominated by giant international chemical companies based in the United States or Europe. Union Carbide, Koppers and Borden, Solvay, and Rhone Poulenc were all major producers. They sold their products to local companies who would use polyvinyl chloride (PVC) to make plastic containers, or nylon fibers to produce textiles, or formaldehyde resins to make plywood. Other buyers were multinationals. The auto industry, for example, was a major customer for the final products of the industry. Between the outputs of Petrobrás's refineries and the developing market for plastics, synthetic rubber, and other final products there was an unfilled gap. Basic and intermediate petrochemical products still had to be imported. The most likely candidates to fill the gap were either Petrobrás, by integrating forward, or the multinationals, by integrating backward.

Petrobrás was primarily concerned with the search for new reserves; its efforts at exploration absorbed vast amounts of capital and personnel. For the multinationals, importing inputs was hardly a disaster. As long as they had parent companies interested in exporting and as long as none of their competitors threatened to set up facilities for local production, they were in a comfortable position. In addition, the ambiguous nature of Decreto/Lei 2,004 (the law creating Petrobrás) made the multinationals wary of making major investments in petrochemicals. The limits of the monopoly were unclear. A multinational that put itself heavily into basic petrochemicals ran the risk that the government might decide that these were to be considered part of the legally defined Petrobrás monopoly. With the increasing nationalism of the early sixties, such fears seemed even more justified.

The military coup of 1964 did not break the impasse, but it set the stage. In 1965, soon after the coup, there was an explicit statement that petrochemicals would be the domain of private enterprise. Union Carbide stepped forward and proposed the construction of a naphtha cracker with a capacity of 120,000 tons per year of ethylene, double Brazil's consumption of polyethylene, polystyrene, and PVC combined. The cracker would use the Wulff process, the most advanced in the world according to Union Carbide. Most of the ethylene produced by the Wulff crackers would be used by Union Carbide itself in the production of roughly 90,000 tons of polyethylene.

A local group also decided to try to fill the gap. The "Capuava" or "Soares/Sampaio" group, which was led by Paulo Fontainha Geyer, started with one of the small, locally owned refineries. Despite its small size (about 25,000 barrels per day), the group's

Capuava refinery was the largest of the private refineries and the only one located in the industrial center of São Paulo. The Capuava group realized that, while their base in the refining business gave them a foot in the door, they did not have sufficient strength to enter into production of basic petrochemicals on their own. Their first attempts to attract a powerful partner centered on multinationals. They tried to interest two giant petroleum companies, Gulf and Phillips, neither of which was very heavily involved in Brazil at the time. Phillips decided to join the project and help build a naphtha cracker with an initial capacity of 167,000 tons per year of ethylene, later to be expanded to 300,000. The Capuava group also brought in other local capital, including the financial group headed by Walter Moreira Salles.

The most interesting of the Capuava group's overtures, however, was to the state. They wanted Petrobrás, on whom they would depend for their supplies of naphtha, to become a partner in the project. Petrobrás could not do this. It was legally prohibited from entering joint ventures on a minority basis. After considerable negotiation, a solution was discovered. In December of 1967, a new state-owned company, Petroquisa, was created. Though it was a wholly owned subsidiary of Petrobrás, Petroquisa was legally able to enter joint ventures as a minority member. The Capuava group's petrochemical complex would be Petroquisa's first joint venture. The new state partner had some ambivalence, however, about entering a joint venture with foreign capital. In the end Phillips "decided not to proceed" (UNIDO, 1969b:4).

The entrepreneurial efforts of the Capuava group did not end with pulling together a coalition to build the central Petroquímica União organization. In order for the complex to be profitable, they needed customers, more customers than were currently available. The group went out and recruited multinational associates who could become users of the chemical feedstocks produced by Petroquímica União. Four companies were set up to buy Petroquímica União's output. One of them was wholly owned by the Capuava group and its local allies. Three of them were joint ventures with multinationals, and one of them was a three-way split with multinationals, the state (Petroquisa), and local capital all participating. In addition, another joint venture with a multinational was brought in to supply chlorine, which, in combination with ethylene, is a prime ingredient in making vinyl chloride.

Later, the Capuava group and their most important local allies (the Moreira Salles group) joined Hanna Mining in a holding company, UNIPAR. The complex of companies surrounding Petroquímica União became known as the UNIPAR group. At the time it was created in the late sixties, this group represented an almost unique example of local capital, state capital, and multinationals bound together by buying-and-selling relationships and equity interlocks, to form a single interdependent system of companies. Figure 5.1 illustrates schematically the structure of the UNIPAR group.

The most surprising thing about the sequence of events that led to the creation of the UNIPAR group is that the entrepreneurial impetus came from local capital. Paulo Geyer and the Capuava group are universally acknowledged, by both Brazilians and foreigners in the industry, to have taken a risk that few multinationals would have dared, despite their greater resources. The creation of Petroquímica União was not just daring, it also turned out to make sense in terms of what was needed for the development of the industry at that time. Several companies explained to me that, at the time Petroquímica União came onstream, they had reached the limits of what they could do with the outmoded processes they were then employing and that, without the new supplies of ethylene and other basic inputs that Petroquímica União provided, they would have been stymied (cf. UNIDO, 1969a).

The second lesson of the Petroquímica União experience is

FIGURE 5.1 The UNIPAR Group, 1971

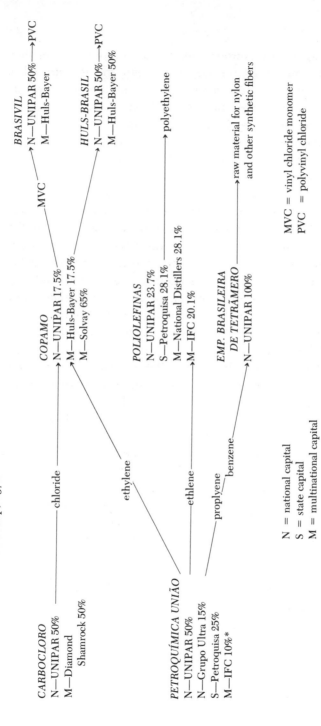

CARBOCLORO
N—UNIPAR 50%
M—Diamond
    Shamrock 50%

PETROQUÍMICA UNIÃO
N—UNIPAR 50%
N—Grupo Ultra 15%
S—Petroquisa 25%
M—IFC 10%*

COPAMO
N—UNIPAR 17.5%
M—Huls-Bayer 17.5%
M—Solvay 65%

POLIOLEFINAS
N—UNIPAR 23.7%
S—Petroquisa 28.1%
M—National Distillers 28.1%
M—IFC 20.1%

EMP. BRASILEIRA
DE TETRÂMERO
N—UNIPAR 100%

BRASIVIL
N—UNIPAR 50%——→PVC
M—Huls-Bayer

HULS-BRASIL
N—UNIPAR 50%——→PVC
M—Huls-Bayer 50%

chloride ——————— MVC

ethylene ——————→ polyethylene

ethlene

proplyene

benzene ——————→ raw material for nylon
                  and other synthetic fibers

N = national capital
S = state capital
M = multinational capital

MVC = vinyl chloride monomer
PVC = polyvinyl chloride

* Participation by the IFC is purely financial and involves no active involvement in the company. There is a small participation by Hanna Mining in UNIPAR itself which is of a similar nature.

Source: Banas, Brasil Industrial, 1972, Vol. III (São Paulo: Editora Banas, 1972), p. 137.

that local private enterprise, even in its most ambitious form, was under no illusions about entering an industry like petrochemicals on an independent basis. It should be noted that the state entered, not because Petrobrás was anxious to take over the petrochemical industry, but because the private sector was anxious to gain its participation. Neither empire-building on the part of state technocrats nor any ideological commitment to state participation brought the Brazilian state into the petrochemical industry; rather, it was the logic of the situation, a logic that was even clearer to the "national industrial bourgeoisie" than it was to the state itself.

The development of the petrochemical industry in the sixties was characterized by an impressive initiative on the part of local capital and by the entry of the state. Neither of these developments prevented multinational firms from continuing to hold a central position in the industry, but the main thrust in the industry's transformation came through the creation of the Petroquímica União complex and the UNIPAR group. In the beginning of the seventies, the importance of Petroquisa began to increase while both the pioneering multinational (Union Carbide) and the pioneering local group (UNIPAR) ran into difficulties that dislodged them indefinitely from positions of real leadership.

The first startling development was the failure of Union Carbide's Wulff cracker. What had been considered "start-up difficulties" in Wulff units wherever they were tried (UNIDO, 1969b:4) turned out to be fundamental flaws. Wulff crackers just did not work. In Brazil, millions of dollars of investment had to be simply written off, and the technology had to be abandoned. The multinational entrant had lost on the ground that should have been its forte—the ability to supply sophisticated technology. Union Carbide ended up dependent on Petroquímica União to supply it with ethylene for its polyethylene operations, and Harold Walker was transferred back to the United States. While it remained, and will remain in the future, one of the largest chemical companies in Brazil, Union Carbide lost the central role in the petrochemical industry that it might have had if the Wulff technology had worked.

The decline of the UNIPAR group was less sudden but more thorough. The group's problems started with the inevitable delays, cost overruns, and other difficulties associated with the construction of the Petroquímica União complex, which made the costs of the products produced higher than anticipated. In addition, despite the UNIPAR group's best efforts, the downstream markets for its output were not all ready by the time the plant came on-stream. Petroquímica União had to pay the price of being a pioneer. But in 1974, only two years after Petroquímica União had come on-stream, the market for basic petrochemical products had grown so much that it was time to double the output. The Capuava group's banking operations were not going well. In addition, the Moreira Salles group, which had the other major share of the stock of UNIPAR, decided it no longer wanted to be involved in petrochemicals. One way out might have been to expand the Capuava group's profitable refining operation, but this would have meant reversing the long-standing policy that oil refining should be a state monopoly. The UNIPAR group was in difficulty, and the only escape was to turn to the multinationals or Petroquisa.

By mid-1974, the pioneering local group had been dethroned. Petroquisa took over Petroquímica União, leaving UNIPAR only a minority holding, and Orfilo Lima dos Santos arrived to take charge. The original base, Refinaria União, was made part of Petrobrás itself. The Moreira Salles shares of the UNIPAR holding company were sold to an Italian group, and Capuava also lost its banking operations. Entrepreneurship was not enough to gain local capital a central place in the petrochemical industry. At the end of 1974, the only thing the Capuava group had left of its petrochemical empire was voting control of the UNIPAR holding company, and even this was maintained by only a slim majority.

Petroquisa had moved into a central position. Its importance was reinforced by other transformations outside the sphere of the UNIPAR complex of companies. Phillips Petroleum decided to get out of the nitrogenous fertilizer business in Brazil, and Petroquisa, in what was generally considered to be a "rescue operation," ended up as a major partner in Ultrafertil, Brazil's largest producer of ammonium nitrate, DAP, and sulphuric acid. An earlier decision by Petrobrás to maintain exclusive control of synthetic rubber production led Firestone to give up its major interest in the production of styrene, and Petroquisa took this over as well. The state may have been drawn into the petrochemical industry by private interests in 1967, but by 1974 it was a ubiquitous participant in the vast petrochemical complex that had grown up around São Paulo.

The activity in São Paulo turned out to be only a dry run for an even more ambitious effort on the part of Petroquisa. In 1972, Petroquisa created a new subsidiary of its own, Copene (Petroquímica do Nordeste, S.A.) (Copene, 1974; U.S. Dept. Commerce, 1974) and began to draw up plans for an entirely new petrochemical industry to be located in the northeast of Brazil. That it was willing to try to implant a full-blown petrochemical industry thousands of kilometers from the major markets of São Paulo and Rio, in the middle of the backward northeast, was an indication of the new state company's growing self-confidence. That private firms, both local and multinational, were willing to join in the venture showed that Petroquisa's capability was highly rated by others as well.

Organizationally, Petroquisa, through Copene, was to play the same role in the Polo do Nordeste that the Capuava group had played in the creation of the Petroquímica União complex. Copene itself would be in charge of the central cracking unit supplying ethylene, propylene, benzene, etc. It would also supply steam and electric power. Copene was also responsible for putting together a set of user companies to surround the central unit. These companies in combination would become owners of 50% of the stock in Copene itself. The tripartite alliance of multinational, state, and local capital that had been tried in São Paulo became the *modus operandi* for the new complex.

In two years of negotiations, Petroquisa managed to put together a set of companies which, once they all go on-stream, should double the size of Brazil's petrochemical industry and constitute the biggest single impetus to industrialization that has been attempted in the northeast region. Surrounding the Copene central complex, twenty processing units have been planned, organized into eighteen firms. Eleven of them follow the tri-pé form. They are three-way alliances between state capital, local capital, and multinational firms. Five others involve two types of capital (local and multinational, or state and multinational); one is controlled by local private capital, and one is wholly state-owned.

The linkages established in the new northeast complex do more than bind state, local, and multinational capital. They also bring together foreign capital from different center countries. A dozen multinationals based in at least six developed countries are involved in the ownership of the Polo do Nordeste. In addition to the dozen multinationals who are owners, fourteen others are involved as licensors of production processes. In one company, for example, the stock is shared among a European multinational, a Japanese firm, and two local firms; the process they will use is licensed from an American firm. In another case, ownership is divided among a Japanese firm, Petroquisa, and a Brazilian firm. The Brazilian firm, in turn, has two major American firms as shareholders; the process to be used is licensed from still another American firm.

Integration and Differentiation Inside the Tri-pé

If the Polo do Nordeste is successfully implanted, it will be an impressive demonstration that it is possible to harness the multinationals to a project in which capital accumulation is defined in essentially nationalist terms. All participants in the Polo do Nordeste recognize that it is a risky venture that will produce returns only over the long run. Otto Vincente Perrone, the Petroquisa executive who was the key figure in organizing this new petrochemical complex, saw it as important in large part because it would contribute to regional development. His description of the project (Perrone, 1972) is in terms of comparisons with regional development strategies in Europe.

For the private sector in São Paulo, the aim of developing the northeast could not in itself justify participating in the project. For each of them individually, investments in São Paulo or in the vicinity of São Paulo made sense. The inputs, markets, and services were all in São Paulo. The penalties of being a pioneer in the northeast were likely to be great. At the same time, they recognized that São Paulo was being choked by its own development. Continuing increases in the demand for inputs like water and electricity were creating strains. Transportation facilities were under pressure. The private sector could see that starting at a fresh location could enhance long-run possibilities for profitable operation. Petroquisa bridged the gap between the long-run logic of accumulation and the problems of the individual firm. It provided assurances that the move to Bahia would be a collective one. There would be others there to attract a skilled labor force, and to provide inputs and perhaps even markets for outputs. Most important, Petroquisa itself would carry a major part of the burden of risk.

In the eyes of its partners, the role of Petroquisa took many forms. Petroquisa's participation gave them confidence that the other private partners would not give up in the face of difficulties, leaving them without complementary plants and others to share the overhead. The state was seen as a potential disciplinarian. As one participant put it, "If you have a policeman for a partner, he may only have 3% of the equity but he has a gun." Petroquisa also took the major responsibility for the parts of the project that were most likely to take losses in the early stages. Electrical generators, water supplies, the central cracking unit itself, had to be ready when the downstream plants began to reach completion, otherwise they would not be able to operate at all. Yet, until all the downstream plants were operating at close to full capacity the central facilities were likely to lose money. This had been one of Petroquímica União's problems in São Paulo, and in the isolated pioneering environment of Bahia it was likely to be even worse. Having Copene take charge of the central facilities meant that no individual private investor had to shoulder these risks.

Relations with Petrobrás were another area of uncertainty where Petroquisa seemed likely to be a valuable partner. Petrobrás is a looming presence in the operations of any petrochemical firm in Brazil. Access to raw materials depends on Petrobrás, which, along with the National Petroleum Council and the Interministerial Price Council (CIP), also determines the prices at which the raw materials will be available. Dealing with Petrobrás is not always easy. As one multinational manager put it, "When Petrobrás doesn't live up to a contract there isn't too much you can do about it. You just don't sue Petrobrás." Doing business with Petrobrás was also compared to "sleeping with an elephant," something that you only do carefully. It is not that Petrobrás was viewed as pathologically inefficient or anti-foreign, only that it was very powerful and therefore had to be handled with extreme care. Having Petroquisa as a partner is the closest a multinational can come to a guarantee that Petrobrás will be on its side.

Beyond Petrobrás, there are the other parts of the state apparatus to be considered. Multinational managers are well aware of the extent to which their profits depend on favorable treatment by the state. The head of one multinational said that he considered Brazil a socialist country because the state was so heavily involved in the economy. Another said, "It's like doing business with the Russians: you have to play by their rules." A third felt he needed every ally possible within the state apparatus in order to protect his technology, open the possibility of remitting profits back to the United States, and protect him in general from damages that might be inflicted by other parts of the state apparatus. Even when you are in a joint venture with Petroquisa and have the full support of the government in principle, he said, "it's a formidable bureaucratic wall you face."

For companies participating in the Bahian complex, the question of the treatment they receive from the government as individuals is perhaps less important than the treatment that the Bahian project as a whole receives. Without full backing from the state over the long term, the future of the whole northeast petrochemical complex would be jeopardized. Petroquisa's participation provides insurance that the state apparatus will continue to stand behind the venture.

The participation of the multinationals in the project is almost as crucial to Petroquisa as Petroquisa's participation is to them. Technology is, of course, one of the multinationals' prime contributions. It would have been possible to purchase most of the technology, but buying technology has disadvantages. An engineering firm does not have the same interest in future profits that a partner does. Once a plant is constructed the engineers are not there to deal with problems. Getting technology from a partner whose local profits depend on its efficient operation is the best way to insure that it will work. Petroquisa was looking for full, continuous access to the most advanced technology available; taking on multinational partners was the best way to get it.

Having multinational partners also made it easier to raise the estimated three-quarters of a billion dollars (U.S. Dept. Commerce, 1974) necessary to finance the Polo do Nordeste. Independently of the direct contributions of the individual partners (either from parents or from retained earnings of Brazilian subsidiaries), the participation of the multinationals helped to legitimate the raising of funds on international capital markets.

Despite Petrobrás's enormous capacity to accumulate capital, its resources were stretched by other activities, such as continued exploration.

The problem of stretched resources also applies to Petrobrás in the area of management. Petrobrás is known in the industry as a "school for petrochemical management." The Brazilians it has trained not only staff its own operations, but also fill important positions in the private sector, where there is a heavy demand for competent Brazilian executives. This, combined with the creation of Petroquisa and the diversification of Petrobrás's operations, puts considerable pressure on managerial as well as financial resources.

Both the multinationals and Petroquisa gain from their alliance, but the partner that gains the most may well be the national bourgeoisie. According to the analysis of Araújo and Dick (1974), local firms contributed only about 5% of the capital and almost none of the technology, yet they ended up with about 30% of the equity. Once again, the bargaining power of the local bourgeoisie appears stronger than one would expect on the basis of traditional economic analysis. The combination of integrative skills and political legitimacy has carried at least certain representatives of the local bourgeoisie a long way.

One effect of the tri-pé has been to bring local groups into the petrochemical industry that have no obvious reason for being there. The construction firm, Carmargo Correa, which has a share along with Mitsubishi and Petroquisa in Ciquine Química, is one example of an unlikely entrant into petrochemicals. The Coimbra Bueno group, which became a partner in Polibrasil S.A. along with Royal Dutch Shell and Petroquisa, is another. Euvaldo Luz, who was Dupont's partner in Salgema, is a third.

Local partners like these may create problems, as Dupont's Salgema project illustrates. In the first five years of the project's life, it experienced several difficulties due in part to the fact that Dupont and Luz "did not see eye to eye" (*Business Latin*

America, 1975:145). Completion of the plant, scheduled for 1974, was delayed and the costs of construction mounted. The state-owned portion of this project was originally held by the Banco Nacional de Desenvolvimento Econômico. In mid-1975 it was reported that Dupont "would warmly welcome a partnership with Petroquisa." According to this report, Dupont felt that Petroquisa "could make a valuable technical contribution and that Petroquisa's links to other official agencies would facilitate complicated transportation arrangements . . ." (*Business Latin America*, 1975:146). Within a few months, Luz was out, Petroquisa was in, and the project was expanded to include the production of dichlorethylene in addition to caustic soda and chlorine.

Local partners who prove to be liabilities are one of the risks inherent in the tri-pé. Their presence can be justified only in terms of larger political strategy and the importance of strengthening the local bourgeoisie, or at least maintaining legitimacy in its eyes. As long as they are content with a nonoperational role, these unlikely partners are not a disadvantage; but their presence can be seen more as a subsidy to local capital than a positive move toward resolving problems of accumulation.

Local capital, if it is to be a working partner, must bring a certain strength of its own into the venture. If local groups can offer some relevant industrial experience and familiarity with the local environment of bureaucratic regulations and incentives, then the effect of their participation is different. They may reinforce Petroquisa in cases of conflict between the multinational logic of global accumulation and the nationalist logic of local accumulation. They may offer useful assistance to the multinational partner, along the lines suggested in the last chapter. By giving such groups a chance to participate in ventures that they could not otherwise enter, the tri-pé strengthens them and, of course, separates them further from other local capital.

The number of local groups who can take advantage of the

tri-pé is not large. It includes primarily the very largest groups whose private alliances with the multinationals were discussed in Chapter 3. It also includes some smaller, newer groups who are not as diversified as the groups considered in Chapter 3 but who have strong positions in petrochemicals. They are the "cutting edge" of local capital in petrochemicals in the early seventies, just as the Capuava group was in the sixties. Two good representatives are the "Grupo Ultra" and the Peixoto de Castro group.

The Grupo Ultra began with the Peri Igel family's successes in the distribution of bottled gas. Its transformation into a sophisticated industrial conglomerate is, however, the work of Hélio Beltrão. Beltrão's career was not that of a typical industrialist, but it was one that prepared him well for the epoch of the tri-pé. Entering Getúlio Vargas's civil service in the thirties, he made himself a reputation as one of Brazil's foremost "functionários públicos." When the military government came to power it called on him to head the commission for civil service reform. He was also minister of planning under Costa e Silva. As president of the Ultra group he has diversified its holdings through alliances with both the multinationals and the state.

By the mid-seventies the companies associated with the Grupo Ultra were involved in everything from fertilizer production to supermarkets. Ultragaz continued to be a major power in the distribution of bottled gas. Ultrafertil had become a partnership with Petroquisa instead of with Phillips Petroleum, but the Ultra group retained its interests in Ultrafertil. Ultralar, which produced appliances, was mounting a chain of supermarkets and "hypermarkets." It was now in partnership with a Dutch firm. Oxiteno S.A., which produced glycols, ethers, and ethanolamines was, along with the UNIPAR companies, one of the pioneering examples that proved that the tri-pé could work in São Paulo. In Oxiteno the Grupo Ultra allied itself with Petroquisa, Lokab (another local chemical group), and Scientific Design, a North American firm that provided the technology. One

of Oxiteno's principal customers is Atlas S.A., a partnership between the Grupo Ultra and ICI (more specifically, ICI's North
American subsidiary). Melamina Ultra is the only case in the Polo
do Nordeste of national, private capital on its own. It will be the
first melamine producer in Latin America. Oxiteno S.A. will also
have a plant in the Polo do Nordeste, planned to be three times
as large as its plant in São Paulo.

The Grupo Ultra's participation in the petrochemical industry
depends on alliances. It also depends on personnel who have
been trained in state enterprises. Aside from Beltrão with his experience in the state apparatus, there are perhaps a dozen executives trained by Petrobrás, including Paulo A.G. Cunha, who is
vice-president of the group's holding company, Cobrapar. The
Grupo Ultra still does not rank with Matarazzo or Ermírio de
Moraes, but it is a good example of the way in which aggressive
local capital can take advantage of the space created by the state
to grow and to gain a strategic position among the multinationals.

Another local group that has been highly successful in the petrochemical industry is the Grupo Peixoto de Castro. Like the
Capuava group, it grew out of one of the National Petroleum
Council's original, pre-Petrobrás private refinery concessions
(Cohn, 1968:100). Manguinhos Refinaria S.A. near Rio de Janeiro
provided the group with a profitable base from which to expand
In the sixties they moved into the production of methanol and
formed Prosint S.A. Later they bought out Synteko, a local firm
and one of their principal customers. With the purchase of Synteko they became involved in the Polo do Nordeste as partners in
Metanor, which will have a methanol capacity about twice as
large as their Rio operation. The other partners in this venture
are Petroquisa and Paskin (a local chemical group based in
Bahia). Peixoto de Castro is not allied with multinationals as the
Grupo Ultra is, but, like the Grupo Ultra, it has been able to take
advantage of the state-sponsored Polo do Nordeste to strengthen
its position in petrochemicals.

The Grupo Ultra and the Grupo Peixoto de Castro illustrate that the role of local capital in petrochemicals did not end when Petroquisa took over Petroquímica União. Neither of these groups will ever dominate the industry, but they are not simple satellites either. Peixoto de Castro will have an independent base as long as it is allowed to keep its refinery. The Grupo Ultra is more entangled with powerful partners, but its entanglements give it leverage and a basis for expansion. Like the Azevedo Antunes group, it has made the formation of alliances the basis of its growth.

Petroquisa has not been able to create an industrial bourgeoisie out of whole cloth. Many examples show just the opposite. When the state has been forced to rely on partners like Euvaldo Luz, the result has been not to create a modern, nationally owned chemical firm, but to strain the tri-pé itself. The tri-pé is successful when it takes sophisticated and aggressive local firms, separates them further from the bulk of their locally owned competitors, and brings them into closer collaboration with the multinationals. Like the private alliances discussed in Chapter 3, it differentiates the local bourgeoisie, and widens the gap between the elite and the rest.

The main effect of the tri-pé is to reinforce the integration of the state apparatus, the multinationals, and those few locally owned firms able to participate. The petrochemical industry provides a natural context for such integration. The tri-pé only solidifies an interdependence that was obvious to the major producers in the industry from the beginning. In the sixties and early seventies most products were supplied by only one or two firms. Cooperation among competing firms was seen as necessary for survival. In the case of PVC, for example, a Solvay subsidiary, Eletro Cloro, was producing about half Brazil's output. Vulcan S.A., currently a subsidiary of Occidental Petroleum, was, and still is, one of Eletro Cloro's biggest customers. At the same time Plavinil, another Solvay subsidiary, was Vulcan's biggest competitor. Seeing the necessity of living in the industry together with Vulcan over the long run, Solvay has been willing to reduce the amount of PVC it supplies to its own subsidiary in order to make sure that Vulcan does not suffer excessive shortages.

Locally owned firms as well as multinationals have been aware of the importance of cooperation. Oxiteno, for example, is the source of the major inputs for Atlas S.A., its joint venture with ICI. Atlas was allowed to set up its plant on an adjacent location, but the Grupo Ultra has tried to be extremely scrupulous in not giving Atlas any other advantage that might alienate the three or four other multinationals that are Ultra's major customers. One of the reasons Ultra did not join with a partner in its melamine venture in the Polo do Nordeste was that it was afraid that an alliance with any one of its major customers might have alienated the others.

The tri pó did not create integration out of atomized competition. It institutionalized the cooperation that already characterized the petrochemical industry. The small number of buyers and sellers of basic products helped make this cooperation possible. So did the fact that at least through 1974, petrochemicals was a seller's market. Firms usually faced the problem of producing enought to satisfy regular customers, not the problems of competition from other producers. Difficulties in maintaining supplies made mutual interdependence all the more obvious. In mid-1974, for example, Carbocloro had trouble with one of its transformers and had to reduce its output of chlorine. Lacking the chlorine from Carbocloro, Copamo had to reduce its output of vinyl chloride monomer by 50%. This in turn created problems for Brasivil, which had relied on Copamo's output in order to produce PVC (cf. Figure 5.1).

Complementing the tendencies toward integration inherent in the structure of the industry itself is the conviction on the part of public and private sector managers that they take a common view of the aims of management. The ideological similarity between the executives of state enterprises and those who direct the multinationals is striking. The members of the state bourgeoisie who work in the joint ventures already operating in São Paulo see themselves as "hardnosed" and having a strong interest in the "bottom line." Their private counterparts see them the same way; Petrobrás and Petroquisa personnel are recognized as having a "strong profit orientation." The technical competence of the state managers is also recognized by their private sector counterparts. No one, for example, questioned the ability of Orfila Lima dos Santos to run the Petroquímica União cracking operations as efficiently or more efficiently than any manager from the private sector would have done.

Just as the tri-pé reinforced the structural interdependence that already existed in the industry, it also reinforces the ideological cohesiveness of the state bourgeoisie and the multinational managers. Some of them have worked together now for a number of years, confronting problems together and in most cases resolving them successfully. Especially for North American executives, who have less contact with public sector industrialists at home, the experience has unquestionably been educational. A final factor reinforcing cohesion is the movement of individuals from Petrobrás and Petroquisa to the private companies, a movement which is likely to continue as long as Petrobrás provides good training and private sector salaries remain superior.

There are some perceived differences between the public and private partners within the tri-pé. The general policies of Petrobrás and Petroquisa are viewed as being willing to give up dividends if necessary to ensure the highest possible levels of output. Petrobrás as a monopoly is seen as having certain obligations that a private firm would not have—for example, to make sure that there is gasoline distribution along the Transamazônica, even if these operations are unprofitable. State managers may be characterized as less aggressive and more "team players" than private managers.

Members of the state bourgeoisie themselves still feel a certain distinctiveness, but there is no sense of inferiority. Those who were trained in the Petrobrás "school" generally feel that the Petrobrás system is as good as or better than the administrative methods of any international firm. That they have been sent to rescue important private producers obviously enhances their feelings of competence. The members of the state bourgeoisie have gained confidence, partly as a result of participation in tri-pé ventures, in their own ability to run any industrial operation, no matter how complex or technologically advanced.

The self-confidence of the state bourgeoisie seems to have created only minor frictions up to this point. North American engineers with long experience in construction may resent the arguments they get from young Petroquisa engineers over questions of equipment or plant design. But this sort of friction is unlikely to disrupt the tri-pé. The confidence of the state managers will make a difference only if serious policy differences between the state and the multinationals arise in the future. In the unlikely event of serious conflict, however, the experience that the state bourgeoisie is gaining in the context of the tri-pé will make it a more formidable opponent for the multinational managers.

While the tri-pé is most obviously a mechanism for integration, it fits in well with preexisting patterns of differentiation. So far, it has been restricted to a specific area of the petrochemical industry, fostering partnerships that fill the old gap between the state monopoly in refining and the private "third and fourth generation" firms three or four links along the path to the final consumer. In a few basic products, notably synthetic rubber and fertilizers, the state participates in ventures that are closer to the consumer. But even when the state does become involved in an enterprise, like Ultrafertil, that sells part of its production directly to consumers, there is a tendency to let the private partners focus on the commercial aspects of the operation.

While the state has generally refrained from moving too close to the consumer, some multinationals have begun to place greater emphasis on consumer goods. These goods are subject to looser price controls and may therefore offer better profitability. Multinationals also prefer to concentrate on more specialized, technologically exotic chemicals, the "filet mignon" of chemical production. This pattern of differentiation fits in nicely with the "product life cycle model." The areas multinationals have chosen for themselves correspond to Moran's findings on the circumstances that give the multinationals the best bargaining position. The division of labor that has developed around the tri-pé in the petrochemical industry fits the needs and interests of the multinationals very well. It allows them to concentrate on product differentiation and new technology, the sources of their greatest strength.

The differentiation that has developed around the tri-pé has another facet. Participation is voluntary. The division between participants and nonparticipants follows nicely along the lines of the discussion presented in the last chapter. Newcomers, anxious to break into the market, are most likely to have an interest in participating. The Japanese chemical combines Sumitomo and Mitsubishi are two such newcomers. For them and for other Japanese giants, the tri-pé has been a means of entering a market in which they had little previous base. Shell and Dupont also took advantage of the tri-pé to expand what had previously been a restricted participation in chemicals. Established companies like Union Carbide and Rhone-Poulenc saw no need to participate. Some newcomers, like Dow Chemical, decided to try to break into the market without utilizing the tri-pé.

Overall, the tri-pé in the petrochemical industry has succeeded in involving multinational capital in a nationalist agenda for the local accumulation of capital, while at the same time allowing them considerable leeway to exploit those areas of the industry in which they have the strongest leverage and expertise.

The multinationals are in general quite content with the role that Petroquisa has played and is playing. Petroquisa can take some pride in having strengthened Brazil's basic industrial capacity and having taken a major step in the direction of improving the industrial position of the northeast. Nor can local capital raise complaints about the tri-pé in petrochemicals. For the best-prepared local firms the tri-pé has provided an opportunity to participate in enterprises from which they would otherwise have been excluded, and to diversify in ways that would otherwise have been difficult.

Other Attempts at Alliance-building: The CVRD, CEME, and the BNDE

Viewed from inside, the growth of the Brazilian petrochemical industry appears synonomous with the creation of triple alliances. Does the model of the tri-pé extend beyond petrochemicals or is it peculiar to the history and structure of that industry? To some degree petrochemicals is unique. Even though the government has indicated that the tri-pé will "serve as a model" for the capital goods, raw materials, and mining sectors (*Business Latin America*, 1977:144), the tri-pé will probably never penetrate other industries to the extent that it has petrochemicals. In industries where there are no strong state enterprises, the tri-pé can only be a financial arrangement. In addition, there are few industries in which buyer-seller relations can be used to reinforce shared ownership as effectively as they have been in petrochemicals. Nonetheless, joint ventures involving the state have proliferated well beyond the confines of the petrochemical industry.

The best nonpetrochemical examples of joint ventures linking the state and the multinationals are the subsidiaries of the Companhia do Vale do Rio Doce. The CVRD is second only to Petrobrás among state-owned industrial enterprises and is one of the two hundred largest corporations in the world outside the United States. It is responsible for most of Brazil's iron ore exports, which, since iron ore has become a major export product, makes the CVRD a crucial factor in determining Brazil's trade balance. Like Petroquisa, the CVRD has tended to set up joint ventures with companies that are its customers, but since its production is for export, its partnerships have a different character.

Growing directly out of the CVRD's export business are a number of joint ventures in plants for pelletizing iron ore. In the mid-seventies eight pelletizing plants were projected. All of them were to be operated by the CVRD but four were to be jointly owned by CVRD's foreign customers. Two were joint ventures with Japanese capital and were slated to export all of their output to Japan. One was a Brazilian-Italian operation whose output is to go to Italsider, Italy's state-owned steel company. One was a joint venture with the Spanish National Industrial Institute and will export its output to Spain. In all four of these ventures the CVRD has 51% of the equity.

From its profitable position in iron ore, the CVRD has begun a steady course of diversification into a wider and wider range of activities. Its interest in mineral extraction will soon be expanded to include phosphates. The phosphates will be used by a new CVRD subsidiary, Valefertil, to produce tri-superphosphate fertilizer, amonium phosphate, and phosphoric acid. In Minas Gerais the CVRD has gotten into steel making. Together with the government of Minas and a collection of local and foreign private capital, it has set up Acominas. In Maranhão, a steel plant is projected at Itaqui that would use the iron ore from the Carajás deposits. The CVRD has also been involved in the attempts of the state of Minas Gerais to gain an equity position in the Companhia Brasileira de Metalurgua e Mineracao, a private joint venture between U.S. and Brazilian capital to mine niobium.

The plans to exploit the bauxite deposits on the Trombetas River in the Amazon basin provide a good illustration of the

CVRD's approach to joint ventures (see *Business Latin America*, 1972:226; 1974:16). The bauxite was originally discovered by Alcan, which was hoping to mount a wholly owned export operation. By 1972 it was clear that Alcan would not be allowed to control the venture by itself and that Brazil wanted to set up some industrial facilities along with the mining operations rather than simply export raw bauxite. By 1974 a joint venture called Mineração Rio do Norte had been set up in which Alcan retained only 19% of the equity. The largest owner was the CVRD with 41%, while the Companhia Brasileira de Alumínio, owned by the Emírio de Moraes group and Alcan's oldest competitor in Brazil, held 10%, giving Brazilian interests the controlling share. The remainder was split among a variety of European companies.

To provide the industrial facilities that were to complement the bauxite mining operations, the CVRD turned to Japanese capital. In September of 1974 an accord was signed with the Light Metals Smelters Association projecting a complex that would produce 600,000 tons of aluminum a year. The agreement also included plans for a hydroelectric plant on the Tocantins River to supply the aluminum complex with power. If the CVRD succeeds in bringing this project to fruition, an area slated at the beginning of the seventies to be a classic foreign-owned "export enclave" will have been transformed into a major industrial venture controlled by local capital. Unfortunately, doubts have arisen about the willingness of the Japanese to go ahead with it (*Economist, Qrtly. Rev.*, 1975, no. 4).

Further diversification of the CVRD's holdings is represented by Cenibra, a giant cellulose/forestry project in Minas Gerais. The foreign partners in this venture are again Japanese, in this case eleven paper companies combined to form Japan-Brazil Pulp Resources Development. At the time it was initiated, the $800 million project was "the largest Japanese-Brazilian investment that had been made in Brazil" (*Business Latin America*, 1974:58). While the product is different, the underlying model for the venture is very similar to CVRD's iron ore alliances. All of the output will be exported; three quarters of it will go to the CVRD's Japanese partners.

The burgeoning empire of the CVRD is characterized by entrepreneurship and alliances, but the alliances are of a different ilk than those created by Petroquisa. The discussion of bargaining power and joint ventures in the last chapter provides a basis for understanding the differences. Control over raw materials is the state's strong point. The CVRD has more leverage than Petrobrás for two reasons. First, the raw materials it controls are Brazilian. Petrobrás controls access to petroleum but depends on the international market for most of its own supplies. Second, the multinationals need the raw materials the CVRD can provide not just for expansion at the local level but as part of their global strategies of accumulation. At the same time, the technology of mineral extraction and processing is accessible. In this field the multinationals do not have their usual important source of leverage.

The CVRD cannot be faulted in its aggressive pursuit of the nationalist policy of maximizing local accumulation. It has exercised considerable entrepreneurship in the construction of its empire. It is accumulating profits (and foreign exchange) at the rate of $100 million a year. It has used its position to exert continuous pressure on others to process the minerals before sending them out of the country. The preference of multinationals for keeping their processing operations in the center has historically been the bane of third world mineral exporters. The CVRD has not been content to export ore but has already started pelletizing it and will eventually be turning more of it into steel. Alcan would have been happy to export bauxite; the CVRD wanted to export aluminum.

The contribution of the CVRD to alliance-building is more ambiguous. It has been quite successful in forming alliances with Japanese and European firms, but some of its major American partners have been reluctant to share control to the degree demanded by the CVRD. Alcan reportedly almost pulled out of the joint venture in bauxite because it did not like the prospect of having a minority share in the equity (*Business Latin America*, 1972:226; 1974:17). U.S. Steel was willing to take a minority position in the $3.5 billion Carajás iron ore project but wanted to retain veto power on the board of directors. Since CVRD was unwilling to allow this, it may have to buy out U.S. Steel's share.

The future of the Carajás project will test the extent to which a state enterprise can ignore the requirements of the triple alliance and attempt to act "for itself." The opinion of the international business community is that "Brazil would have difficulties financing and developing the project on its own without the assured markets that partnership with foreign firms would guarantee . . ." (*Business Latin America*, 1977:140). Other multinational partners may yet come forward, but the CVRD clearly runs the risk of being unable to push forward its entrepreneurial aims because it has underestimated the value of alliances.

The CVRD also appears much weaker when it comes to forging alliances with the local private sector. It has not played anything like the supportive role that Petroquisa has played. Why have local firms not been included as they were in petrochemicals? One explanation is the lack of local customers for iron ore. The share of Brazilian private capital in the steel industry is small and shrinking as Table 5.2 indicated. The CVRD's most important local customers are state-owned companies; the two largest private customers are both foreign. This explanation is, however, partial at best. The CVRD might have drawn Aços Villares of the Villares group or Siderúrgica Barra Mansa of the Ermírio de Moraes group into a tri-pé arrangement, but it has not done so. Petroquisa also faced a lack of local partners and forged ahead with the tri-pé anyway. Is the exclusion of local partners a consequence of the CVRD's stronger position vis-à-vis the multinationals? Are members of the state bourgeoisie likely to try to bring in their private counterparts only when they feel they need the extra leverage of political support from private capital? The contrast between the CVRD and Petroquisa points in this direction.

There is another contrast between the CVRD and Petroquisa in their relations with the "national industrial bourgeoisie." The CVRD competes with some of the largest local economic groups. The Azevedo Antunes group's Minerações Reunidas Brasileiras is the CVRD's biggest competitor in the area of mineral exports. Once the Carajás operation is underway there will thus be two giant alliances in the area of mineral exports: one based on the CVRD and the other combining Antunes and Bethlehem Steel along with other foreign capital. In the paper industry, the CVRD's new cellulose project will begin by exporting its output to its partners, but it is potentially a prime competitor for the Klabin group, which owns the biggest company in the industry.

The CVRD combined entrepreneurship and alliances but has not adopted the tri-pé as its model. Its formula does not involve the connection between the expansion of the state role and opportunities for local capital that the tri-pé provides. Nor does it offer the same potential for integrating local, state, and multinational capital. The CVRD example suggests that Brazilian private capital has the best chance of being included when the balance of power between the state and the multinationals is not clearly on one side. When the state is in an exceptionally strong position, as it is in the area of mineral exports, the state bourgeoisie has less reason to include its local private counterparts. By the same token, an industry where the multinationals are clearly dominant provides little opportunity for the creation of alliances. The pharmaceutical industry illustrates this nicely.

In the pharmaceutical industry the state lacked every source of leverage that it enjoyed in petrochemicals and mineral extraction. It controlled no significant natural resources relevant to pharmaceuticals. Raw materials were not only imported, they were produced by the multinationals themselves in their center country facilities. Control by the multinationals over new technology gave them a further and overwhelming advantage. The industry was also a difficult one for the state to enter because its products are sold to customers rather than to other industries. Medications being important for the welfare of the population, it would have been awkward for the state to make profits selling drugs. All the reasons that made the state generally reluctant to become involved in the commericalization of consumer goods applied in force to pharmaceuticals.

The denationalization of the industry was another factor that made it inhospitable to tri-pé arrangements. Finding locally owned partners for a tri-pé would have been extremely difficult. There were no equivalents of the Grupo Ultra or the Grupo Peixoto de Castro. Locally owned firms were not strong enough to make good allies, but they could not be left out either. For the state to have gone into a partnership, say with Pfizer to manufacture tetracycline, would have immediately raised cries that the state was contributing to denationalization. Finally, of course, there was no historical foundation to build on in pharmaceuticals. In petrochemicals and iron ore exports, the state bourgeoisie could build on firms with decades of experience. In pharmaceuticals there was nothing.

Despite the obvious problems, the state created two agencies in 1971 that could have developed into a major example of state entrepreneurship—the Central de Medicamentos (CEME) and the subsequently elaborated Plano Diretor de Medicamentos (Directive Plan for Medications). Given the difference in the initial context, however, it is not surprising that the CEME's experience had little in common with that of the CVRD or Petroquisa. Nor is it surprising that CEME did not in the end share the success of other state ventures. CEME's difficulties began with the fact that it was based on welfare and distributive considerations rather than on a rationale related to the process of accumulation.

CEME was created to fill what was considered to be a major gap in public medical assistance. The Instituto Nacional da Previdência Social (INPS) provided hospital care and also enabled poor patients to consult physicians on an out-patient basis, but the patients often lacked the money to buy the medications the doctors prescribed. CEME was intended to make basic drugs available to those who could not afford to buy them at commerical prices. The Plano Diretor de Medicamentos began with a quote from then President Médici: "I will not allow anyone to become sick because of lack of prevention, or to die from lack of assistance." From the beginning, the justification of CEME was in welfare terms.

CEME's productive base was not impressive relative to the powerful multinationals that dominated the pharmaceutical industry. It was primarily an administrative organization designed to bring together the production capabilities of twenty publicly owned pharmaceutical laboratories already in operation at the time it was formed. The combined value of the production of all of these laboratories in 1973 was not equal to one of the top ten multinationals (cf. CEME, 1974:35). The gap between CEME and the leading multinationals was even greater in terms of technological sophistication. The repertoire of products produced in CEME's laboratories did not include the newest, most advanced antibiotics, steroids, or hormones. Of the thousands of pharmaceutical products available in Brazilian pharmacies, CEME's *Momento Terapêutico* included only eighty.

The restriction of CEME's product line is not simply a sign of weakness. It is to a large extent deliberate and consistent with the enterprise's welfare objectives. CEME's projected product line is based on the National List of Essential Medicines (Relação Nacional de Medicamentos), which contains between three and four hundred medications. The aim is to concentrate on the distribution of a limited number of medicines that will help cure the most common illnesses of the poor. The restriction of the product line and the attempt to promote specialization among the twenty laboratories in the CEME system helps to make production more efficient despite the small scale of the individual production units.

CEME's definition of its "market" is almost the mirror image of the market as seen through the eyes of the private sector. CEME is supposed to distribute its medications without charge to those whose family income does not exceed the minimum wage. (Pregnant women, nursing mothers, and children under five were also included in theory, but in practice low income is the defining characteristic of the population served by CEME.) The contrast between CEME's "market" and the private sector's market is highlighted by looking at the difference in regional terms. Private marketing estimates have assumed that almost half the total Brazilian market is in the states of São Paulo and Rio/Guanabara and that no more than 15% was in the northeast (cf. Ayres and Miranda, n.d.). In CEME's market, two-thirds of the "customers" in 1973 lived in the northeast and no medications at all were distributed in the state of São Paulo since it was assumed that the state government was capable of handling the task on its own.

Other differences between CEME and the private sector make it not surprising that the economics of production in CEME's laboratories are very different from those of private sector plants. As was mentioned in Chapter 2, industrial costs may represent as little as one-third of total costs for a foreign subsidiary and raw materials is the largest item within the category of industrial costs. For the public laboratories that produce for CEME, over 60% of total costs are industrial costs, and labor is the most expensive element among them. In the private sector commercialization is the biggest factor in nonindustrial costs, whereas the nonindustrial costs of public laboratories are composed only of administrative costs (see CEME, 1973:62, 65).

The disjunction between CEME and the private sector in the

area of research and development has already been touched upon in Chapter 4. For the private sector, research and development are aimed at new products. CEME is not interested in further product differentiation, but one of the goals of the Plano Diretor de Medicamentos is to reduce the proportion of pharmaceutical raw materials being imported. To this end, CEME was supposed to spend between $2 and $3 million a year promoting the investigation of methods of synthesis for pharmaceutical raw materials (CEME, 1973:525). In 1973 it sponsored research at five different universities, spending about half a million dollars to support work on synthesizing half a dozen pharmaceutical raw materials (CEME, 1974:79). Since pharmaceutical raw materials were a major item on Brazil's import bill, the research made sense from a nationalist perspective. From the point of view of the multinationals, however, such work was not only without benefit but might be considered threatening. The research sponsored at the Federal University of Bahia on "the synthesis of analogs of nitrofurans" could hardly have been seen positively by Eaton Laboratories (Norwich-Morton) for whom nitrofuracin had been a profitable exclusive product for years.

In pharmaceuticals there was no basis for the sort of ideological cohesion that unites the state bourgeoisie and the multinational managers in the petrochemical industry. CEME and the multinationals defined the "bottom line" in different ways. As long as its aim was free distribution, CEME could not talk about profits. CEME nonetheless thought of itself as efficient and was proud of its productive and distributive apparatus. From its perspective, the private sector was not "efficient" in that it produced too many different products, devoted too large a proportion of its resources to sales efforts, and did not work hard enough at cutting down imports. At one point, CEME's President, João Felício Scárdua (1974:15) said that his organization would be able to produce medications for 40% of the prices charged by the multinationals. The multinationals, of course, considered such statements indicative of a lack of understanding of the true conditions existing in the industry.

Objectively, CEME was not a threat to the private sector and particularly not to the multinationals. It was never likely to be able to produce the sophisticated products that were the mainstay of the muntinationals' profits. It was not competing for the private sector's customers. The people who received its medications would not for the most part have been able to purchase drugs on the private market. One might even argue that CEME's operations should have the effect of eventually expanding the private pharmaceutical market by acquainting a large segment of the population with a range of medications that they may some day be in a position to purchase. Most important, CEME itself is a major new customer for private producers. One-third of the drugs distributed by CEME in 1973 could not be produced in its own laboratories but had to be purchased from the private sector (CEME, 1974:35). Rather than taking customers away from the multinationals, CEME's purchases added $3½ million to the market.

This situation was not enough to turn the multinationals into CEME's ally. CEME defined the purposes of the pharmaceutical industry in a threatening way and was looked upon by the multinationals as a potential competitor in the long run. As long as turning the industry over to local entrepreneurs was the only alternative nationalists could provide to denationalization, the multinationals felt they had little to fear from the state. But if CEME were able to prove itself as a producer, the nationalists would have another alternative. CEME was ominous because it raised the possibility of an antidenationalization alliance between the state and local capital. Such a coalition would have been almost impossible in practice, but the laws that created CEME seemed to raise it as a theoretical possibility.

The decrees regulating CEME all included protestations of support for local capital. The National Directive Plan for Medications (Plano Diretor) spoke of CEME (1973:448) as a "source of hope" for "genuinely Brazilian" firms. Decree No. 72.552 (July 1973) talked of "participation of industrial chemical-pharmaceutical firms of exclusively Brazilian funds, in the production system of the Central de Medicamentos." Some multinationals took this to mean that only locally owned firms were going to be allowed to sell to CEME. In fact, CEME purchased its drugs from both local and foreign firms and its president was quoted as saying that it would be illegal for CEME to give preference to local groups (Scárdua, 1974). Nonetheless, the possibility of CEME restricting its purchasing to locally owned firms, like the possibility of its entering into production on its own, remained threatening to the multinationals.

Brazilian-owned firms were less negative toward CEME than the multinationals but CEME offered them little in the way of profitable opportunities. The products they produced were those which CEME was most likely to produce for itself. The products CEME bought from the outside were made mainly by multinationals. The largest sale by a local laboratory to CEME in 1973 was of penicillin. The seller, Laboratories Majer Mayer, does not itself produce penicillin and probably purchases it from an American subsidiary. Willingness to accept a lower margin of profit may have allowed the local firm to get the CEME contract, but occasional opportunities to resell materials bought in bulk from multinationals hardly represent an exciting "source of hope" to local firms.

In the beginning of 1974 there was a move to expand CEME's role as an industrial organization by turning it into a public corporation (Kucinski, 1975). President Geisel did not go along with the idea. By the end of the year, when CEME's president João Felício Scárdua was asked about the possibility of CEME's becoming a "Medibrás" he replied that it would be "stupidity for the government to enter directly into an area of production that was so sophisticated" (Scárdua, 1974:16). By mid-1975 CEME had been dismembered. Instead of remaining directly under the presidency as it had been since its creation, it was split into two parts, each under a different ministry. The job of distributing drugs was given to the Welfare Ministry. Research activities were transferred to the Ministry of Industry and Commerce (Kucinski, 1975:70). The possibility of a state-owned corporation in pharmaceuticals analogous to Petrobrás, the CSN, or the CVRD no longer existed.

The history of CEME shows that the growth of state enterprise is not so inevitable as it might appear from the examination of other industries. CEME's demise also suggests that a successful state enterprise cannot be built around welfare or distributive concerns, especially if there is no complementarity between multinationals and the state-owned corporations. Entrepreneurship is not enough. Nor is potential contribution to a nationalist model of accumulation. CEME, had it been allowed to engage in the production of basic pharmaceutical raw materials, would have made a contribution to improving Brazil's balance of payments just as Petroquisa was designed to do. But any contribution that it might have made would have threatened the profits of the multinationals without offering them any compensating advantages. And while it provided them with support in principle, CEME did not offer locally owned firms any real possibility of entering profitable new areas or gaining better leverage vis-à-vis the international drug companies. The only people who received unequivocal benefits from CEME were its "customers." In the Brazilian political context, there was no possibility of using their support as a bargaining chip in the fight for an expanded role.

The demise of CEME showed the difficulty of building state enterprise around any aim other than accumulation. In addition, CEME's experience revealed the obstacles that the state would face if it tried to redress the balance between local and foreign capital in industries thoroughly dominated by the multinationals. Along with its welfare rationale, CEME was clearly intended as a mechanism for combating denationalization. President Scárdua (1974) defined the agency's goal as "not statism but nationalization, a gradual nationalization." CEME was supposed to strengthen locally owned companies not only by buying their products but also by encouraging them to modernize and merge together. CEME's activities had, however, no noticeable effect. In the end, local pharmaceutical firms were left to seek aid from the various financial agencies that the state has set up to indicate its concern for local capital

Companies like Petrobrás, the CSN, and the CVRD epitomize the state's emerging role as an industrial entrepreneur. State entrepreneurship in the financial sector is perhaps best exemplified by the National Development Bank (BNDE), which is larger than any other financial institution in the country except the Bank of Brazil. A pamphlet discussing the plight of local pharmaceutical firms in the late sixties listed half a dozen different BNDE-sponsored financial programs to which they could turn for help (Mendes Alves, 1969). Having expanded far beyond its original task of financing public investments in infrastructure, the BNDE now plays a variety of roles. An increasing proportion of its loans are going to the private sector, and in this capacity it has been an important auxiliary to the tri-pé. It provided the financing for the central servicing unit of the Polo do Nordeste complex. It was the BNDE that lent Euvaldo Luz the capital that allowed him to become Dupont's partner in the Salgema scheme. At the time, the BNDE was already the major shareholder in this project.

One of the most highly publicized aspects of the state's role as a financier has been its support and protection of local industrialists. This has not been an easy job. The state has acted as a financial partner in industries where it would not have been able to play a directly industrial role, but as the case of the pharmaceutical industry illustrates, financial support is insufficient to reverse the most serious cases of denationalization. Just as Petroquisa could not create modern chemical firms simply by taking on local partners, the BNDE has been effective only when there were additional circumstances favoring the survival of local capital. In industries like textiles, where the "comparative advantage" of local capital is greater, financial support from the state may have more effect. The Companhia Progresso Industrial-Bangú, one of Brazil's oldest and best-known textile firms, is an example. In the late sixties, it had entered on hard times and seemed likely to go the way of America Fabril and Corcovado, textile giants in decline. The BNDE came in with financing for renovations, making managerial reorganization a condition of the loan. By 1974, Progresso Industrial was exporting 50% of its output, had formed a joint venture with a Dutch company to produce apparel, and was allied with a Japanese trading company to help in its international marketing.

The BNDE eventually found itself with 80% of its projects in the private sector and only 20% in the public sector. In 1974, three new agencies were formed under its auspices. Like their predecessors, IBRASA, FIBASA, and EMBRAMEC were designed to keep local companies from having to sell out to foreigners or go out of business because they lacked capital. They tried to limit their involvement in the management of the firms they assisted by taking their share of the equity in the form of nonvoting shares. At the same time, the BNDE agencies were supposed to be helping companies that were considered leaders in their region or branch of industry. Like any investor, they wanted to make sure that their funds were going to be used effectively.

Attempts to aid the local private sector seemed to be having the unanticipated result of turning local firms into subsidiaries of the BNDE. Local capital, no more anxious to relinquish control over its ventures than the multinationals would have been, resisted this trend. According to *Business Latin America* (1975:114), "Companies have shied away from using these mechanisms [IBRASA, FIBASA, and EMBRAMEC] because of some of the conditions imposed, such as the number of government representatives required on boards of directors." In 1975, under pressure from some sectors of private capital to play a less visible role, the BNDE shifted toward loan rather than equity financing and lowered the interest rates on its loans (*Business Latin America*, 1975:113). In 1976, under the same kind of pressure, support for local capital was expanded still further with the introduction of a new "Special Program for the Support of Capitalization of National Private Capital" (PROCAP). By channeling government funds through private investment banks rather than applying them directly to individual firms, this new program decreases the degree of government intrusion even more.

If equity participation by the BNDE is threatening to the triple alliance because it raises the possibility of the BNDE turning into a giant holding company, strategies like the PROCAP are equally threatening for those interested in maximizing the rate of accumulation. They raise the specter of state funds being used not for investments but for subsidies to local capitalists. Unless financial assistance from the state requires or at least provokes reorganization or modernization, it cannot be the instrument of a real strengthening of local capital, to say nothing of enhancing the rate of local accumulation. Yet, resistance of local firms makes it harder for the BNDE agencies to play an active part. The entrepreneurial role that is possible for Petroquisa or the CVRD is taken away from the state almost completely in the PROCAP program. The ability of the state to direct the process of accumulation is diminished, and support for the local private sector comes closer to being another subsidy.

The final ironic twist occurs in the case of enterprises that are locally controlled but contain a substantial amount of foreign capital. The state occasionally appears to be subsidizing the expansion of the multinationals under programs designed to prevent denationalization. Sifco, for example, was looking for a way of expanding its jointly owned Brazilian auto parts subsidiary. It finally hit upon the idea of taking a minority position and thereby making it possible to finance its multimillion dollar expansion plans through IBRASA (*Business Latin America*, 1975:389).

The financial tactics of the BNDE have their limits, as have the other strategies that the state has employed. The tri-pé depended on a quite specific structural context for its success, and thus the CVRD's model of alliances depended on the extremely strong bargaining position of the state in the area of mineral exportation. Financial incentives require at least some local entrepreneurial strength, and thus are more successful in textiles than pharmaceuticals. Even in the industries where it can be applied, state financing is susceptible to degenerating into subsidies that give the state little more opportunity for entrepreneurship than normal fiscal incentives.

The expansion of state enterprise up to the mid-seventies has not been based on a smooth overall plan. It has been pragmatic and uneven, based on reactions to bottlenecks and problems. Sometimes, as in the case of CEME, the state has overextended its limits and been forced to retreat. Nonetheless, each of the enterprises considered illustrates a different situation in which the only way of maintaining the rate of accumulation and preserving some semblance of local control seems to be through increased initiative on the part of the state. Future bottlenecks will unquestionably generate new lines of expansion for state enterprises. The real question is how much further the state can expand without disrupting the pattern of alliances that has been established. Even the alliances of the mid-seventies contain seeds of potential conflict. Preventing the conflicts from getting out of control may require a dampening of future state entrepreneurship. By the same token, future state entrepreneurship may be possible only at the expense of increased conflict between the present allies.

Politics and the Triple Alliance

One of the military's aims in 1964 was to "abolish politics," which meant in practice eliminating popular input into the political process. The "bourgeois autocracy" (see Chapter 1 and Fernandes, 1975) that resulted allowed the regime to define problems of growth and welfare as resolvable in technocratic terms. The regime legitimated itself on the basis of technocratic efficiency. It could impose the order necessary for the process of accumulation to continue.

As we have seen, the sector that benefited most from defining accumulation as a technocratic problem was the state sector. The doubling of the share of state enterprises in the ownership of the largest manufacturing firms is a most dramatic structural change in the economy (see Table 5.2). Most of the expansion of state enterprises has not only been linked to pushing the process of accumulation forward but also to breaking through bottlenecks that neither the multinationals nor local capital were able to handle. Despite the benefits of state expansion to the private sector, however, fears of the state acting "for itself" have grown along with the growth of the state sector.

When the Capuava group sold out to the government there were those who said that Petrobrás had deliberately squeezed out the local group, both by refusing to let them expand their refinery and by not paying higher prices for Petroquímica União's products. Whether or not this explanation for the Capuava group's fall has any truth in it, the fears that it illustrates have a real basis. The potential is there for the state to use its position in infrastructure or basic products to squeeze either the multinationals or local capital.

The potential for friction is much more apparent when the state steps out of its complementary role. At the beginning of the seventies, Petrobrás decided to expand its activities in the area of distribution. The expansion seemed motivated by a desire for profitable new areas to offset expensive and at that time relatively unrewarding drilling operations. Petrobrás's new filling stations did little to enhance the economy's overall rate of accumulation or strengthen its industrial base. But they did create a crisis for the multinationals that had previously dominated the distribution area. By 1974 Petrobrás controlled 30% of the distribution of gasoline, and its new subsidiary, Petrobrás Distribuadora, had larger sales than either Shell or Exxon. Rumors circulated that Exxon would pull out of Brazil if Petrobrás expanded any further.

The example of Petrobrás's expansion into distribution is a particularly apt one. There is no reason to believe that it was an effort designed primarily to foster accumulation in general. Its obvious aim was to foster the profits and expansion of Petrobrás in particular. Once state-owned enterprises begin to place primary emphasis on their own growth and profits rather than on carrying out their part in the overall development project as constructed by the state apparatus, they become more of a "state bourgeoisie" than members of the state bureaucracy. Recent indications that the central state apparatus is having trouble controlling state enterprises reinforce this view. There were reports, for example, that some state enterprises had refused to turn over their books to the Ministry of Finance (see Baer, Newfarmer, and Trebat, 1977).

What these examples suggest is that there is an organizational logic to the behavior of state managers just as there is to the behavior of multinational managers. Arthur Stinchecombe (1974) has underlined the necessity of providing bureaucrats with careers, that is, predictable possibilities for future promotions, in order to ensure their effective performance in state enterprises. Yet clearly, once a manager has a career and begins to identify his future with the future of his company, he begins to take a proprietary interest in the future of the firm, regardless of who owns the stock. In fact, the analyses of "managerial capitalism" that appear dubious when applied to large private firms (cf. Zeitlin, 1974) may be much more apt when applied to the executives of state-owned firms.

When the executives of state enterprises take on a "privatized" perspective that favors their immediate corporate interests at the expense of either the interests of the state apparatus as a whole or the private sector, then they indeed begin to look like a "state bourgeoisie." To transform themselves into a "classlike" group however, state executives would need an ideology that goes beyond seeing themselves as skilled technocrats implementing a general project. Recent evidence suggests that, despite the confidence in their own administrative capacities mentioned earlier, they lack the necessary legitimating ideology.

Survey work conducted by Luciano Martins and his colleagues among executives of state-owned firms indicates that even they continue to see local private capital as the most appropriate instrument for Brazil's development. Once again, the peculiar political strength of the local bourgeoisie is striking. Private enterprise continues to hold sway ideologically despite both its objective limitations and the immense objective power of state enterprise.

The ideological hegemony of private enterprise is nowhere better illustrated than in the recent "anti-estatização" (anti-statism) campaign. The Estado de São Paulo and Visão, two of the most influential components of the Brazilian news media, are the main public mouthpieces of the debate. Their argument is interesting in that it inverts part of the logic of the tri-pé. Those who advocate restricting state enterprise do not see the tri-pé as a means of using the power of the state to prevent the multinationals from overrunning local partners or of making it easier for local capital to enter large-scale, technologically advanced ventures. Quite the contrary, they portray the state as squeezing out local capital by allying itself with the multinationals. Visão, for example, argues that state enterprises are "joining hands with the multinationals" at the expense of local capital. To prove this point, Visão collected numerous examples of the government giving preference to foreign firms in cases where "dozens of genuinely Brazilian private companies" could have provided the services required perfectly well (Visão, 1976:86).

What complicates the interpretation of the antistatism campaign is that it is not simply a campaign on behalf of local capital.
It is also a campaign on behalf of the idea of private enterprise in
general. The accusations of inefficiency, senseless expansion of
payrolls, and overbureaucratization that are leveled against public enterprises are very much in the old North American tradition
of defending free enterprise. The Mesquita family which owns
the Estado de São Paulo, and Octávio Gouvea de Bulhões, who is
president of Visão's editorial council, are adherents of a brand of
classic economic liberalism that is hard to find in the ranks of
politicians, state personnel, or even entrepreneurs in contemporary Brazil. This liberalism also includes political elements. In
their attacks on statism they cite Castello Branco's argument that
"in democracies, governmental action should stimulate the private sector."

Since political and ideological factors are important in determining the bargaining position of the local bourgeoisie, it is not
surprising that the antistatism campaign has become linked to
pressure for democratization and a return to civilian rule. If 1976
was the year of the "anti-estatização" debate, 1977 became the
year of the "democratização" debate. The issues are parallel.
Both have to do with the ability of the local bourgeoisie to use its
political and ideological leverage to claim a larger share of the
economic pie. At least some segments of the bourgeoisie have
discovered that the autocratic side of "bourgeois autocracy" may
be turned against them.

The seriousness with which the government has taken this
campaign reflects the political strength of the local, private capital. Once again, the strength of the private bourgeoisie derives in
part from their social ties with the rest of the dominant class.
Business Latin America notes (1977:144) that decision makers
within the regime have "been very careful not to underestimate
the business community's strength and its ties with like-minded
military men." In a country where 50% of the graduates of the

War College (Escola Superior de Guerra) are civilians (see Stepan, 1971), no general, even one who is president, can afford to ignore the demands of local capital.

Despite the parallelism of the "anti-estatização" and "democratização" movements, there is an obvious contradiction in the demands of the local bourgeoisie that reflects a contradiction in their objective situation. The support of the state is an essential element in their defense against the multinationals. They need a strong state. Most important, they need the very state-owned enterprises whose growth they are beginning to find threatening. As the analysis of the tri-pé makes clear, partnership with state enterprises is the only route for entry into sectors that would otherwise be unambiguously dominated by the multinationals. Unless they are willing to give up their state-owned partners, local capital must learn to live with the expansionist tendencies that are inevitable in any large-scale corporation, no matter how irksome or even threatening this expansionism may be.

For the multinationals the situation is less ambiguous. They have no particular interest in "democratização" and they have a much stronger interest in "anti-estatização." As the expansionism of state-owned enterprises becomes more aggressive, the image of state capital as the "handmaiden" of private expansion is undermined. By the mid-seventies Brazil was being accused by *The New York Times* (e.g., 9/13/76) of moving toward state capitalism. *The Times* compared the intrusion of the Brazilian state in the economy to Chile under the Allende regime and said, "The government denies switching policies but the foreign investors are complaining."

A country with $30 billion in foreign debts, a trade deficit of $3 to $4 billion a year, and foreign reserves shrinking at the rate of $1 billion a year cannot afford to take the disenchantment of the international business community lightly. Nationalist policies must occasionally be set aside as a sign of good intentions. In October 1971 the Geisel government decided to let foreign oil com-

THE STATE AND THE MULTINATIONALS

panies engage in exploration for oil on a contract basis. This reversed one of the most sacrosanct nationalist policies—the maintenance of the state monopoly in oil exploration. Shortly before the decision was made, Roberto Campos, whose sympathies for market solutions and for the multinationals are well known, apparently told Geisel that Brazil's credit standing in London was weakening. The admission of foreign oil companies was interpreted as an attempt to "show the international financial community that Brazil welcomes foreign currency, loans and capital investment" (*Economist, Qrtly. Rev.*, 1975, no. 4).

Geisel's action was not in itself a serious threat to Petrobrás's power. The bid for contracts implied only service contracts and not control over the oil that might be found. Nonetheless, given the central importance of "Petróleo é nosso" as a nationalist slogan, the decision was a serious one politically. The "hardline" within the military as well as representatives of the local industrial bourgeoisie, such as Minister of Industry and Commerce Severo Gomes, were reported to be upset.

The strong nationalist reaction to this minor infringement of the Petrobrás monopoly is indicative of the contradictory nature of the "anti-estatização" campaign. As a campaign on behalf of free enterprise, it immediately becomes suspect lest it be a promultinational campaign. Even though those who foment the campaign always stress the damage that state expansion does to local capital, their models of private sector efficiency are often multinationals. If Petroquisa, the Compania do Vale do Rio Doce, the CSN, or any other major state enterprise were returned to the private sector the most likely buyers would be foreign. Any overt participation by the multinationals in the antistatism debate would of course increase the likelihood that it would be interpreted as a "promultinational" campaign. As the Brazilian-American Chamber of Commerce (1976:4) put it in their news bulletin, "the controversy has inevitably placed foreign businesses in a delicate position."

The reticence of the multinationals is indicative of their lack of political legitimacy, but it also reflects their interests. While they, like local capital, are threatened by the expansionism of state enterprise, they are also beneficiaries of the triple alliance. State enterprises play a crucial role in a system of accumulation that has been extremely profitable for them. State enterprises are their partners in joint ventures, their suppliers, and their customers. The interests of the multinationals have become linked with those of state enterprises in much the same way that the interests of large oligopolistic competitors are connected in any advanced capital industry.

The antistatism and democratization furors have made plain, if there was ever any doubt, that the triple alliance must be a political alliance as well as an economic one; but they have also revealed the strength of the alliance more clearly. Matarazzo, Azevedo Antunes, and Hélio Beltrão were not the leaders of the fight against state expansionism; rather it was led by representatives of those parts of the local bourgeoisie which have not been incorporated into the tri-pé. In a few instances, like Villares and Bardella, they represent substantial local holdings, but Papa Junior and the Federation of Commerce are more typical of the base of support for the campaigns.

The political tensions of the mid-seventies are in part due to the expansionist tendencies of state managers, but they reflect even more the split of the national bourgeoisie into an elite that can participate in the triple alliance and lesser local capital that must make its own way. Without discounting the trouble-making potential of small capital, the strength of the participating elites must be underlined. Severo Gomes, the representative of small capital in the Geisel cabinet, was forced out and replaced by the head of the Bank of Brazil. Neither the autonomy nor the expansion of state enterprises have been curtailed.

The major response of the regime to the demands of the dissident representatives of local capital has been an increased emphasis on policies restricting the uncontrolled expansion of the multinationals. In the computer industry, for example, entry by multinationals was made contingent on their willingness to share both equity and technology, thereby excluding companies like IBM (*Business Latin America*, 1977:193, 307). The aim is apparently to try to foster some local "tri-pés" in the computer field. In short, the immediate response to political pressure is more likely to strengthen the triple alliance than to weaken it.

Both the strengths and the potential weaknesses of the triple alliance are more clearly revealed by examining the state sector. The undisciplined expansionism of individual state firms represents a potentially disruptive factor. An ideological stance that privileges the local private sector may be a political force with equal potential for disrupting the functioning of the alliance, especially if "like minded military men" are drawn in behind this ideology. Despite both these developments, cooperation among state enterprises, the multinationals, and the elite segment of local capital continues, the stable carapace of dependent development.

6.

Dependent Development in Perspective

IN April 1975 Reuben W. Hills III and Jorge Wolney Atalla had a meeting (see Louis, 1977). They were a rather unlikely pair. Hills was a solid member of the San Francisco elite, a Stanford graduate, a member of the Pacific Union Club, and a former advisor to the State Department. Atalla's grandfather, like Francisco Matarazzo, had immigrated to Brazil at the end of the nineteenth century. But he came from Lebanon rather than Italy and he became the owner of a coffee plantation rather than an industrialist. Atalla himself might easily have ended up as a member of the "state bourgeoisie." He started his career as a petroleum engineer with Petrobrás and was at one time superintendent of the Petrobrás refinery at Cubatão. But, instead of following a career like that of Orfila Lima dos Santos, he went back to run the family coffee plantation. Coffee was what brought Hills and Atalla together. Hills Brothers coffee was the fourth largest processor of coffee in the United States and Atalla's family was the owner of 12.5 million coffee trees in São Paulo.

The events that succeeded the meeting were more unlikely than the meeting itself. Within a year Atalla, on behalf of Copersucar, the São Paulo sugar cooperative, had engineered the purchase of Hills Brothers. The fourth largest U.S. coffee processor was transformed into a subsidiary of a Brazilian firm, a dramatic reminder that the evolution of dependent development within Brazil has ramifications in the center.

If the purchase of Hills Brothers was symbolic of the fact that Brazil was no longer the underprivileged coffee producer of the past, the behavior of coffee prices at the same time was no less so.

Taking advantage of a natural disruption in supply, the Brazilians managed to push coffee prices up to 300 percent of their 1974 levels. The multinationals involved in roasting and processing pushed the retail prices up in proportion to the rise in the cost of green coffee so as to maintain their profits. Center country consumers were the losers. The resemblance to the practices of the oil-producing states and the oil companies in cooperating around a strategy of price increases was striking. Equally notable was the difference between the way coffee prices behaved in the seventies and the way that they had behaved in the period of classic dependence.

Dependent development, even in the limiting case of Brazil, has not reached the point where the periphery is in a position to "turn on her civilizer," but the case of Hills Brothers does bring us back again to Hobson and his nightmare. The task of trying to understand the triple alliance and its implications is not one only for Brazilianists or even only for "dependentistas." It is a task for anyone who wants to understand the contemporary structure of international capitalism. Our analysis of the triple alliance should help us see clearly what is happening in Brazil, but also take us beyond Brazil.

The Brazilian Model of Dependent Development

Our initial model of dependent development consisted mainly of statements about the interrelation among the multinationals, local capital, and the state. It would be an exaggeration to say that the model has been "proved." Nonetheless, even in the absence of the systematic, precise evidence that would constitute proof of the model, it is not an exaggeration to say that most of the assertions have been substantiated by an examination of the details of Brazilian development. Beyond that, a number of them have been refined and modified, and some additional propositions have been added.

We started out with the proposition that the global rationality of the multinationals seriously detracted from their natural contribution to local accumulation, but that the contradictions between their global strategies and local priorities were resolvable by bargaining. From the Visconde Mauá's reluctant partners in the railway industry, through the frustrations of sales representatives trying to get foreign headquarters to see the profitability of investing in local manufacturing facilities in the 1920's, to the inability of Farquhar to find a willing international steel firm in the 1930's, the historical failure of international capital to conform to the entrepreneurial model has been repeatedly illustrated.

A more analytical approach to the problem, focusing on the issue of the multinational's contribution to local technological capacity, shed further light on the entrepreneurial limitations of the international firm. The reluctance of multinationals to invest in local facilities for technological innovation made perfect sense in terms of their own global logic, but not in terms of a "nationalist" logic that placed a priority on local rather than global accumulation.

The issue of local research and development also illustrated the possibilities for modifying the behavior of the multinationals. Even in an industry like pharmaceuticals, where the multinationals' bargaining position is extremely strong, and even on a relatively amorphous issue like research and development, the multinationals could not afford to ignore political pressure. While the response was limited, it was encouraging from the nationalist point of view in at least one respect. It seemed that each change in behavior provided the basis for further incremental change. Insofar as the incremental nature of changes in multinational strategy is a generalizable phenomenon, bargaining victories are likely to cumulate over time.

Examining attempts to pull the multinationals more deeply into the process of local accumulation also made clear how much the probability of modifying the multinationals' behavior varied by industry and issue. In pharmaceuticals, pressure for local production of basic inputs did produce the desired response from the multinationals; but on the issue of local R & D, similar pressure had no effect. The best examples of local pressure resulting in increased multinational involvement in Brazilian industrialization came from industries where concrete alliances between multinational firms and state-owned enterprises were possible.

The triple alliance within the petrochemical industry provided the archetype of the multinational drawn into basic industrialization. The partnerships of the CVRD aimed at promoting local processing of Brazil's mineral exports were equally illuminating. Even in areas where the partnerships were with local rather than state-owned firms, as in synthetic fibers, the possibility of getting solid entrepreneurial efforts out of the multinationals was demonstrated. As long as the contributions of the multinationals are seen as negotiable, rather than natural, responses to market conditions, then the possibility of harnessing international capital to local accumulation exists.

Precisely because the participation of the multinationals is negotiated rather than natural, the issue of control is a recurring theme. Shared control of any venture made a commitment to strategies emphasizing local accumulation more likely. In the case of research and development, for example, even 10% local equity participation increased the probability that a firm would report local R & D efforts. Of course, modifications of multinationals' strategies and the existence of local equity participation cannot be treated as though they were independent of each other. Both depend on bargaining. Bargaining in turn depends on the strengths and weaknesses of local capital and the state.

The initial model of dependent development stressed the central role of the state in fostering accumulation. This emphasis appears amply justified in the light of the data subsequently examined. The discussion focused primarily on state enterprises rather than on the regulatory role of the state or its capacity for extracting surplus from the rest of society. But, even without a thorough examination of these other aspects of its role, the centrality of the state to the process of accumulation is undeniable.

State enterprises emerged as the most effective instruments for the promotion of a nationalist logic of accumulation, that is, one that gives local accumulation priority over global maximization. The growth of the state sector was the most substantial structural change in the ownership of industry during the period of the "miracle." In quantitative terms the state has become the most important source of investment capital. More crucially, state enterprises played key roles in breaking through bottlenecks that local capital was unable to tackle and foreign capital was unwilling to embark on independently. State initiatives in petrochemicals have been used here as the main example of breaking bottlenecks, but other examples, such as state entrepreneurship in building up electrical generating capacity are no less telling.

Along with its entrepreneurial contribution, the state has been fundamentally important in the construction of alliances. Again the petrochemical tri-pé is the most striking example. But even state enterprises less oriented toward alliances, such as the CVRD, have built important ties with multinationals. Finally, of course, pressure from the regulatory side of the state apparatus has been important in fostering joint ventures between local and foreign capital even when state enterprises are not directly involved as partners.

The ability of state enterprises to enter into alliances with both the multinationals and the national bourgeoisie arises in part from the recognition by the private partners that the state's contribution is valuable to them, not only in terms of the actual capital provided but also in terms of security. Partnership with state enterprises usually improves relations with the rest of the state apparatus and also offers a potential means of disciplining other private partners.

The possibility of state participation in alliances with private partners is also enhanced by the apparent correspondence between the ideological views of the members of the "state bourgeoisie" and those of the private sector. Ideological cohesion among these groups is not only at the abstract level of a shared interest in accumulation, but exists more concretely at the level of a shared faith in corporate growth and profitability as measures of success. Because they agree on the meaning of the "bottom line," state managers, local capitalists, and multinational managers can get along. The absorption of traditional corporate ideology by state managers has, however, some other consequences for the role of state enterprises that were not adumbrated in the initial model.

On the more abstract level, the adoption of what is essentially a private sector ideology leaves state managers without a specific ideological legitimation for the role of the public sector. They must see local private capital as the ideal instrument for fostering accumulation, and the strong presence of state enterprise as a "second best" alternative required by the force of circumstances.[1] This leaves them particularly vulnerable to political attack from the local private sector.

The absorption of traditional capitalist ideology also leads state managers to see expansion of individual state firms as their primary goal. This produces expansionist corporate policies that may easily be viewed as threatening by the private sector, provoking exactly the kind of political attack to which the state sector is vulnerable. It also produces resistance to discipline from the central state apparatus. Insofar as state firms become more "privatized" in their behavior, the coherence of overall national development policy is threatened. In the longer run, the ability of state firms to play the kind of distinctively "nationalist" role that they have played to date may even be endangered.

---

[1] This conclusion is based in part on my interpretation of preliminary research results reported (orally) by Luciano Martins. When Professor Martins and his colleagues complete their research, we will have a much more thoroughly elaborated picture of state sector executives.

In the initial model, a great deal of attention was devoted to the organizational logic of the multinationals, but very little to the organizational logic of state-owned firms. The behavior of state-owned firms was assumed to be determined by the interests of the state apparatus as a whole. In retrospect this appears no less naive than assuming that a simple market model is sufficient to predict the behavior of multinationals. The ability of state enterprises to collaborate with private firms is the linchpin of the triple alliance. Yet, this same ability has implications that potentially undermine the model of dependent development. A deeper look at the organizational nature of state enterprises is necessary to unravel these contradictory implications. For the present, however, the dominant contribution of state enterprises to dependent development remains the centrally important one of combining entrepreneurship and alliances.

The possibility of forming alliances with state enterprises was postulated initially as an important source of strength for the local industrial bourgeoisie. But analysis of the position of local capital revealed other sources of strength and confirmed suspicions that traditional analyses of dependence have seriously underestimated the strengths of the local capital. It is true that the analysis has done nothing to refute the assumption that local capital remains the weakest of the three partners. But, having said that, it was the strength of local capital that was most surprising and impressive.

One way in which local capitalists have been underestimated is by portraying them as traditional, more interested in the "good life" and maintaining control over their property than in entrepreneurship and expansion. The local bourgeoisie contains representatives of the "traditional" type without doubt. But, if the cases that have been examined here are at all representative, it also contains others who are anything but quiescent. Even in an industry where denationalization has resulted in extreme marginalization of local capital, pharmaceuticals, there were striking examples of local entrepreneurship. The aggressive export activities of local textile firms were equally impressive. Perhaps most striking was the key entrepreneurial role of Paulo Geyer and his associates in the petrochemical industry.

Local capital also appeared to have a special "comparative advantage" in situations where integration with the local social structure was the key to business success. The contact networks of traveling salesmen in the pharmaceutical industry and the astute extension of credit to small apparel manufacturers and retail stores that is necessary in the textile industry require an embeddedness in the social structure that only long-established international capital is likely to attain. The role of individual members of the local bourgeoisie in tying together foreign firms in the electrical industry was another example of integrative capacity.

More significant in terms of giving local capital some influence over the process of accumulation were the examples of integrative ability seen in some partnerships of local firms with multinationals and the state. The Paulo Geyer group was not only an exemplar of entrepreneurship but also of alliance-building. Multiple alliances with multinationals of diverse national origins have enabled certain of the largest local groups, like Matarazzo and Antunes, to build extremely powerful positions. In discussing the tri-pé in the petrochemical industry it was suggested that local capital was able to use its integrative role to gain benefits quite out of proportion to its contribution of capital or technology.

Recognition of the strengths of local capital does not change the fact that, in gross quantitative terms, the multinationals and the state are gradually expanding their control over the Brazilian industrial establishment at the expense of local capital. Nor does it negate the fact that the bourgeoisie depends on the state for capital and the multinationals for technology and can therefore make only a complementary contribution to the process of accumulation. It does not revive the national bourgeoisie as the hero of industrialization. It does, however, indicate that certain representatives of local capital have the ability both to influence the shape of the process of accumulation and to claim a share of the surplus that it generates, and that neither of these is likely to erode away in the foreseeable future.

The implications of this analysis of the position of local capital are very different depending on which group is under consideration: the elite (the very largest local economic groups who are able to participate in the triple alliance), or the vast majority of the local bourgeoisie. The one inescapable conclusion that emerges is that local capital cannot be analyzed as a single homogeneous entity.

For most local capitalists, the existence of special strengths or "comparative advantage" implies only that there are certain industries and certain niches within other industries in which they will be able to operate profitably as long as profit levels overall remain buoyant. For some, the niches may be extremely profitable. On average, the niches of local capital are likely to command a less than proportionate share of the surplus.

For elite local groups the implications are different. Their possession of special abilities or "comparative advantage" prevents their relegation to the status of "compradores." In the process of deciding what goes on within Brazil, their subordination to their multinational partners cannot be assumed; rather their strategies are constrained by their incorporation into a set of relations with international capital in general. They must "play by the rules" of international capital in the same way that any capitalist must play by the rules deemed appropriate by his class. It is the elite who are members of the "transnational kernel" or the "internationalized bourgeoisie."

The split between the incorporated elite and the rest of the local bourgeoisie facilitates the functioning of the triple alliance. The multinationals themselves represent a tiny elite in proportion to the capitalist classes of their home countries. The participation of a small elite of capitalists on the Brazilian side continues this pattern. Any attempt to integrate a larger proportion of the local bourgeoisie into the alliance directly would create extreme problems of coordination, not to mention difficulties over the division of the spoils.

The exclusion of the majority of the Brazilian bourgeoisie from participation in the triple alliance makes practical sense, but it also weakens the political foundations of dependent development. Those who have been excluded still have a general interest in the defense of private property and a high rate of local accumulation. But since they are rather marginal to the central thrust of the process of accumulation, they cannot discount the possibility that even nationalist strategies of accumulation will leave an increasing share of the surplus in the hands of the multinationals, the state, and the incorporated local elite at their expense.

The concerns of the excluded segment of the local bourgeoisie are not exactly "nationalist" in the sense that the term has been used here (emphasizing local rather than global accumulation). They must focus instead on the particularistic question of their own share of the surplus, regardless of what effect increasing their share would have on the overall rate of accumulation. Their most effective resource is political legitimacy. Because they are both national and private they represent the ideologically ideal instruments of local accumulation. Their claims to a larger share of the surplus must be enforced by political means. But their success depends on undermining political support for the triple alliance and, insofar as they are successful, not only the triple alliance but the strategy of dependent development itself would be undermined.

Some hints of the potential for political disruption that exists within the current model can be seen in the "antistatism" and "democratization" campaigns. Recognition of this potential, however, should not distract attention from the fact that the combination of differentiation and integration that has emerged in the period of the mid-sixties to mid-seventies has been highly profitable for all three kinds of capital. The current division of labor reflects the relative strength, both economic and political, of the different kinds of capital involved. It also provides a context within which bargaining over control and profits can take place in a way that reinforces rather than disrupts the triple alliance.

The crude outlines of the division of labor among the multinationals, state enterprises, and local capital form exactly the pattern that would be expected. Industries in which the most important thing is access to universally applicable, rapidly changing technology that cannot be obtained on an open market are the domain of the multinationals. Marketing technologies, as epitomized by the tobacco industry, are no less important than production technologies, as exemplified by certain specialized branches of the chemical industry. In areas where the multinationals have firm control over access to necessary technology, like pharmaceuticals, they are able not only to dominate overall but also successfully to resist sharing control over their own enterprises within the industry.

"Traditional" sectors, such as leather goods, apparel, and wood products, where competition is more intense and profits likely to be lower, are left to local capital somewhat by default. The multinationals could displace local firms in these industries simply by using their superior financial power, but the costs, both economic and political, would outweigh the benefits. Other industries where production tends to be already regionally decentralized and therefore less susceptible to centralization, such as cement and beer, have also remained largely in the hands of local capital. Strong economies of scale, however, resemble rapidly changing technology and a high degree of product differentiation, in being associated with foreign domination.

In addition to "technical" factors, there continues to be a historical element in the determination of the division of labor. Industries whose implantation in Brazil antedates the rise of the multinational corporation, such as food and textiles, are less foreign-dominated than those which originated under the aegis of foreign capital, such as the auto and rubber industries. These historical factors seem to be growing less important, as indicated by the intrusion, on the basis of scale economies and product differentiation, of multinationals into cotton textiles and certain branches of the food industry.

Local capital, either state or private, seems to have the best bargaining leverage vis-à-vis the multinationals where the fundamental sources of profits are relatively easily monopolized local raw materials, such as mineral deposits. In these industries, the exclusion of multinationals unless they are operating in partnership with local or state capital, has special political legitimacy. The multinationals have been unable to bargain for anything more than minority partnerships.

The special niche of state capital is large, lumpy, long-term-return investments. These include steel and other intermediary products as well as electrical energy and infrastructure financing. Only state enterprises are able to take the nationalist logic of external benefits and long-range returns seriously enough to undertake such investments. In addition, the political logic of legitimate exclusion of foreign capital applies to certain intermediate products, such as refined petroleum, as strongly as it does to extractive enterprises.

Finally, in those endeavors in which technology and scale are not of overriding importance and the ability to develop an extensive network of suppliers and/or customers is the most crucial element of success, only the long-established multinationals can compete with the more efficient representatives of local capital. Local dominance of retail trade is the most obvious example, but local successes in textiles and pharmaceuticals are also illustrative.

Without a division of labor that leaves each kind of capital with its own redoubts, the organization of the triple alliance would be much more difficult. But most branches of industry are not the preserves of any one kind of capital. Within these "disputed areas" or "buffer zones" integration on the basis of joint ventures is necessary. The petrochemical industry, lying between the state-dominated extractive and intermediate sectors and the multinational-dominated chemical industry, is an obvious case in point. The synthetic fibers side of the textile industry is another. Control over productive technology gives multinational newcomers bargaining leverage, while well-developed commercial expertise does the same for established local firms. Partnerships between them are the result.

Neither the technical characteristics of an industry nor the terms of bargaining between locals and multinationals are static. Even in the brief period between the military coup and the mid-seventies, bargaining has changed substantially. In the mid-sixties, Hanna Mining was still hoping for independent access to the Aguas Claras mineral deposits. By the mid-seventies, the computer industry, which on the basis of its technical features should have been a multinational preserve, was defined as an area in which multinational participation would be allowed only in partnership with local capital.

The terms of bargaining shifted partly because of incremental changes produced by experiences within Brazil. Once partnerships were successfully imposed in some areas they seemed more plausible in others. State managers and local executives gained confidence in their ability to protect their interests within a partnership. Multinational managers learned that partnerships could be profitable ventures. Equally important for the multinationals were demonstrations from outside Brazil, both of the feasibility of partnerships and of the potential dangers of trying to operate without local allies.

In the end, these shifts in the bargaining situation helped make possible the forging of the triple alliance. Similarly, an earlier shifting of local definitions of what kinds of economic pressures were politically legitimate had been crucial to inducing the multinationals to participate in the ventures that made dependent development possible in the first place.

Initially, the idea that a triple alliance among multinationals, the state, and a segment of local capital was essential to dependent development seemed a reasonable hypothesis. Certainly it was as reasonable as explaining industrialization on the periphery as the outcome of conflict between the national bourgeoisie and imperialism. Now that the details have been fleshed out and the necessary refinements and modifications made, the basic model seems more than plausible. Reviewing the characteristics of each kind of capital, it is clear than none alone could have sponsored the kind of dependent capitalist development that occurred in Brazil during the late sixties and early seventies. Even more incontrovertible is the evidence that collaboration among all three kinds of capital has taken place and that it has had the effect of deepening and diversifying Brazil's industrial capacity.

Since the main emphasis throughout has been on the success of the triple alliance as a strategy for accumulation in a dependent context, it is important to close this review of the model with a reiteration of the limitations of dependent development. Among all the evidence that the triple alliance has spoken successfully to issues of accumulation, there has been an equally significant lack of evidence that it can speak to issues involving the welfare of the mass of the population.

Collaboration among the three partners is based on a common respect for the logic of profitability. The Central de Medicamentos (CEME) was the state enterprise most conspicuously unable, first of all, to form alliances with the multinationals and, ultimately, to guarantee its own survival. CEME's role was conceived in welfare terms and its contribution to accumulation was indirect at best. Thus, even though CEME was no threat to the profits of the private sector, either foreign or local, it was not a potential ally and was dismembered.

The discussion of local R & D revealed the same disjunction

between the logic of the triple alliance and the citizens' welfare. Bargaining over whether technologically innovative activities would be done locally did not touch on the question of whether the content of innovation would serve the needs of the local populace. Whether products were developed locally or abroad, by multinationals or local firms, they were developed in response to perceived opportunities for profits, which given the skew of Brazilian income distribution, is hardly synonymous with the satisfaction of needs.

Unfortunately, the bargaining that goes into the construction and maintenance of the triple alliance is not simply irrelevant to questions of welfare. The nature of the immediate contradictions within the triple alliance is such as to exacerbate the exclusionary side of dependent development. Division of the surplus among the partners is the first concern. The participation of the multinationals is contingent on their receiving at least what they consider their fair share. The state bourgeoisie wants its share both out of "nationalistic" desires to promote accumulation in general and out of particularistic desires to expand individual firms.

The only way to ease the strains of distribution within the alliance is to increase the absolute size of the surplus. Increasing the rate of accumulation is one way of doing this. Shifting returns from labor to capital is the other. Only one kind of redistribution is likely under the triple alliance, redistribution from the mass of the population to the state bourgeoisie, the multinationals, and elite local capital. The maintenance of the delicate balance among the three partners militates against any possibility of dealing seriously with questions of income redistribution, even if members of the elite express support for income redistribution in principle (cf. McDonough, 1977).

Inability to deal with questions of welfare is not the only limitation of the triple alliance. As this summary has indicated, the local elite structure contains at least two serious internal contradictions that may ultimately limit its ability to deal even with questions of accumulation. The first of these is the political contradiction created by the exclusion of a large portion of the local bourgeoisie. The local private sector has ideological legitimacy, at least among the bourgeoisie as a whole. They also have a potentially powerful set of allies in the form of those members of the military who define "nationalism" in terms of local autonomy more than in terms of local accumulation. Should excluded local capital become sufficiently disenchanted as to attempt seriously to upset the triple alliance, and should they be able to persuade equally disenchanted "nationalists" to join them, the combination of cultural legitimacy and access to the means of violence could be quite hazardous to the survival of the triple alliance.

The second potentially disruptive internal factor is of a more economic type and flows from the reemergence within the state sector of the traditional capitalist contradiction between the interests of individual firms and the overall necessities of accumulation. If the central state apparatus is unable to discipline privatistic expansionist tendencies among state-owned enterprises, the effects on the confidence of both the multinationals and the local private sector could be extreme. Neither private partner could tolerate a situation in which state enterprises availed themselves freely of the privileges of their special position to engage in "cutthroat" competition and the untrammeled pursuit of corporate growth.

The other face of both these contradictions is the possibility that those parts of the state apparatus most sensitive to political pressure from the local bourgeoisie would react by redistributing the surplus to the local bourgeoisie, along the lines of a more loosely controlled and expanded PROCAP or perhaps more primitively on the basis of "corruption." This would reduce the political disaffection of the local bourgeoisie, but only at the expense of accumulation. Since a continued high rate of local accumulation is the sine qua non of the triple alliance, subsidizing the excluded members of the local private sector is as dangerous as risking their political disaffection.

Neither of these internal contradictions represents the most important limitation of the strategy of dependent development. Dependent development is viable only if it has support from the larger system of imperialism. The entire success of the dependent development is predicated on multinationals willing to invest, international bankers willing to extend credit, and other countries willing to consume an ever increasing volume of Brazilian exports. The emphasis here has been on the internal elite structures that made the triple alliance possible. Yet the formation of these internal structures could not have taken place in the absence of an environment in which international capital, both financial and industrial, was anxiously pursuing new opportunities in the periphery and in which Brazil stood out as an ideal investment climate. The process of accumulation in Brazil is still vulnerable to the effects of disruptions in the international economy, and that vulnerability constitutes the most obvious limitation of the triple alliance.

Like classic dependence, dependent development will eventually reach its limits and be superseded by new social structural forms. The fact remains that the triple alliance has transformed Brazil internally and changed its relations to both the center and the rest of the periphery. The economy produced by dependent development was the base from which Jorge Atalla could go to New York and plausibly decide to buy out Reuben Hills. The question remains, to what extent may developments in Brazil be repeated in other dependent countries, and to what extent are they the product of a unique national environment?

Situating the Brazilian Model

The initial discussion of dependent development made it clear that the model was not intended for application to most third world countries; rather it was intended to characterize the few among them that have managed to capture some control over their own surplus and embark on attempts at industrialization.

The most promising starting point from which to begin systematically differentiating such countries from the rest of the third
world is Wallerstein's concept of the "semi-periphery." Unfortunately, the theoretical definition of what constitutes the semi-
periphery is still imprecise. Wallerstein (1974c) speaks of it as oc-
cupying a "third structural position" within the world economy
and as being characterized internally by a division of labor that
includes some more advanced (higher wage) industry (Wallerstein, 1976). Using these hints to identify a distinctive category
of countries is difficult, as recent attempts like that of Daniel
Chirot (1977) indicate.[2]

Until the idea of the "semi-periphery" has been specified
theoretically and the characteristics of "semi-peripheral" countries have been better elaborated, using the term is primarily a
way of asserting that there is a distinct category of countries that
cannot be simply considered "peripheral" and yet are structur-
ally distinguishable from center countries. Our purpose is to determine whether the elite structure of at least one subset of these
countries—traditionally considered part of the third world—can
be described in terms of the triple alliance.

In the absence of well-defined, theoretically grounded means
of designating the members of the "semi-periphery," a simpler,
interim measure is necessary to single out some potential members. Sheer scale is the most obvious candidate. If scale is measured in terms of gross national product, then the major countries
of the capitalist center stand nicely apart from other nations.

---

[2] Chirot's is one of the few recent empirical works that appears fully committed
to the concept of the semi-periphery, yet even he at times seems to accept the
more conventional "three worlds" format which assigns Spain, Italy, and Ireland
to the "capitalist core." Yet sometimes (e.g., p. 214) these countries are treated as
part of the "semi-periphery." Likewise, Chirot labels Brazil, Mexico, India,
Egypt, Nigeria, Indonesia, Iran, China, Saudi Arabia, Turkey, and North Viet-
nam as simply parts of the "third world" at the end of his book. But in the text (pp.
145, 205-211, 214, 250) these countries are identified as part of the "semi-
periphery."

Likewise, one of the requirements for the kind of transition that Brazil has experienced is a certain minimum economic scale. Scale is a crude stand-in for the kind of structural analysis that would be necessary to provide a theoretically convincing rationale for categorizing countries. Nonetheless, the classification provided in Table 6.1 fits quite nicely with intuitive notions of center, periphery, and semi-periphery.

Most of the countries of the third world are poor and tiny. As long as there is a periphery they are likely to be in it. Table 6.1 relegates 120 such countries to cell number 8. Specific features of the Brazilian case may be relevant to these countries. The areas in which local capital has a "comparative advantage" may well be the same. The relative possibilities for state entrepreneurship may well vary in the same way from sector to sector, even if the overall possibilities for state enterprise are much less. The state and the local bourgeoisie are likely to have much less bargaining power vis-à-vis the multinationals in smaller and poorer states, but the relative dimensions of the bargaining should be similar. The possibilities of enforcing a priority on local accumulation are less, but the lines of conflict between nationalist and global rationality should be the same. In short, the possibility of transposing certain elements from the analysis of the Brazilian case to the analysis of the "real" periphery is great, but the overall model is unlikely to apply.

The most interesting part of Table 6.1 for our purposes are cells 3 through 6 which contain a very disparate collection of about 40 countries. They range from Italy, which might easily be considered part of the center, to Thailand, which would seem clearly part of the periphery. They include small rich countries, like Sweden and Belgium, and large poor countries, like India and Indonesia. They contain a large number of socialist bloc countries, ranging from the Democratic Republic of Germany to Bulgaria. They also contain countries, like Spain, which were once part of the center and countries like Venezuela and Mexico

TABLE 6.1 Crude Classification of the International System circa 1970

	Per Capita GNP Greater than $900	Per Capita GNP Less than $900
	(1)	(2)
GNP greater than $100 billion	U.S. U.S.S.R. Japan Germany (Fed. Rep.) France United Kingdom	China
	(3)	(4)
GNP between $30 billion and $100 billion	Italy Canada Germany (Dem. Rep.) Poland Spain Sweden Czechoslovakia Australia	India Brazil Mexico
	(5)	(6)
GNP between $5 billion and $30 billion	Belgium Switzerland Denmark Romania Finland Norway Netherlands Hungary Greece Austria New Zealand Venezuela Argentina Israel etc.	South Africa Yugoslavia Pakistan Iran Turkey Indonesia Korea Philippines Chile Colombia Egypt Nigeria Peru Bulgaria Thailand Taiwan
	(7)	(8)
GNP less than $5 billion	Ireland Iceland Luxembourg Hongkong Kuwait etc.	Roughly 120 third world countries.

Based on IBRD, 1973.

that were once firmly peripheral and can no longer be comfortably considered that way.

While it would be interesting to explore the applicability of the Brazilian model to former center countries like Spain or socialist countries like Yugoslavia, the subset to which the model is likely to apply consists of those countries which have both traditionally been considered part of the third world and can now reasonably be considered part of the "semi-periphery." Since theories of imperialism and dependency have usually lumped all third world countries together, it is the distinctiveness of "semi-peripheral" third world countries as opposed to the rest of the periphery that is primarily at issue. Nothing indicates this distinctiveness more clearly than the way in which international capital has acted toward "semi-peripheral" third world countries.

Table 6.2 compares U.S. investment in the seven "developing" countries containing the largest amount of manufacturing investment with U.S. investment in all other developing countries as of 1974. The extent to which manufacturing investment is concentrated is striking. Brazil and Mexico together contain almost exactly half of total U.S. direct investment in manufacturing. The seven countries in combination contain over 75%. For the rest of the developing world, direct investment in manufacturing represents only about 12% of total direct investment. For most third world countries foreign capital continues to be involved in exporting primary products. Economically, the model of classic dependency comes closer to describing their situation than does the model of dependent development.

The differentiation between third world countries experienceing dependent development and other third world countries has increased sharply in the period since World War II. Table 6.3 replicates the calculations of Table 6.2 for the year 1950. What is striking about this table is that the average percentage of manufacturing investment in the seven developing countries is only slightly higher than the percentage of manufacturing investment

TABLE 6.2   U.S. Manufacturing Investment as a Proportion of Total
U.S. Direct Investment in Third World Countries Containing the
Largest Amounts of Manufacturing Investment, 1974

	Total Investment*	Total Manufacturing Investment*	Manufacturing Investment as a % of Total
Brazil	3,658	2,502	68%
Mexico	2,825	2,146	76%
Argentina	1,155	772	67%
Venezuela	1,772	659	37%
Colombia	629	375	60%
Philippines	727	340	47%
India	345	234	68%
Total for Countries with Largest Manufacturing Investment	11,111	7,028	63%
Total for Other Third World Countries	17,368	2,094	12%
Total for All Third World Countries	28,479	9,122	32%
Countries with Largest Manufacturing Investment as % of Total	39%	77%	

* In millions of current $US.
Source: Lupo and Freidlin, 1975·Table 13.

for the third world as a whole. Only in Brazil, Argentina, and
Mexico did manufacturing investment reach over 20% of the total. Twenty-four years later, manufacturing remained a tiny proportion of total investment in most of the third world, but for the
select few it had become the predominant kind of investment.
Investment overall had become more dispersed by 1974, but
manufacturing remained highly concentrated.

It might be argued that manufacturing investment is not the
proper measure of differentiation within the third world because
it ignores the importance of oil and other primary commodities.
To be sure, having a resource base is central to dependent de-

TABLE 6.3   U.S. Manufacturing Investment as a Proportion of Total U.S. Direct Investment in Third World Countries Containing the Largest Amounts of Manufacturing Investment, 1950

	Total Investment*	Total Manufacturing Investment*	Manufacturing Invest-ment as a % of Total
Brazil	644	285	40%
Mexico	415	133	32%
Argentina	356	161	45%
Cuba	642	54	8%
Chile	540	29	5%
Colombia	193	25	13%
Venezuela	993	24	2%
Total for Countries with Largest Manu-facturing Investment	3,783	711	19%
Total for Other Third World Countries	1,952	135	7%
Total for All Third World Countries	5,735	846	15%
Countries with Largest Manufacturing Invest-ment as % of Total	66%	84%	

* In millions of current $US.
Source: Pizer and Cutler, 1960:Table 3.

velopment, but manufacturing investment remains a crucial indicator of relation to the international system, even for those countries in which primary exports remain most important. Venezuela is a case in point. Despite the overriding importance of oil in the Venezuelan economy, the rise in the proportion of foreign investment in manufacturing between 1950 and 1974 is more dramatic in Venezuela than in any other third world country.

If the investment decisions of U.S. multinationals reflect changes in the structure of the international economy, then it is clear that certain countries have become differentiated from the rest of the third world. Equally clear is the fact that these countries are a critical group as far as the evolution of imperialism is concerned. As manufacturing becomes more important, but continues to be concentrated, the role of these countries becomes increasingly central to the overall growth of the imperialist system. It is to this distinctive and critical subset of third world countries, which we are calling for lack of a better label the "semi-periphery," that the Brazilian model of dependent development should apply.

The Brazilian Model and the Semi-Periphery

To exclude those countries of the "semi-periphery" which are not also part of the third world reduces the heterogeniety of the category. But even so, the amount of variation is imposing. Table 6.4 gives some indication of the range of the variation. The production figures presented in this table also confirm our initial assertion that Brazil represents the limiting case of dependent development.

The selection of commodities presented in Table 6.4 makes evident the extent to which Brazil has become separated from other third world countries. Even the one commodity whose production declined in Brazil between 1965 and 1974, cotton fabrics, identifies Brazil as having an industrial structure more like the center than the periphery. It seems somehow especially appropriate that cotton textiles, which were so intimately associated with the original industrial revolution in England, should now have become an industry of the periphery. In 1970 Europe began to import more cotton textiles than it exported (UN, 1974:1044). Brazil's exports continued to grow, but the decline in its total production mirrored declines taking place in the United States, Britain, and most European countries.

In the case of steel, India and Mexico both produced amounts in the same range as Brazil, but no other third world country even came close. The Democratic Republic of Korea came near-

TABLE 6.4　Production of Selected Commodities in Larger Third World Countries, 1965 and 1974*

Commodity	Country					
	Brazil	Mexico	India	Iran	Egypt	Nigeria
Cotton fabrics	(in millions of square meters)					
1965	1508	793	9135	505	575	86
1974	1292	977	9900	576	850	276
1974 as % of UK	284%	215%	2180%	127%	187%	61%
Steel (crude ingots)	(in millions of metric tons)					
1965	2.9	2.4	6.4	—	0.2	—
1974	7.5	5.0	6.6	—	0.3	—
1974 as % of UK	34%	23%	30%	—	1%	—
Synthetic fibers	(in thousands of metric tons)					
1965	10	8	1	—	0.2	—
1974	69	82	15	—	0.3	—
1974 as % of UK	35%	41%	8%	—	0%	—
Refrigerators	(in thousands of units)					
1965	260	113	31	39	20	—
1974	1038	375	102	257	55	—
1974 as % of UK	86%	31%	8%	21%	5%	—
Passenger cars (including assembled from imported parts) (in thousands of units)						
1965	113	67	35	4	3	—
1974	562	259	47	51	10	—
1974 as % of UK	37%	17%	3%	3%	0.6%	—

* Data for last available year have been substituted for 1974 data in cases where 1974 data were missing.
Source: UN, 1976:579, 632, 631, 477, 446, 349, 179.

est with a total production less than half of Brazil's. Mexico and the Republic of Korea both produce more synthetic fibers than Brazil, but in consumer durables like passanger cars and refrigerators not even Mexico was a close competitor.

How far across the range of countries tentatively labeled as "semi-peripheral" is the Brazilian model of dependent development likely to be a useful frame of reference? If it does not apply to Mexico, the most obviously similar nation, then the overall model that has been presented here must be considered descriptive of an idiosyncratic case. The elements it contains may find analogies in other instances of dependent development, but the model as a whole would not be applicable. If, on the other hand, the model applies not just to Mexico but to Nigeria, then its generalizability must be considered impressive. Nigeria is not only one of the least industrialized countries in the group but also one whose primary qualification for semi-peripheral status is its oil wealth. Brazil and Nigeria represent opposite poles within the range of third world countries that might be considered members of the "semi-periphery."

While a systematic examination of other countries of the "semi-periphery" would obviously be preferable to comparisons with Mexico and Nigeria alone, the latter, more limited, endeavor is more feasible and should suffice to give some hint of the degree to which the idea of the triple alliance as the structural underpinning of dependent development is generalizable.

The degree of similarity with Mexico is, not unexpectedly, encouraging.[3] The case of Monsanto in Mexico provides a nice illustration of how much elite structures there can resemble those in Brazil. In 1972, Brazil was not the only country where Monsanto's local position did not seem commensurate with its global strength. In Mexico, Monsanto's wholly owned subsidiary was not growing and Monsanto's lack of alliances was part of the reason. According to the *Wall Street Journal*, Monsanto's response to the situation was as follows:

Without government cooperation, growth was impossible. So Monsanto did what the government hoped it would do—it

[3] My perspectives on the Mexican case are largely based on the work of others who have done primary research in Mexico. I have benefited from collaboration with Susan Eckstein and from the work of Susan Kaufman Purcell and John Purcell. Discussions with Gary Gereffi, as well as access to his excellent work on the steroid hormone industry, have also been very important in the development of my ideas. Perhaps most influential of all has been the work of Doug Bennett and Ken Sharpe. Of course, none of these people should be held responsible for the way in which I have interpreted or may have distorted their ideas.

"Mexicanized." In essence it joined forces with Mexican investors to form a new company, 38% owned by Monsanto, controlled by a Mexican holding company called DESC. Since Monsanto took on its Mexican partners doors have been opening. And in just three years, profits of the concern have soared over 200%. (11/5/76:36).

In Mexico, as in Brazil, alliances between multinationals and a small number of the largest economic groups are increasing. In both countries, the state and state-owned corporations are centrally involved.

The similarities between the alliances behind industrialization in both Mexico and Brazil are more significant because there are reasons to expect the two countries to be different. Mexico, by virtue of sheer proximity, should be more dependent on the United States. U.S. investors account for a much larger share of total direct foreign investment in Mexico than they do in Brazil. The United States also accounts for a much larger share of Mexico's foreign trade. Oligopolistic competition that pits multinationals from different center countries against each other has been important in the evolution of industrialization in Brazil. Mexico should have had a more difficult time using this source of leverage.

Compensating for Mexico's greater economic dependence on the United States is its greater success in the institutionalization of stable, centralized political control. Out of the chaos of Mexico's revolution came a political structure remarkably well suited to the needs of capital accumulation. During the forties, fifties, and sixties, while Brazil searched for an effective political formula, Partido Revolucionario Institucional was able to maintain control and limit redistribution and at the same time provide institutionalized political access for most of the local bourgeoisie and some representatives of the organized working class. If the local Mexican bourgeoisie is as well or better off than its Brazilian counterpart, it would seem to owe its position to the political apparatus created by PRI (cf. Eckstein and Evans, 1978).

There are other obvious differences between the two countries. Mexico has half as many people and a somewhat higher per capita income. The indigenous cultural traditions and community structures that characterize the rural areas of the two countries are dissimilar, as is the ethnic structure of the urban areas. Brazil's Indian population, unlike Mexico's, was largely destroyed; Mexico had no postcolonial flux of European immigration comparable to Brazil's. Despite these differences, the pattern of alliance between the state, the multinationals, and elite local economic groups in Mexico is much like the one that has already been described in Brazil.

Nowhere are the similarities more evident than in the distribution of multinational, state, and local capital by sectors. In both Brazil and Mexico capital of different origins gravitates towards different branches of industry. In Table 6.5 the distributions that have already been considered for Brazil are juxtaposed with those for Mexico. Brazil is as similar to Mexico as Brazil in 1966 is to Brazil in 1972 (cf. Newfarmer and Mueller, 1975:108, 110). Indeed, the distributions for Brazil and Mexico are no more different than distributions for Brazil taken from different sources (cf. Chapter 3).

Scale, technology, and commercial strategy operate to separate multinational and local capital in Mexico in much the same way that they operate in Brazil. State capital in Mexico is more dispersed than Brazilian state capital, but primary metals, the most important sector of state participation in manufacturing in Brazil, also contains the highest proportion of state capital in Mexico. Chemicals, the other sector of significant state activity in Brazil, is also a major area of activity for the Mexican state. Petroleum exploration and refining is another area of strong state involvement in both countries. The pattern of differentiation in the two countries is more alike for private capital than for state capi-

TABLE 6.5   The Shape of Investment in Brazil and Mexico, 1972

| | % of Assets among the Top 300 | | | | | | % of "Joint Ventures"* among U.S. Multinational Affiliates | |
| | Foreign | | State | | Local Private | | | |
Industry	Brazil	Mexico	Brazil	Mexico	Brazil	Mexico	Brazil	Mexico
Food	32	26	0	7	67	67	36	37
Textiles	44	5	0	22	56	73	***	20
Paper**	29	51	0	10	71	39	33	83
Chemicals	69	68	12	20	19	12	30	34
Rubber	100	100	0	0	0	0	33	25
Stone, Clay, Glass	22	32	0	2	78	66	30	69
Primary Metals	23	41	51	24	25	35	46	48
Electrical Machinery	78	60	0	16	22	24	27	26
Transportation	82	79	4	13	13	8	0	36
Total Manufacturing	51	52	15	16	35		29	39

* Firms that are less than 90% owned by the U.S. multinational.
** In Brazil this is paper, wood and furniture.
*** Not disclosed.
Source: Newfarmer and Mueller, 1975:55, 73, 108, 126.

tal, but even in the case of state capital the similarities are strong.

If Brazil and Mexico are close to identical in their differentiation of capital, Mexico is more advanced when it comes to the integration of the three kinds of capital. In at least three sectors, (paper, transportation, and nonmetallic minerals) there are significantly higher proportions of joint ventures in Mexico, while there are no sectors in which the proportion of joint ventures is significantly higher in Brazil. Overall, the proportion of North American affiliates that are joint ventures is a third higher in Mexico than in Brazil. These differences are not surprising. The Mexican state was publically advocating "Mexicanization" long before the Brazilian regime began to push alliances. There is still no explicit, general doctrine of "Brazilianization." Despite the greater prevalance of joint ventures in Mexico, however, the alliances that have been formed have much in common with their Brazilian counterparts.

In Mexico, as in Brazil, participation in alliances with the multinationals is limited primarily to a few large, sophisticated "grupos economicos." Bennett and Sharpe (1978) have argued that the primary effect of Mexicanization has been to increase the concentration of economic power at the local level. Most local capitalists cannot raise the capital necessary to participate in Mexicanization. The largest local economic groups, like their counterparts in Brazil, participate in multiple partnerships with a variety of multinational partners.

As in Brazil, state and local capital have been particularly successful in sectors like mining where profits are based on natural resources rather than technology. American Smelting and Refining, for example, had to sell a majority interest in its Mexican subsidiary to a local group. This same local group is also involved in a joint venture with the state in copper. Another local group has joined with two different state-owned corporations plus two different multinationals (Phelps Dodge and Anaconda) in another copper mining venture. This latter sounds very much like the tri-pé model developed in the Brazilian petrochemical industry. In discussing it, Mexico's minister of national properties mentioned explicitly that a "triumverate" of state, multinational, and local private capital was the desired model in mining projects. (*Business Latin America*, 1974:356)

Bennett and Sharpe (1978) suggest that a dozen or so of the largest "grupos" are the prime beneficiaries of "Mexicanization" and point out the diversity of the alliances that bind these companies to the multinationals. One example is the group around Bruno Pagliai, which has joint ventures with Alcoa, Hughes Tool, Taylor Forge and Pipe, Yamaha, S.K.F., and Renault. A second is built around the Banco Nacional and has alliances with Westinghouse, Celanese, Union Carbide, Kimberley Clark, Scott Paper, and Rolls Royce. Like Azevedo Antunes, Matarazzo, and Monteiro Aranha in Brazil these groups are not simply "junior partners" to a single multinational. They are participants in the networks that bind international capital together. Their participation in these networks separates them from the vast majority of local capitalists.

In Mexico, as in Brazil, the multinationals have found that the formation of alliances with elite local capital is generally advantageous. *Business Latin America* (1973:155) cites Kimberley Clark as an example of a company which "felt that its very success in Mexico argued for a majority local ownership as an appropriate way to guarantee a clear road for continued expansion and diversification." Westinghouse found its joint venture with the private Banco Nacional and the state-owned Nacional Financeira a very successful vehicle for expansion into a diversified set of electrical equipment and component manufacturing ventures. Monsanto's Mexican partner also has joint ventures with Phillips Petroleum and Dana Corporation and both companies are earning 24% return on investment according to the *Wall Street Journal* (11/5/76:36).

The shape of the compromise between the nationalist logic of the state and the global perspective of the multinationals looks the same in Mexico as it does in Brazil. The multinationals have been given generous incentives and good opportunities for future profits. In return they share control and returns with a few elite members of the local bourgeoisie. In Mexico as in Brazil the state has tried to push the multinationals into doing local research and development. Royalty payments for foreign technology are limited and a National Registry for Transfer of Technology was created by the 1973 law on the transfer of technology. In the petrochemical industry, the government has made it clear that "firms which engage or intend to engage in the development of local R & D will be given preference" (Goldmark, 1976).

Politically, the bargaining between the multinationals and the state is slightly less limited in Mexico than in Brazil. Gereffi's

(1978) analysis of the steroid hormone industry provides a nice example. The state has some leverage in steroid production because the raw material base, barbasco root, is found in Mexico. But the multinationals have control over channels of export marketing. When the state-owned corporation, Proquivemex, tried to force a substantial increase in the price paid by the multinationals for barbasco, the multinationals responded by relying on stockpiles, leaving Proquivemex without buyers. Proquivemex in turn organized the peasants, who collected barbasco and sold it to the state firm, to back the demand for nationalization of the steroid hormone industry.

The multinationals rallied allies of their own. Cocamin, the National Industrial Confederation, came out in opposition to the state corporation's tactics, which it claimed "put social tranquility in danger" (Gereffi, 1978). At the same time the National Chamber of Chemical Pharmaceutical Firms attacked Proquivemex for its production of finished products, which they claimed would displace private local production. The state corporation was outmaneuvered. Other segments of the state apparatus stepped in and began trying to work out a compromise acceptable to the multinationals.

The differences between the case of CEME in Brazil and the Proquivemex confrontation with the multinationals in Mexico exemplifies the differences in the political position of state corporations in the two countries. CEME was never able even to attempt confrontation based on mobilization in the way that Proquivemex did. In part, of course, CEME was weaker because it had no natural resource to use as leverage, but more significantly, it was weaker because the Brazilian political system left it no way of using its constituency (families making less than the minimum wage) as a political resource. It would have been unthinkable for CEME to have organized rallies against foreign drug companies or attempted in any way to organize mass support behind itself.

In Mexico, populism may not be a winning strategy for the state bourgeoisie, but it is a possible strategy. In Brazil it is out of the question. The possibilities for confrontation between the state bourgeoisie and the multinationals are correspondingly greater in Mexico. At the same time, the possibility of popular mobilization creates greater impetus for alliances between local groups and the multinationals. The Mexican bourgeoisie is aware of the advantages of appearing nationalistic, but, when a state corporation poses the issue in terms of peasants versus multinationals, local capital has little choice. "Social tranquility" must be defended and therefore the local bourgeoisie must side with the multinationals.

The conflict between Proquivemex and the multinationals is no more typical of Mexico than CEME is typical of Brazil. It does, however, illustrate the possible consequences of trying to include nonelite participants in the bargaining process. As long as participation is limited to elite local capital and the state, nationalism means maximizing local accumulation. With broader participation, questions of distribution and welfare are more likely to come to the fore. Local capital is "nationalistic" as long as "nationalism" means putting primacy on local rather than global accumulation. If nationalism takes on a broader meaning, then the common interest of local capital and the multinationals in accumulation makes their differences over the exact strategy of accumulation relatively unimportant.

The Proquivemex case is interesting because it suggests that state capital in Mexico may be willing to entertain definitions of nationalism that place more weight on distribution and welfare. An alliance between the state bourgeoisie and nonelite groups appears completely out of the question in the Brazilian context. It is highly implausible in Mexico as well, but the Mexican context has at least provided an instance that raises the issue. At the same time, the inability of the triple alliance to speak to issues of welfare and redistribution is thoroughly reconfirmed by this example. If the state bourgeoisie is tempted to step out of line, their private partners will combine to remind them of the rules.

The internal alliances that lie behind dependent development are similar in both Mexico and Brazil. So are the difficulties involved in sustaining the process of accumulation. In the mid-seventies, Mexico, like Brazil, was faced with disturbingly large trade deficits for which, in both countries, imports of intermediary and capital goods were primarily responsible. By 1976 they shared the distinction of being the only less developed countries in the world with $25 billion of foreign debt. The devaluation of the peso in 1976 signaled the failure of control over inflation, which had been the hallmark of Mexico's growth in the fifties and sixties. Mexico's ability to stem inflation had seemed a significant indication of differences between Mexico and Brazil (cf. Eckstein and Evans, 1978). By 1976 those differences had largely evaporated.

Like Brazil, Mexico has found that dependent development requires a mass of imported inputs even larger than the exports it generates and that even when the multinationals cooperate in the promotion of local accumulation they still ship more capital back to the center than they bring in. Mexico's newly discovered oil reserves may alleviate its balance of payments problems, but Mexico still reinforces the lessons of Brazil. Dependent development does not correct the imbalances in semi-peripheral relations with the center; it replaces old imbalances with new ones.

A final characteristic that joins Brazil and Mexico is the exclusion of the mass of the population from the benefits of economic growth. The mass of Mexicans may not have been subjected to the harsh declines in real incomes that the earners of the minimum wage experienced in the late sixties in Brazil, but the share of income of the bottom 80% of the population is no larger in Mexico than it is in Brazil. The superior political apparatus of PRI has, in the past, limited the need for direct, violent repression of the sort that the Brazilian military has resorted to. But even differences in this regard may be shrinking. PRI has been willing to engage in brutal repression when it seemed necessary, and desperate actions on the part of the bottom 80%, such as the recent peasant land invasions, may well force PRI to become more openly repressive in the future.

External imbalances threaten the rate of local accumulation. Lower rates of local accumulation make it less likely that local elites will be willing to make any serious attempts to redistribute the surplus. Continued misery for the mass of the population and increased use of repression combine to make dependent development look less than attractive, whether it is seen from Brazil or from Mexico. But the consequences of dependent development for the bottom 80% will not in themselves undermine the model. The real question is whether accumulation can be sustained at sufficient levels to generate the profits necessary to maintain the current alliance.

To apply the model to Mexico is easy. To use it for Nigeria is more of a challenge.[4] In some ways, Nigeria barely deserves to be considered part of the "semi-periphery." Except for the oil industry, which is a classic enclave, it is primarily an agricultural country. The manufacturing investment it contains is a fraction of that which international capital has chosen to locate in Brazil and Mexico. Yet, the international business community is beginning to discuss Nigeria the way they discussed Brazil at the beginning of the seventies—as a potential member of the "semi-periphery."

The attraction of Nigeria to the multinationals was summed up nicely by *Forbes* magazine in 1976:

Nigeria, population 70 million to 80 million, is far and away the most populous nation in Black Africa, and also thanks to its oil

---

[4] My interpretation of the Nigerian case owes a great deal to the work of Paul Lubeck. I am grateful for having been able to benefit not only from his written work but from a number of provocative discussions on the contemporary political economy of Nigeria, and hope that he will not find my own discussion too far off the mark.

revenues, the richest. It is not yet rich as South Africa but soon will be . . . Nigeria's economy is growing at a fast 9% a year. This year Nigeria's gross national product will be about $27 billion, about 10% less than South Africa's. Sometime next year or in 1978 at the latest, Nigeria's economy will overtake South Africa's (Flanigan, 1976:51).

Nigeria already has more foreign investment than any other country on the continent except South Africa (see Rood, 1975:22), and according to *Business International* (1977:231), "profits in most foreign-owned companies have been high." It is no wonder that Nigeria has been called "the Brazil of Africa."

To call Nigeria the "Brazil of Africa" underlines the differences between the two continents as much as it does the similarities between the two countries. In an African context the structure of the Nigerian economy may appear relatively advanced; in a Latin American context it would appear anachronistic. From the role of the state to the position of the multinationals, the structure of the Nigerian elite is in many ways more suggestive of the period of classic dependence than of the current period of dependent development in Brazil and Mexico. In both Brazil and Mexico the central state apparatus has succeeded in imposing its authority on regional elites. In Nigeria this process is just beginning. The degree of regional integration that characterizes contemporary Nigeria resembles that of Mexico in the days before PRI or Brazil during the old republic.

Nigeria's trade relations with the outside world are also more characteristic of the period of classic dependence than of dependent development. Being the world's fifth largest petroleum exporter makes the exchange of raw materials for manufactured products relatively painless, but the fact remains that Nigeria's imports and exports are in the same category as Brazil's imports and exports at the end of the nineteenth century. The oil companies import almost all their supplies "right down to the mops used to swab their platforms" (see Lubeck, 1977:11). Even products made from petroleum, like gasoline, a large proportion must be imported.

The overwhelming importance of oil exports makes Nigeria's relations to the multinationals more like those of Venezuela than of Brazil or Mexico, but current relations with the multinationals still bear a strong resemblance to the situation in Latin America in the earlier phases of import-substituting industrialization. For the present, the multinationals see Nigeria primarily as a good market for goods produced either in the center or in more advanced countries of the "semi-periphery." *Business International* (1976:229) summed it up by saying, "Nigeria is likely to maintain its enormous appeal as an export market for the next five years and beyond." At the same time, it reports that "foreign investment has been concentrated in manufacturing over the past several years, a trend that will continue."

Some investment in manufacturing is designed to preserve Nigeria as a market. *Forbes* (Flanigan, 1976:61) reports, for example, that "the 3M Company is producing Scotch tape in a plant outside Lagos in return for the right to bring its hundreds of other products to Nigeria's market." But the investment in manufacturing has gone far beyond "tokenism." As far back as 1965, 60% of all manufacturing firms with ten or more employees were foreign-owned (Nafziger, 1977:58).[5]

Since the manufacturing sector is very small and concentrated in "traditional" industries like food processing and textiles (Lubeck, 1977:17) and since what industry there is is dominated by foreign-owned companies, it follows that "national industrial bourgeoisie" is almost nonexistent. Successful indigenous entre-

---

[5] This figure may be slightly misleading because a large number of smaller manufacturing establishments are considered "foreign-owned" since they are owned by "Levantines" (Lebanese, Greeks, Cypriots, Syrians, and Palestinians). This is, of course, quite different from being controlled by multinationals (see Nafziger, 1977:63).

preneurs are concentrated in commercial and other nonindustrial activities, and there are no "captains of industry" on the order of Ermírio de Moraes, the Villares brothers, or the Conde Matarazzo.

Clearly, Nigeria is not an exemplar of dependent development as the term has been used to describe Brazil. It is a country groping its way out of classic dependence. Yet as a background against which to interpret the kinds of changes that are currently taking place in Nigeria, the Brazilian model is surprisingly useful. The evolution of the role of the state, the shape of alliances with the multinationals, and even the emerging position of local capital seem to be moving toward a tripartite elite structure which, while it may never replicate the Brazilian triple alliance, will certainly resemble it.

The central state apparatus is on the ascendent and its preeminence is greatly enhanced by its control over oil revenues (Lubeck, 1977:2). In its relations with the international oil companies the Nigerian state has been the beneficiary of the struggles of the other OPEC countries. It was able to secure majority control early in its career as a major exporter rather than forced to bargain for half a century as Venezuela was (see Tugwell, 1975). Oil revenues, in combination with the new norms for relations between international capital and third world states that have been pioneered in countries like Brazil and Mexico, have enabled the Nigerian state to enter into partnerships with multinationals outside the petroleum industry as well.

Despite external trade relations and an internal economic structure that resemble classic dependence more than dependent development, the Nigerian state is already thoroughly immersed in concrete alliances with the multinationals. The sectors the state has chosen for itself are largely the ones in which the Mexican and Brazilian states have successfully operated. Obviously, the state is interested in participating in the development of intermediary products based on petroleum. Like the

Brazilian and Mexican states, it has entered petroleum refining and the petrochemical industry. It has also become involved in the iron and steel industry. The factors that lead state enterprise to focus on intermediary products seem to transcend both differences in level of industrialization and the effects of having an economy dominated by oil exports.

There is, of course, a difference between the kind of partnerships that are possible for the Nigerian state and those formed by the Brazilian and Mexican states. In Brazil and Mexico, technicians and executives had almost a generation to develop expertise within the state sector before becoming seriously involved in joint ventures with the multinationals. Precisely because it has been able to form joint ventures at an earlier stage of its development, Nigeria enters them at a disadvantage. Lubeck (1977:16) summarizes the situation by saying, "While the ownership of the industries may rest upon the Nigerian state, Nigerians will not control the production process." Control over equity does not provide the Nigerian state with the same bargaining leverage within joint ventures that it does the Brazilian state, at least not at present.

Perhaps the most interesting parallel between the elite structures of the two countries is the fact that in Nigeria as in Brazil, the local bourgeoisie has not been left out. Given the objective weakness of local private capital in Nigeria and low likelihood of its making a significant contribution to industrialization, it would be reasonable to expect a dualistic battle between the state and the multinationals rather than a triple alliance. But, far from being excluded, the local private sector has done extremely well for itself. Relative to its resources, it has probably done better than local capital in Brazil.

"Indigenization," the Nigerian equivalent of "Mexicanization," requires a minimum of 40% Nigerian ownership in any industry (see *Business International*, 1976:219; 1977:51; Rood, 1976). Small-scale manufacturing and retail trade are reserved exclusively for Nigerians and a broad intermediate set of industries is reserved for majority ownership by Nigerians. In addition, several agencies have been set up to perform the support functions performed in Brazil by the BNDE and its associated agencies (Lubeck, 1977:19). Every attempt is being made to stimulate the growth of the local private sector so that it can play its assigned role in the triple alliance.

As an economic strategy aimed at fostering accumulation, the attempt to stimulate the growth of an indigenous entrepreneurial class is a dubious venture. The possibility that support for the local bourgeoisie will degenerate into subsidies that are not only irrelevant to but run directly counter to the project of accumulation is greater in Nigeria than in Brazil. Nothing illustrates this better than the famous "cement scandal." In 1975 the Nigerian government ordered ten times the amount of cement estimated as necessary according to the development plan, at prices that ended up almost double the going international price. All of it had to be imported. According to Terisa Turner (1977:220), "nearly one out of every four oil dollars earned by Nigeria in 1975-76 were diverted through the cement racket," roughly $2 billion. The result was a bonanza from the point of view of certain well-placed members of the Nigerian commercial bourgeoisie and their foreign allies who supplied the cement, but a large loss from the point of view of maximizing the rate of accumulation.

It would be a negation of the Brazilian historical experience and a theoretical embarrassment if Nigeria were able to step smoothly from classic dependence to dependent development, replicating the Brazilian version of the triple alliance without difficulty. That the Nigerian case appears suitable to formulations of the triple alliance at all is impressive. In fact, the prospects for Nigeria moving successfully in the direction of the triple alliance seem good. Thirty years ago Brazil had no petroleum engineers; thirty years from now Nigeria should have a class of state-sector executives quite like the men who run Petrobrás or PEMEX.

Whether Nigeria will be able to develop a local industrial class equivalent to its counterparts in Brazil and Mexico is more questionable. But if the local private bourgeoisie's current ability to appropriate a share of the surplus is any indication, private local capital is no more likely to be wiped out in Nigeria than it is in Brazil or Mexico.

The Brazilian model does not provide a description of the current structure of the Nigerian elite, nor is it necessarily a blueprint for the future. The perspective provided by the Brazilian experience does offer a framework that helps to make sense of the contemporary Nigerian social structure. On the basis of the close analogies between the Brazilian model and the Mexican case and the usefulness of the model in the more distant Nigerian case, it seems reasonable to view the model of dependent development derived from our analysis of Brazil as applying in varying degrees to a range of countries, third world members of the semi-periphery. Their number is not large but they occupy a crucial position within the international economic order. Their future relations with the international economy, which are conditioned and constrained by the internal structure of the triple alliance, will affect both the rest of the periphery and the center itself.

Strategies for Dependent Development

Trade balances are not a problem for the "real" periphery. During the period of classic dependence Brazil's balance of trade was always favorable. A look at Paraguay, Uruguay, or Bolivia in the mid-seventies reveals the same sort of positive trade balances. It is when a country begins to move from classic dependence to dependent development that the balance of trade becomes a problem. Even oil producers like Nigeria cannot afford to ignore this issue. In Nigeria, not only have imports of manufactured goods increased several times over, but imports of food have increased in an even more surprising fashion. Between 1970 and

1976 Nigeria's food imports increased by a factor of twenty (Lubeck, 1977:26).

Dependent development is import intensive and cannot be otherwise. Strategies that put autarchy ahead of accumulation are not permitted to countries in which the triple alliance dominates the political and economic scene. Strategies of change based on redistribution and on less import-intensive industrial technologies are not plausible choices for countries like Brazil, Mexico, and Nigeria. No segment of the internal elite has a vested interest in such strategies. International creditors also find them threatening. Redistribution is so far a hypothetical threat; relations with the international economy are the actual principal bottleneck to the maintenance of high rates of accumulation. In order to survive, the current elite alliance must continue to transform its relations with its external environment.

Import substitution was a keystone in the construction of dependent development. The extension of import substitution to capital goods must be a central facet of attempts to resolve the external imbalances that dependent development has created. Local production of capital goods would give both state and local capital new possibilities for expansion. The multinationals would be more ambivalent, since this could mean relative decline in exports from the center in favor of local production over which they would have only partial control; but they would probably go along. Local production of capital goods is, however, no more a panacea than local production of consumer goods was. The past ten years have seen dramatic increases in the proportion of capital goods produced locally but the share of capital goods in the import bill has not declined.

Even if Brazil succeeds in decreasing its dependency on imported capital goods, they will remain substantial in the near future. Imports of intermediary goods will continue to grow at least as fast as the overall rate of growth of the economy. Looking at overall trends in Brazil's foreign trade, ECLA (1976:223) concludes, "The recent trend indicates that for every 1% growth of the product, the volume of imports must increase by over 2%." In addition, of course, there are mounting costs in interest payments and amortization of international debt. Already by 1973, the cost of amortization and interest payments required foreign exchange equal to about a third of Brazil's export earnings (ECLA, 1976:222-223).

Even if it offered more secure hope for the alleviation of balance of payments difficulties, concentration on local production of capital goods would still be a problematic strategy. The semiperiphery's role as a market for foreign capital goods has been one of the major attractions of dependent development from the point of view of the center countries. The U.S. Department of Commerce, for example, saw the Polo do Nordeste not so much as a project that might cut down on future American exports of basic and intermediary chemicals to Brazil, but as a potential market for a quarter of a billion dollars worth of imported equipment (U.S. Department of Commerce, 1974:23). On a recent trip to France in search of financing, General Geisel discovered that the French were willing to provide loans for the purchase of French equipment but were not interested in schemes where the equipment was to be made in Brazil (*Business Latin America*, 1976:163).

Like any strategy aimed at autarchy, the creation of a local capital goods industry will meet with an ambivalent reaction at best from international capital. The only way to generate real enthusiasm for the construction of a local capital goods industry would be to allow the multinationals to dominate it (as they were allowed to dominate the automobile industry in the fifties), and this is politically impossible at the current stage of development of the triple alliance. Increased local production of capital goods will be part of the future of dependent development, but only part.

The import bill will rise as long as the process of accumulation continues. In view of this, Brazil's alternatives are either to choke off its own growth in order to solve its balance of payments problems or to expand its exports at least as rapidly as it has been expanding them over the past ten years. Strategies for the expansion of exports can be divided into three categories. To apply some slightly pejorative labels, they might be called the "neoclassical dependence strategy," the "subimperialism strategy," and the "export platform" strategy. A combination of all three is necessary, and each of them has its limitations.

The first, the "neoclassical dependence strategy," emphasizes renewed attempts to export primary products. From soybeans to iron ore, Brazil has tried to use increased exports of primary products as a way out of its recent balance of payments difficulties. Between 1968 and 1973, increases in the value of such exports accounted for three-fifths of the total increase in exports (ECLA, 1970:59). The return of coffee as Brazil's preeminent export in the mid-seventies illustrates both the attractions and the pitfalls of the "neoclassical dependence" strategy. On the one hand, the rise in the price of coffee in 1975 and 1976 played a central role in alleviating Brazil's balance of trade problems, just as favorable trends in the prices of sugar, soybeans, and beef had done earlier (cf. ECLA, 1976:78). At the same time, the prospects are that, just as the price of sugar dropped to a fraction of its 1974 high soon afterwards, coffee prices must come down again by the end of the seventies, leaving a hole in Brazil's export volume even more substantial than the one created by the fall in sugar prices.

Increased primary exports must be complemented by increased exports of manufactured goods. Even with favorable price trends and expansion of output in the primary sectors, primary products represented a declining share of total exports in the 1968-1973 period. Without a sevenfold increase in exports of manufactured goods, Brazil's performance as an exporter would have been weak. Now that manufactured and semimanufactured goods account for about a third of all exports, expanded external markets for manufactured products must play an even greater role in any Brazilian strategy for future growth.

One way of expanding manufactured exports is to take over markets in the periphery now supplied by exports from center countries (the "subimperialism" strategy). The differences between Brazil's industrial capacity and that of the smaller, poorer peripheral countries is clearly sufficient for Brazil to give serious consideration to this idea. Brazil's trade statistics for the seventies are suggestive. While its trade balance with center countries is negative, its trade balance with peripheral countries is highly positive. If only the volume of trade with the periphery were equal to the volume of trade with the center, the outlook would be rosy. During the period of the miracle Brazil made substantial efforts to expand its trade along "subimperial" lines, as Table 6.6 shows. Between 1969 and 1974, exports to smaller,

TABLE 6.6 Destinations of Brazilian Exports, 1969-1974

Country or Area	Exports[1] 1969	Exports 1974	% Increase in Exports 1969-1974	% of Total Increase in Exports Accounted For by the Area
Latin American Free Trade Association	254	918	261	11.8
Bolivia	4	82	1950	1.4
Paraguay	7	98	1300	1.6
Africa	24	417	1638	7.0
Angola	0.3	6	2900	0.1
Mozambique	0.2	6	1900	0.1
EEC Countries[2]	782	2,434	211	29.0
U.S.	760	1,737	128	17.3
Total[3]	2,311	7,950	244	

[1] All figures are in millions of current $US.
[2] Figures include exports to Britain in 1969 as well as 1974.
[3] Because individual totals are included only for selected area, individual figures will not add to total.
Source: IBGE, *Anuário Estatístico*, 1972:279-282; 1975:359-361.

poorer members of the periphery increased much more rapidly than exports overall. Paraguay and Bolivia now take more than 20% of Brazil's exports within the Latin American Free Trade Area, whereas in 1969 they accounted for less than 5%. Africa now takes more of Brazil's exports than England, as Brazil makes every effort to benefit from the expulsion of the Portuguese from their African colonies. It was one of the first western countries to recognize Angola and later offered the newly independent country a substantial loan.

The subimperialism strategy of increasing exports may be complemented by capital investments. Brazil has agreed to help Bolivia in the development of its iron ore, build a gas pipeline (which will transport natural gas to Brazil), and construct a cement factory. With Paraguay, Brazil is constructing the huge Itaipu hydroelectric project. Not surprisingly, state enterprises are playing a central role in the rudimentary beginnings of the Brazilian "subempire." Embraer, the aircraft company, is already selling light aircraft to other Latin American countries. An even more interesting example is Petrobrás's recent endeavors in Iraq. Braspetro, the exploration division of Petrobrás, invested $30 million in explorations there and claimed to have discovered fields that might produce up to 600,000 barrels a day, 20% of which would belong to Petrobrás. More recently, local private capital has begun to join state enterprises. One of Chile's oldest electronics firms was recently bought out by a private Brazilian company (*Business Latin America*, 1977:200).

Even when the possibility of import-saving foreign investments like Petrobrás's arrangement with Iraq are added to export promotion in smaller client nations on the periphery, subimperialism in itself is not enough. The figures in Table 6.6 are inescapable. If exports to Bolivia were to double, the increase could be wiped out by a 5 percent drop in exports to the United States. The best markets for manufactured goods are still in the center. Unless access to these markets can be maintained and expanded, balance of payments problems are likely to impede local accumulation. The "export platform" strategy must be added to the "subimperialism" and the "neoclassical dependence" strategies.

Brazil's attempts at exporting manufactured goods to the center have been no less serious than the other developments just outlined. Shoes are the most spectacular success story. Between 1969 and 1976, shoe exports went from less than $2 million to $200 million. Eighty percent of this hundredfold increase went to the United States (see *Business Latin America*, 1977:80). The overall increase of over $2.5 billion in Brazil's exports to the U.S. and Europe between 1969 and 1974 is some indication that shoes are by no means an isolated case. But the future success of the export platform strategy, even more than the future success of the other methods of export expansion, depends on support from multinationals and ultimately on the reactions of center country states.

Dependent Development and Center Countries

Whether countries like Brazil expand their exports by developing "hinterlands" in the periphery or whether they try to sell their wares in the center itself, they will be in competition with the industrial plant located in the center. From the viewpoint of the multinationals this is an opportunity more than a threat, but the same is not true of the center country taken as a whole. The periphery is not the only arena in which global rationality may conflict with a "nationalist" logic of accumulation; increasingly the center itself has become the scene of struggles between "nationalist" politicians and the multinationals.

For the Ford Motor Company the "threat" of Brazilian auto exports to Nigeria displacing U.S. exports is not a threat unless the cars exported from Brazil are Volkswagens rather than Fords. Otherwise producing the exports in Brazil is as profitable, if not more so, as producing them in the United States. Since overall returns on manufacturing investments by multinationals in Brazil and Mexico run about 50% higher than returns on large manufacturing investments in the United States, producing in Brazil represents an opportunity for increased profitability for the multinational.

Multinationals may also find that they get more generous support from the state apparatus when they export from the "semi-periphery." The J.I. Case Company, a subsidiary of Tenneco, provides a good example:

> . . . in Nigeria, Case markets its own brand of tractors and construction equipment from both its U.S. and Brazilian plants. Sourcing from Brazil is attractive because the Brazilian government, through Cacex (similar to the U.S. Export-Import Bank), provides better credit terms than the U.S. Under the aegis of Eximbank, U.S. banks could offer three-year financing to Case's Nigerian dealer, but the Brazilian agency is able to guarantee as much as five years of credit—at about the same interest rates (*Business International*, 1976:204).

The availability of specific subsidies, in combination with the general incentive of higher overall profit rates, make the expansion of export activities from the "semi-periphery" attractive from the point of view of the multinationals.

From the perspective of center societies, the prospect is not so pleasant. The profits of a few corporations may increase, but other groups within the society, such as labor, are likely to suffer. For the center, perhaps the most important consequence of dependent development is the creation of a split between the interests of center country states and their own multinationals. As the alliance between the state and the multinationals has been strengthened in the "semi-periphery," relations between the multinationals and the state in the center have become much more constrained. The increasing constraint can be seen even in the changing tone of public documents analyzing relations between the United States and Latin America.

In 1969, Nelson Rockefeller was sent on a special mission to South America by President Nixon. He returned to report (Rockefeller, 1969:89) that one of the central problems in Latin America was the "failure of governments throughout the hemisphere to recognize fully the importance of private investment." His recommendation was that "the United States should provide maximum encouragement for private investment throughout the hemisphere." Five years later, in 1974, the Center for Inter-American Relations sponsored a commission on U.S.-Latin American relations. This commission recommended (Commission on U.S.-Latin American Relations, 1975:53) that "relationships between United States investors and Latin American countries are best conducted on a direct basis with a minimum of U.S. government involvement."

Both reports were attuned to the problems of internationally oriented American corporations but the 1974 commission report did not see increased support from center states as the way to improve the multinationals' position. The Rockefeller report was strongly in favor of OPIC (The Overseas Private Investment Corporation) and suggested a variety of roles it might play, including (1969:93) "the power to contract with private companies in the Western Hemisphere to create production facilities necessary to meet an important need which is not being filled by private investors." The commission report recommended (1975:54) that OPIC "could be modified appropriately to further reduce governmental involvement in private investment matters." In the view of the commission, "large private investors can assess and assume risks on their own."

The Rockefeller report expressed concern (1969:75) over the need for a "system of tariff preferences for all developing countries." The commission report favored increased access for imports from Latin America based on tariff preferences granted by the U.S. government, but it emphasized tolerance of the actions of peripheral states, specifically (1975:47) the "temporary use of export subsidies by developing nations." The Rockefeller report is more open in its support of center country corporations, specifically stating that (1969:89) "the United States should not, for narrow domestic reasons, apply tax rules to U.S. private overseas investment which controvert efforts by developing nations to encourage private investment and promote joint ventures." The commission report called only for "adjustment assistance" to aid workers displaced by imports coming from less developed countries.

The two reports convey two very different images of the periphery. The 1969 Rockefeller report reads like a description of classic dependence:

Just as the other American republics depend upon the United States for their capital equipment requirements, so the United States depends on them to provide a vast market for our manufactured goods. And, as these countries look to the United States for a market for their primary products whose sale enables them to buy equipment for their development at home, so the United States looks to them for raw materials for our industries on which depend the jobs of many of our citizens (Rockefeller, 1969:38).

The Latin America described in the 1974 commission report sounds much more dominated by the triple alliance. While the report notes growing inequality and the prevalence of bureaucratic authoritarian regimes, it also notes that

Latin American countries have become more self-confident and technically competent in their dealings with the multinational corporations. . . . Correspondingly the potential for direct and irreconcilable conflicts of interest is diminished as foreign firms see the advantages of the large and growing Latin American market and recognize the desirability of responding constructively to host country concerns (1975:52).

Accompanying the change in the image of the periphery is a corresponding change in the role envisaged for the center country state. The commission report projects an essentially passive role for the American government. It assumes that overt official support from the federal government is likely to do the multinationals as much harm as good in the periphery. All the commission asks of the center state is that it not become protective of its own parochial interests in a way that might impede accumulation in the periphery. The multinationals' acceptance of this more passive posture on the part of the center state comes in part from greater confidence on their part that they can deal with the more important states in Latin America on the basis of alliances such as the ones that have been described in Brazil. But, reluctance to call on center states also arises from questions as to how far the government in the center can be counted on.

Luciano Martins (1975:99) has argued that the recent evolution of the international economy has made it "much more difficult for multinational corporations to present their private interests as being the 'general interest' of the United States." An examination of the implications of dependent development for the center helps make clear why this is so. The returns from the dependent development are even more concentrated in the center than they are in the periphery itself. Newfarmer and Mueller (1975:43) estimate that twenty-five firms control over half of all U.S. manufacturing investment in Latin America. Twenty-five corporations, no matter how powerful or well-connected, are not a very broad political base. The multinationals still get supportive treatment from the United States government, but they must compete with other domestic groups. When an electronics plant closes down in New Jersey because a multinational can produce televisions more profitably in Taiwan, or when a former employee of the New England shoe industry finds Brazilian shoes on the display racks at Sears and Roebuck, the question of costs and benefits becomes a political question in the center.

Organized labor was among the first to present a critique of the role of the multinationals in the evolution of the U.S. economy. In the late sixties, the AFL-CIO began to argue that foreign direct investment was costing somewhere between a quarter of a million and half a million American workers their jobs. Labor also came up with a number of suggested legal changes that would have resulted in a substantial withdrawal of tax and other privileges currently enjoyed by the multinationals. Supporters of the multinationals responded with figures showing that, because investment by multinationals is "defensive," it actually results in an increase of up to half a million jobs in the United States, but congressional reports have leaned toward a more critical assessment. The work of the Senate subcommittee on multinationals provides some good examples.

One recent report to the Senate subcommittee (Musgrave, 1975:xvi) came to the conclusion "that foreign investment did not greatly effect the level of income or tax revenue but that it did have significant distributional effects working to the detriment of the labor share." If foreign investment does not increase the total national income, but simply shifts income from labor to capital, it is politically hard to justify. With the additional proviso that the returns to capital are actually returns to a very small number of multinationals, political justification becomes even more difficult. The view of the Senate subcommittee is almost a restatement of Hobson's conclusion three-quarters of a century earlier that no democracy that kept good books and had the interests of the majority at heart could justify imperialism.

The report to the Senate subcommittee goes on to argue (Musgrave, 1975:xix) that "the private net rate of return from foreign investment lies above the national rate because foreign taxes paid on U.S. investment income received abroad are lost to the U.S. economy," and that "the net rate of return on investment abroad at the margin and as seen from a national point of view is negative." No wonder that the more sophisticated multinationals are eager to accept the solutions offered by the 1974 commission report. Any attempt to secure the kind of positive governmental support envisaged in the earlier Rockefeller report might well unleash the kind of oppositional measures implied by the conclusions of the Senate subcommittee.

As dependent development proceeds, the political life of the multinationals becomes more complicated both at home and in the "semi-periphery." Domestic capital in the center, threatened by the "export platform strategy," finds common ground with labor. Even individual multinationals may assume a "nationalistic" pose if one of their competitors seems to be taking advantage of opportunities in the "semi-periphery" at their expense. Worst of all, when the center country state is persuaded to take "nationalistic" actions, the multinationals find that their newly constructed alliances in the "semi-periphery" are threatened. A number of examples, from instant coffee to shoes, can be used to illustrate the range of controversy.

In the mid-sixties Brazil began producing instant coffee, and by 1967 Brazilian exports to the United States were already equal to one-seventh of U.S. instant coffee production (Tyler, 1968:95). One of the reasons for the success of Brazilian instant coffee was that the Brazilian government did not apply to instant coffee the tax that it applied to all exports of green coffee. Big producers in the United States like Procter and Gamble and General Foods considered the competition grossly unfair. The more imaginative multinationals took a different route. Tenco, a subsidiary of Coca Cola, bought out a Brazilian producer of freeze-dried coffee so that, as *Business Latin America* (1969:82) put it, Coca Cola would be on the winning side whichever way the dispute was settled.

Another controversy involved Embraer's production of light aircraft. Cessna complained that "Brazilians have not only set up insurmountable import barriers at home but are on the verge of exporting a score of their planes to the United States" (*New York Times*, 9/13/76:31). Cessna was understandably disturbed, having seen its exports to Brazil drop from 400 planes in 1973 to 5 in

1976. Piper Aircraft Corporation, on the other hand, was quite happy with Embraer's success since three-fourths of Embraer's production are Piper models produced under an agreement with Piper.

These disputes over the effects of industrial initiatives on the periphery are largely questions of individual corporations protecting their own parochial interests. General Foods could have bought into the soluble coffee industry in Brazil and Cessna might have gotten to Embraer first if it had been a little more agile. Either of these corporations could have been in a position to benefit directly from the incentives offered by the Brazilian state to promote industrialization on the periphery.

Other controversies cannot be reduced to disputes among individual corporations. The shoe industry is a prime example. The manufacture of shoes is essentially a United States domestic industry and one that has been badly hurt by the influx of imports. Under pressure from both domestic capitalists and labor, the American government persuaded the Brazilian government to eliminate some of the export incentives provided for Brazilian shoe manufacturers. Then the U.S. International Trade Commission proposed additional increases in U.S. tariffs on a quota basis that would cut the amount of Brazilian-made shoes able to enter under the normal tariff to about 60% of what Brazil had hoped to export in 1977 (*Business Latin America*, 1977:80).

This is not a controversy among multinationals, but rather a conflict between domestic U.S. interests and domestic Brazilian interests. Nor is it an isolated case. Duties have also been raised on scissors and may be raised on wool yarn. Brazilians, looking at their already massive trade deficit with the United States, find the attack on their exports unjustified and unreasonable. It was against this background that the Carter campaign on "human rights" met such a violent reaction in Brazil, including the abrogation of the United States-Brazil military cooperation agreement.

For the multinationals it is the worst of all possible worlds. The

American government is not just failing to provide effective support, it is a positive embarrassment, an embarrassment that could have negative consequences for multinational expansion and profits within Brazil. In the aftermath of Brazil's hostile reaction to the Carter administration, *Business Latin America* predicted somberly (1977:92) that one of the consequences would be "a warmer welcome for investors from nations other than the U.S." and a preference for non-U.S. partners in future joint ventures with state enterprises. It is small wonder that the leadership of the more sophisticated multinationals has become concerned over the direction of center country politics.

Concern over politics at home is perhaps best expressed by the Rockefeller-sponsored Trilateral Commission (see Frieden, 1977) in its famous "Report on the Governability of Democracies" (Crozier et al., 1975). The American section of the report was written by Samuel Huntington, known for his work on the military and on political instability in developing countries. Huntington expresses concern that "democratic distemper" in the United States will hinder the ability of the state to perform the functions necessary to the promotion of accumulation and suggests that democracy is not necessarily "optimized when it is maximized."

One of the fears expressed by Huntington is that the excessive democracy currently prevalent in the center countries is likely to "encourage economic nationalism." He cites the example of tariffs against shoe imports and goes on to point out that "a strong government will not necessarily follow more liberal and internationalist economic policies, but a weak government is almost certain to be incapable of doing so" (Crozier et al., 1975:105).

The overall conclusion of Huntington's analysis is essentially that the kinds of economic policies required to implement the global strategies of accumulation pursued by the multinationals are incompatible with continued "excessive" levels of democracy in the center. If Huntington is correct, then his conclusions pose real problems for the triple alliance. Dependent development in Brazil is hardly a major cause of the political difficulties of the multinationals at home. Brazil is only one small contributor. But if "ungovernability" continues to be a problem in the center, and there is no sign that it is becoming less so, then the triple alliance within Brazil will lack the external support on which it relies for its ability to deal with the current imbalances in its trade relations with the rest of the world.

The Brazilian model cannot survive without its allies from the center. If center elites falter, or have to turn their energies inward in order to survive, then Brazil must find a radically different route to follow. The collapse of the current model would not insure a decent life for the mass of the Brazilian population, but there would be at least the hope that another route might emphasize distribution and participation rather than accumulation and exclusion. Had they been aware of the Trilateral Commission's concern, the workers who burned the buses in Brasilia would no doubt have been cheered to discover that "ungovernability" was a worrisome problem for the multinationals at home as well as for the triple alliance within Brazil.

Bibliography

Adelman, Irma and Cynthia Morris, 1973. *Economic Growth and Social Equity in Developing Countries*. Stanford: Stanford University Press.

Aharoni, Yair, 1966. *The Foreign Investment Decision-Making Process*. Boston: Harvard Graduate School of Business Administration.

Amin, Samir, 1976. *Unequal Development: An Essay on the Social Formations of Peripheral Capitalism*. New York: Monthly Review Press.

―――, 1977a. "Capitalism, State Collectivism and Socialism," *Monthly Review* (June), 29(2):25-41.

―――, 1977b. "Self-Reliance and the New International Economic Order," *Monthly Review* (July-August), 29(3):1-21.

Araújo, José Tavares de and Vera Dick, 1974. "Governo, Empresas Multinacionais e Empresas Nacionais: O Caso da Indústria Petroquímica," *Pesquisa e Planejamento Econômico*, 4(3):629-654.

Aronson, Jonathan, 1977. "The Politics of Bank Lending and Debt Rescheduling in Zaire, Indonesia, Brazil and Mexico." Paper presented at the joint meeting of the Latin American and African Studies Associations, Houston, Texas.

Averitt, Robert, 1968. *The Dual Economy*. New York: W. W. Norton.

Ayres, Paulo Filho and Romildo N. Miranda, n.d. "Market Research and Evaluation as a Service Rendered by the Drug Industry to the Doctors and the Drug Store." São Paulo (mimeo).

Bacha, Edmar, 1975. "Recent Brazilian Economic Growth and Some of Its Main Problems," Text for Discussion No. 25, Department of Economics, Universidade de Brasília.

―――, 1976. "Issues and Evidence on Recent Brazilian Economic Growth," Cambridge, Massachusetts (mimeo).

Baer, Werner, 1965. *Industrialization and Economic Development in Brazil*. Homewood, Illinois: Richard D. Irwin.

―――, 1969. *The Development of the Brazilian Steel Industry*. Nashville: Vanderbilt University Press.

―――, 1973. "The Brazilian Boom, 1968-1972: An Explanation and Interpretation," *World Development* (August), 1(8):1-15.

Baer, Werner, I. Kerstenetsky, and A. Villela, 1973. "The Changing Role of the State in the Brazilian Economy," *World Development*, 1(11):23-24.

———, R. S. Newfarmer, and Thomas Trebat, 1977. "On State Capitalism in Brazil: Some New Issues and Questions," *Inter-American Economic Affairs*, 30(3):69-96.

Baker, Jonathan, 1977. "Oil and African Development," *Journal of Modern African Studies*, 15(2):175-212.

Baklanoff, E. N., 1966. "Foreign Private Investment and Industrialization in Brazil," in *New Perspectives on Brazil*, E. N. Baklanoff, ed. Nashville: Vanderbilt University Press.

Banas, Editora, 1969, 1972. *Brasil Industrial*. São Paulo: Editora Banas.

———, 1973. *As Grandes Companhias, 1972-1973*. São Paulo: Editora Banas.

Bandeira, Moniz, 1973. *Presença dos Estados Unidos no Brasil: Dois Seculos de História*. Rio de Janeiro: Editora Civilização Brasileira.

Baran, Paul, 1968. *The Political Economy of Growth*. New York: Monthly Review Press.

Baranson, Jack, 1966. "Transfer of Technical Knowledge by International Corporations to Developing Economies," *American Economic Review* (May), 56(2):254-267.

Barlow, E. R., 1953. "Management and Control of Foreign Subsidiaries," unpublished D.B.A. dissertation, Harvard University.

Barnet, Richard and Ronald Müller, 1974. *Global Reach: The Power of the Multinational Corporations*. New York: Simon and Schuster.

Belli, R. David, 1970. "Sales of Foreign Affiliates of U.S. Firms, 1961-1965, 1967 and 1968," *Survey of Current Business* (October), 50(10):18-20.

Bennett, Douglas and Kenneth Sharpe, 1978. "Controlling the Multinationals: the Ill Logic of Mexicanization," in *Global Dominance and Dependence: Readings in Theory and Research*, Lawrence V. Gould and Harry Parg, eds. Brunswick, Ohio: King's Court Communications (forthcoming).

———, Morris Blachman, and Kenneth Sharpe, 1978. "Mexico and Multinational Corporations: An Explanation of State Action," in *Latin America in the International System*, Joseph Grunwald, ed. Beverly Hills, California: Sage Publications (forthcoming).

Bergsman, Joel, 1970. *Brazil: Industrialization and Trade Policies*. New York: Oxford University Press.

Bernet, Jean, 1971. *Guia Intervest: O Brasil e o Capital Internacional*. Rio de Janeiro: Intervest Editora e Distribuidora Ltda.

Bertero, Carlos, 1972. "Drugs and Dependency in Brazil: An Empirical Study of Dependency Theory, The Case of the Pharmaceutical Industry," Latin American Studies Program Dissertion Series, No. 36, Cornell University.

Blume, Norman, 1968. "Pressure Groups and Decision-Making in Brazil," *Studies in Comparative International Development*, 3(11):205-223.

Boulding, Kenneth, 1964. "R and D for the Emergent Nations," in *Economics of Research and Development*, Richard Tybout, ed. Columbus: Ohio State University.

Bradshaw, Marie T., 1969. "U.S. Exports to Foreign Affiliates of U.S. Firms," *Survey of Current Business* (May), 49(5):34-51.

Brash, Donald T., 1965. *American Investment in Australia*. Cambridge: Harvard University Press.

Brazilian-American Chamber of Commerce, Inc., 1976. *News Bulletin*, 4(84):2-6.

Burns, Tom and G. M. Stalker, 1961. *The Management of Innovation*. London: Tavistock.

Business International, 1976-1977. New York: Business International Corporation.

Business Latin America, 1967-1977. *Weekly Report to Managers of Latin American Operations*. New York: Business International Corporation.

Cardoso, Fernando Henrique, 1964. *Empresário Industrial e Desenvolvimento Econômico no Brasil*. São Paulo: Difusão Europeia do Livro.

————, 1971. *Política e Desenvolvimento em Sociedades Dependentes*. Rio de Janeiro: Editora Zahar.

————, 1972. "Dependency and Development in Latin America," *The New Left Review*, 74:83-95.

————, 1974. "As Tradições de Desenvolvimento-Associado," *Estudos Cebrap*, 8:41-75.

————, 1977. "The Consumption of Dependency Theory in the United States," *Latin American Research Review*, 12(3):7-25.

Cardoso, Fernando Henrique and Enzo Faletto, 1973. *Dependência e Desenvolvimento na America Latina: Ensaio de Interpretação Sociológica*. Rio de Janeiro: Editora Zahar.

Carter, C. F. and B. R. Williams, 1958. *Investment in Innovation*. Oxford: Oxford University Press.

Central de Medicamentos (CEME), 1973. *Plano Diretor de Medicamentos*, Vol. 1: *Análise Diagnôstica*. Brasília: Governo Federal.

————, 1974. *O Empreendimento CEME—Sinópse*. Brasília: Governo Federal.

————, 1974. *Relatório de Atividades—1973*. Brasília: Governo Federal.

Chandler, Alfred D., 1962. *Strategy and Structure*. Cambridge: MIT Press.

Chase-Dunn, Christopher, 1975. "The Effects of International Economic Dependence on Development and Inequality," *American Sociological Review*, 40(6):720-739.

Chiaverini, Vicente, 1968. "Pesquisa Technolôgica na Indústria," in *Pesquisa Technolôgica na Universidade e na Indústria Brasileira*. São Paulo: Editora Pioneira.

Chirot, Daniel, 1977. *Social Change in the Twentieth Century*. New York: Harcourt Brace Jovanovich.

Coats Patons Ltd., 1973. *Annual Report and Accounts, 1973*. Glasgow, Scotland.

Cohn, Gabriel, 1968. *Petróleo e Nacionalismo*. São Paulo: Difusão Europeia do Livro.

Comanor, William S., 1963. "The Economics of Research and Development in the Pharmaceutical Industry," unpublished Ph.D. dissertation, Harvard University.

Commission on U.S.-Latin American Relations, 1975. *The Americas in a Changing World*. New York: New York Times (Quadrangle).

Conjuntura Econômica, 1974. "Os 500 Maiores Sociedades Anônimas Brasileiras," 28(7):76:110. Rio de Janeiro.

Connor, John M. and Willard Mueller, 1977. *Market Power and Profitability of Multinational Corporations in Brazil and Mexico*. Report to Subcommittee on Foreign Economic Policy, U.S. Senate. Washington: GPO.

Cooper, J. D., 1970. *The Economics of Innovation in the Drug Industry.* Washington: American University.

Cooper, M. H., 1966. *Prices and Profits in the Pharmaceutical Industry.* New York: Pergamon Press.

Copen, Melvyn R., 1967. "The Management of United States Manufacturing Subsidiaries in a Developing Nation: India," unpublished D.B.A. dissertation, Harvard Graduate School of Business Administration.

Copene (Petroquímica do Nordeste, S.A.), 1974. "Polo Petroquímico do Nordeste," Rio de Janerio: Copene.

Crozier, Michel, Samuel Huntington, and Joji Watanuki, 1975. *The Crisis of Democracy: Report on the Governability of Democracies to the Trilateral Commission.* New York: New York University Press.

Cyert, Richard and James March, 1963. *A Behavioral Theory of the Firm.* Englewood Cliffs, New Jersey: Prentice Hall.

Davis, Wyndham, 1967. *The Pharmaceutical Industry: A Personal Study.* Oxford: Pergamon Press.

Dean, Warren, 1969. *The Industrialization of São Paulo, 1880-1945.* Austin: University of Texas Press.

Devlin, D. T. and G. R. Kruer, 1970. "The International Investment Position of the United States: Developments in 1969," *Survey of Current Business* (October), 50(10):21-37.

O Dirigente Industrial, 1969. "Os Quinhentos Maiores Sociedades Anônimas do Brasil." (October), 11(2):33-52.

Djerassi, Carl, 1968. "A High Priority?: Research Centers in Developing Nations," *Bulletin of the Atomic Scientists* (January), 26(1):24-25.

Dos Santos, Teotonio, 1970. "The Structure of Dependence," *American Economic Review*, 60(5):235-246.

E. I. Dupont de Nemours & Co., 1966-1974. *Annual Reports.*

Eckstein, Susan and Peter Evans, 1978. "The Revolution as Cataclysm and Coup: Political Transformation and Economic Development in Brazil and Mexico," in *Comparative Studies in Sociology*, R. Tomasson, ed. Greenwich, Connecticut: JAI Press.

Economic Commission for Latin America, 1963. *The Textile Industry in Latin America*, Vol. 2: *Brazil.* New York: United Nations.

————, 1964. "Fifteen Years of Economic Policy in Brazil," *Economic Bulletin for Latin America*, 9 (December).

Economic Commission for Latin America, 1965. *External Financing in Latin America*. New York: United Nations.

————, 1965a. "The Growth and Decline of Import Substitution in Brazil," *Economic Bulletin for Latin America*, 9(1):1-61.

————, 1970-1972. *Economic Survey of Latin America*. New York: United Nations.

————, 1974. *Economic Survey of Latin America, 1972*. New York: United Nations.

————, 1976. *Economic Survey of Latin America, 1974*. New York: United Nations.

Economist Intelligence Unit Ltd., 1974-1976. *Quarterly Economic Review: Brazil*. London: *The Economist*.

Emmanuel, Arrighi, 1972. *Unequal Exchange*. New York: Monthly Review Press.

————, 1974. "Myths of Development versus Myths of Underdevelopment," *The New Left Review*, 85:61-82.

Evans, Peter, 1971. "Denationalization and Development: A Study of Industrialization in Brazil," Ph.D. dissertation, Harvard University.

————, 1972. "The Latin American Entrepreneur: Style, Scale, and Rationality," in *Workers and Managers in Latin America*, Davis and Goodman, eds. Lexington, Massachusetts: D.C. Heath and Co.

————, 1974. "The Military, the Multinationals and the 'Miracle': The Political Economy of the 'Brazilian Model' of Development," *Studies in Comparative International Development*, 9(3):26-45.

————, 1975. "Industrialization and Imperialism: Growth and Stagnation on the Periphery," *The Berkeley Journal of Sociology*, 20:113-146.

————, 1976a. "Continuities and Contradictions in the Evolution of Brazilian Dependence," *Latin American Perspectives*, 3(2):30-54.

————, 1976b. "Foreign Investment and Industrial Transformation," *Journal of Development Economics*, 3(4):119-139.

————, 1977a. "Direct Investment and Industrial Concentration," *The Journal of Development Studies*, 13(4):373-386.

————, 1977b. "Multinationals, State-Owned Corporations, and the Transformation of Imperialism: A Brazilian Case Study," *Economic Development and Cultural Change*, 26(1):43-64.

———— and M. Timberlake, 1977. "Dependence and the Bloated Tertiary: A Quantitative Study of Inequality in Less Developed Countries." Presented at the annual meeting of the American Sociological Association, Chicago.

Fajnzylber, Fernando, 1971. *Sistema Industrial e Exportação de Manufacturados: Análise de Experiência Brasileira*. Rio de Janeiro: IPEA.

Fausto, Boris, 1970. *A Revolução de 1930*. São Paulo: Editora Brasiliense.

Fernandes, Florestan, 1975. *A Revolução Burguesa no Brasil*. Rio de Janeiro: Zahar Editores.

Fernandez, Raul and José F. Ocampo, 1974. "The Latin American Revolution: A Theory of Imperialism, Not Dependence," *Latin American Perspectives*, 1(1):30-61.

Figuereido, Nuno Fidelino de, 1972. *A Transferencia de Tecnologia no Desenvolvimento Industrial do Brasil*. IPEA, serie monografica, No. 7. Rio de Janeiro: IPEA/INPES.

Fishlow, Albert, 1972. "Brazilian Size Distribution of Income," *American Economic Review* (May), 62:391-402.

———, 1973. "Some Reflections on Post-1964 Brazilian Economic Policy," in *Authoritarian Brazil*, A. Stepan, ed. New Haven: Yale University Press.

———, 1974. "Algumas Reflexoes sobre a Politica Economica Brasileira apos 1964," *Estudos Cebrap*, 7(Jan.-Mar.):5-66.

Fitzpatrick, Brian and E. B. Wheelwright, 1965. *The Highest Bidder*. Melbourne: Lansdowne Press.

Flanigan, James, 1976. "Nigeria: Where the Real Action Is," *Forbes*, 118(11):51-61.

Fouraker, Larry and John Stopford, 1968. "Organizational Structure and Multinational Strategy," *Administrative Science Quarterly*, 13:47-64.

Frank, André Gundar, 1967. *Capitalism and Underdevelopment in Latin America*. New York: Monthly Review Press.

———, 1974. "Dependence is Dead, Long Live Dependence and the Class Struggle: A Reply to Critics," *Latin American Perspectives*, 1(1):87-106.

Franko, Lawrence, 1969. "Strategy Choice and the Multinational Corporate Tolerance for Joint Ventures with Foreign Partners," unpublished D.B.A. dissertation, Harvard Graduate School of Business Administration.

338 BIBLIOGRAPHY

Frieden, Jeff, 1977. "The Trilateral Commission: Economics and Politics in the 1970's," *Monthly Review*, 29(7):1-18.

Friedman, Wolfgang and Jean Pierre Béguin, 1971. *Joint International Business Ventures in Developing Countries*. New York: Columbia University Press.

Fundação, ABIF, 1973. *Relatório Anual*. Rio de Janeiro.

Furtado, Celso, 1964. *Development and Underdevelopment: A Structural View of the Problems of Developed and Underdeveloped Countries*. Berkeley: University of California Press.

———, 1965. *The Economic Growth of Brazil*. Berkeley: University of California Press.

———, 1969. *Um Projeto para o Brasil*. Rio de Janeiro: Editora Saga S.A.

———, 1972. *Análise do Modêlo Brasileiro*. Rio de Janeiro: Civilização Brasileiro.

Galeano, Eduardo, 1969. "Denationalization and Brazilian Industry," *Monthly Review*, 21(7):11-30.

Geiger, Theodore, 1961. *The General Electric Company in Brazil*. Washington: National Planning Association.

Gereffi, Gary, 1978. "Drug Firms and Dependency in Mexico: The Case of the Steroid Hormone Industry," *International Organization*, 32(1):237-286.

Gerschenkron, Alexander, 1952. "Economic Backwardness in Historical Perspective," in *The Progress of Underdeveloped Countries*, Bert Hoselitz, ed. Chicago: University of Chicago Press.

Girvan, Norman, 1973. "The Development of Dependency Economics in the Caribbean and Latin America: Review and Comparison," *Social and Economic Studies* (March), 22(1):1-33.

Goldmark, Peter F., 1976. "Report on Meeting with Representatives of the U.S. Petrochemical Industry with Officials of the Mexican Registry of Foreign Investment and Registry of Transfer of Technology." New York: Council of the Americas (mimeo).

Goodman, Louis W., 1975. "The Social Organization of Decision-Making in the Multinational Corporation," in *The Multinational Corporation and Social Change*, D. Apter and L. W. Goodman, eds. New York: Praeger.

Gordon, L. and G. Gommers, 1962. *United States Manufacturing In-*

vestment in Brazil. Boston: Division of Research, Graduate School of Business Administration, Harvard University.

Graham, Richard, 1968. *Britain and Modernization in Brazil: 1850-1914*. Cambridge: Cambridge University Press.

Griffin, Keith, 1969. *Underdevelopment in Spanish America*. Cambridge: MIT Press.

Hall, Clarence, 1964. "The Country that Saved Itself," *Readers Digest* (November):135-158.

Hirschman, Albert, 1958. *The Strategy of Economic Development*. New Haven: Yale University Press.

———, 1965. *Journeys toward Progress*. New York: Anchor Books.

———, 1967. *Development Projects Observed*. Washington: Brookings Institute.

———, 1969. "How to Divest in Latin America and Why," in *Essays in International Finance*, No. 76. Princeton: Princeton University Press.

———, 1970. *A Bias toward Hope: Essays on Development and Latin America*. New Haven: Yale University Press.

——— and Charles E. Lindblom, 1962. "Economic Development, R & D, and Policymaking: Some Convergent Views," *Behavioral Sciences* (April), 7:211-27.

Hobson, J. A., 1938. *Imperialism: A Study*. London: George Allen and Unwin. Originally published 1902.

Hymer, Stephen, 1970. "The Efficiency (Contradictions) of Multinational Corporations," *American Economic Review* (May), 60 (2):441.

Ianni, Octavio, 1970. *Crisis in Brazil*. New York: Columbia University Press.

Illich, Ivan, 1969. "Outwitting the Developed Countries," *The New York Review of Books* (November), 13(8):20-24.

Instituto Brasileiro de Geografia e Estatistica (IBGE), 1968. *Anuário Estatístico do Brasil*. Rio de Janeiro: IBGE.

———, 1972. *Anuário Estatístico*. Rio de Janeiro: IBGE.

———, 1973. *Sinópse Estatística*. Rio de Janeiro: IBGE.

———, 1975. *Anuário Estatístico*. Rio de Janeiro: IBGE.

———, 1976. *Anuário Estatístico*. Rio de Janeiro: IBGE.

Instituto de Planejamento Economico e Social (IPEA), 1973. *Mercado Brasileiro de Produtos Petroquímicos*. Série Estudos para o Planejamento, No. 3. Brasília: IPEA.

IPEA, 1974. *Perspectivas da Indústria Petroquímica no Brasil*. Série Estudos para o Planejamento, No. 9. Brasília: IPEA.

Instituto Roberto Simonsen, 1968. *Pesquisa Tecnológica na Universidade e na Indústria Brasileira*. São Paulo: Editora Pioneira.

International Bank for Reconstruction and Development (IBRD), 1973. *World Bank Atlas*. Washington: IBRD.

Jaguaribe, Helio, 1968. *Economic and Political Development: A Theoretical Approach and a Brazilian Case Study*. Cambridge: Harvard University Press.

Jenkins, Rhys, 1977. *Dependent Industrialization in Latin America*. New York: Praeger.

Jewkes, John, David Sawyers, and David Stillerman, 1958. *The Sources of Invention*. New York: MacMillan.

Johnson, Harry, 1968. *Comparative Cost and Commercial Policy Theory for a Developing World Economy*. Stockholm: Almquist and Wiksell.

———, 1970. "The Efficiency and Welfare Implications of the International Corporation," in *The International Corporation*, C. P. Kindleberger, ed. Cambridge: MIT Press.

Johnstone, Alan W., 1965. *United States Direct Investment in France: An Investigation of the French Charges*. Cambridge: MIT Press.

Kahl, Joseph, 1976. *Modernization, Exploitation and Dependency*. New Brunswick, New Jersey: Transaction Press.

Katz, Jorge, 1974. *Oligopolio, Firmas Nacionales y Empresas Multinationales: La Industria Farmaceutica Argentina*. Buenos Aires: Siglo XXI Argentina Editores, S.S.

Kefauver, Estes with Irene Till, 1965. *In Few Hands: Monopoly Power in America*. New York: Random House.

Kidron, Michael, 1965. *Foreign Investment in India*. Oxford: Oxford University Press.

Kindleberger, Charles P., 1970. *The International Corporation*. Cambridge: MIT Press.

Klein, Burton, 1958. "A Radical Proposal for R & D," *Fortune* (May), 57(5):112-114.

Knickerbocker, F. T., 1973. *Oligopolistic Reaction and Multinational Enterprise*. Boston: Division of Research, Graduate School of Business Administration, Harvard University.

Kornhauser, William, 1963. *Scientists in Industry: Conflict and Accommodation*. Berkeley: University of California Press.

Kucinski, Bernard, 1975. "Pushtherapy in Brazil," in *Hungry for Profits*, R. Ledogar, ed. New York: IDOC/North America.

———— (with the assistance of Robert Ledogar), 1975. "Ambivalent Hosts," in *Hungry for Profits*, Robert Ledogar, ed. New York: IDOC/North America.

Landes, David S., 1966. *Technological Change and Industrial Development in Europe 1750-1914*. Cambridge Economic History of Europe, Vol. 6, Part 2. Cambridge: Cambridge University Press.

Lauterbach, Alfred, 1966. *Enterprise in Latin America*. Ithaca: Cornell University Press.

Layton, Christopher, 1966. *Transatlantic Investments*. The Atlantic Institute.

Leff, Nathaniel H., 1968. *The Brazilian Capital Goods Industry: 1929-1964*. Cambridge: Harvard University Press.

Lenin, V. I., 1966. "Imperialism: The Highest Stage of Capitalism," in *The Essential Lenin*. Bantam Books. Originally published 1916.

Lewis, Cleona, 1938. *America's Stake in International Investments*. Washington: The Brookings Institute.

Louis, Arthur M., 1977. "Brazil's Coffee (with Sugar) Billionaire," *Fortune*, 96(1):83-88.

Lubeck, Paul, 1977. "Nigerian Development in the Seventies: Petroleum, State Capitalism and Regional Hegemony." Paper presented at the joint meeting of the Latin American and African Studies Associations, Houston, Texas.

Lupo, Leonard and Julius Freidlin, 1975. "U.S. Direct Investment Abroad in 1974," *Survey of Current Business* (October), 55(10):43-64.

Mac Ewan, Arthur, 1975. "Changes in World Capitalism and the Current Crisis of the U.S. Economy," *Radical America*, 9(1):1-23.

Magdoff, Harry, 1969. *The Age of Imperialism*. New York: Monthly Review Press.

March, James and Herbert Simon, 1958. *Organizations*. New York: John Wiley and Sons.

Marini, Ruy Mauro, 1972. "Brazilian Subimperialism," *Monthly Review*, 23(9):14-24.

Martins, José de Souza, 1973. *Conde Matarazzo: O Empresário e a Empresa*. São Paulo: HUCITEC.

Martins, Luciano, 1975. *Nação e Corporação Multinational*. Coleção Estudos Brasilerios, #4. Rio de Janeiro: Editora Paz e Terra.

Martins, Luciano, 1976. *Pouvoir et Développement Économique: Formation et Évolution des Structure Politique au Brésil.* Paris: Editions Anthropos.

Marx, Karl, 1963. *The 18th Brumaire of Louis Bonaparte.* New York: International Publishers. Originally published 1852.

McDonough, Peter, 1974. "Foreign Investment and Political Control in Brazil." Paper presented at Conference on Multinational Corporations as Instruments of Development, Yale University, May 9-12.

————, 1977. "Policy Misperceptions and Brazilian Elites," unpublished paper, Ann Arbor: Institute for Social Research, University of Michigan.

McMichael, Philip, James Petras, and Robert Rhodes, 1974. "Imperialism and the Contradictions of Development," *The New Left Review,* 85:83-104.

Mendes Alves, Renato, 1969. "A Indústria Farmacêutica de Capitais Nacionais e seus Problemas," Report to Associação Brasileira da Indústria Farmacêutica, Rio de Janeiro.

Merhav, Meir, 1969. *Technological Dependence, Monopoly and Growth.* New York: Pergamon Press.

Mericle, Kenneth, 1977. "Corporatist Control of the Working Class: The Case of Post-1964 Authoritarian Brazil," in *Authoritarianism and Corporatism in Latin America,* James Malloy, ed. Pittsburgh: University of Pittsburgh Press.

Miranda, Maria Augusta Tiberica, 1963. *Vamos Nacionalizar a Indústria Farmacêutica.* Cadernos do Povo Brasileira, No. 11. Rio de Janeiro: Civilização Brasileira.

Moore, Barrington, 1967. *Social Origins of Dictatorship and Democracy.* Boston: Beacon Press.

Moraes, George S., 1967. "Profile of the Industrial Research System with Case Studies of Successful and Unsuccessful Industrial Research Programs." Paper presented to the Joint Study Group on Industrial Research in Brazil.

Moran, T. H., 1974. *Multinational Corporations and the Politics of Dependence: Copper in Chile.* Princeton: Princeton University Press.

————, 1975. "Multinational Corporations and Dependency: A Dialogue for Dependentistas and Non-Dependentistas," Washington: Johns Hopkins School for Advanced International Studies (mimeo).

Moss, Robert, 1972. "The Moving Frontier: A Survey of Brazil," *The Economist* (September), 244:11-73.

Müller, Ronald, 1975. "Global Corporations and National Stabilization Policy: The Need for Social Planning," *Journal of Economic Issues*, 9(2):181-204.

Murphy, Elmer R. 1924. "The Way to Sell in Brazil," *System, The Magazine of Business*, 28:588-591.

Musgrave, Peggy, 1975. *Direct Investment Abroad and the Multinationals: Effects on the U.S. Economy*. Prepared for the use of the Sub-Committee on Multinationals of the Committee on Foreign Relations, U.S. Senate. Washington: GPO.

Nafziger, Wayne E., 1977. *African Capitalism: A Case Study of Nigerian Entrepreneurship*. Stanford: Hoover Institution Press.

National Science Foundation, 1963. *Research and Development in Industry, 1960*. Survey of Science Resources Series, NSF, 63-7. Washington: GPO.

———, 1974. *Research and Development in Industry, 1972*. Survey of Science Resources Series, NSF, 74-312. Washington: GPO.

Nelson, E. L. and Frederick Cutler, 1968. "The International Investment Position of the United States in 1967," *Survey of Current Business* (October), 48(10):19-31.

Nelson, Richard R., 1959. "The Economics of Invention: A Survey of the Literature," *The Journal of Business* (April), 32(2):101-127.

———, 1961. "Uncertainty, Learning, and the Economics of Parallel R & D Efforts," *Review of Economics and Statistics* (November), 43:351-364.

Newfarmer, Richard S., 1977. "Multinational Conglomerates and the Economics of Dependent Development: A Case Study of the International Electrical Oligopoly and Brazil's Electrical Industry." Unpublished Ph.D. dissertation, University of Wisconsin, Madison.

——— and Willard Mueller, 1975. *Multinational Corporations in Brazil and Mexico: Structural Sources of Economic and Non-Economic Power*. Report to the Sub-Committee on Multinationals, Committee on Foreign Relations, U.S. Senate. Washington: GPO.

O'Connor, James, 1973. *The Fiscal Crisis of the State*. New York: St. Martin's Press.

O'Donnell, Guillermo, 1973. *Modernization and Bureaucratic-Authoritarianism*. Berkeley: University of California Press.

344   BIBLIOGRAPHY

Oliveira, Tarquínio Barbosa de and Paulo Filho Ayres, 1949. "Monografia sobre a Indústria Farmacêutica Brasileira," unpublished paper presented to CIESP, São Paulo.

Pacheco, Mario Victor de Assis, 1962. "Desnacionalização da Indústria Farmacêutica," Revista Brasilense (May-June), 41:12-49.

————, 1968. Indústria Farmacêutica e Segurança Nacional. Rio de Janeiro: Civilização Brasileira.

Pearson, Michael, 1969. The Million Dollar Bugs. New York: G. P. Putnam and Sons.

Pelz, D. C. and Frank M. Andrews, 1963. Scientists and Organizations. New York: John Wiley and Sons.

Pereira, L., 1970. Ensaios de Sociologia do Desenvolvimento. São Paulo: Livraria Pioneira Editora.

Perrone, Otto V., 1972. "A Ação do Petroquisa na Implantação do Polo Petroquímico do Nordeste," Rio de Janeiro: Petroquisa.

Pessoa, Samuel B., 1963. Endêmias Parasitárias da Zona Rural Brasileira. São Paulo: Fundo Editorial Procienx.

Petras, James and Maurice Zeitlin, eds., 1968. Latin America: Reform or Revolution. New York: Fawcett.

Petrobrás, 1967. Centro de Pesquisas e Desenvolvimento, Depto. Industrial. "A Implantação da Pesquisa Industrial no Brasil," Rio de Janeiro.

————, 1968. Relatório de Atividades. Rio de Janeiro.

Phelps, Dudley Maynard, 1936. Migration of Industry to South America. New York: McGraw-Hill.

Pignaton, Alvaro, 1973. "Capital Estrangeiro e Expansão Industrial no Brasil," Text for Discussion No. 10, Department of Economics, Universidade de Brasília.

Pizer, Samuel and Frederick Cutler, 1957. U.S. Investments in the Latin American Economy. Washington: U.S. Department of Commerce.

————, 1960. U.S. Business Investments in Foreign Countries. Washington: U.S. Department of Commerce.

Polanyi, Karl, 1944. The Great Transformation. Boston: Beacon Press.

Portes, Alejandro, 1976. "The Sociology of National Development," American Journal of Sociology, 82(1):55-85.

————, 1977. "Ideologies of Inequality and their Major Types and Evolution in Latin American History." Paper presented at the annual meeting of the American Sociological Association, Chicago.

Prebisch, Raul, 1950. *The Economic Development of Latin America and Its Principal Problems*. New York: United Nations.

———, 1964. "Center and Periphery," in *Leading Issues in Development Economics*, G. Meir, ed. Oxford: Oxford University Press.

Purcell, John and Susan Kaufman Purcell, 1976. "The State and Economic Enterprise in Mexico: The Limits of Reform," *Nueva Politica*, 1(2):229-250.

Queiroz, Maurício Vinhas de, 1962. "Os Grupos Econômicos no Brasil," *Revista do Instituto de Ciências Sociais*, 1(2).

———, 1965. "Os Grupos Multibilionários," *Revista do Instituto de Ciências Sociais*, 2(1).

———, 1972. "Grupos Econômicos e o Modelo Brasileiro," Tese de Doutoramento, University of São Paulo, São Paulo.

———, 1973. "Brasil e Japão: Analogias e Contrastes Históricos," *Debate e Crítica: Revista Semestral de Ciências Sociais* (January-December) (1).

———, Luciano Martins, and José A. Pessoa Queiroz, 1965. "Os Grupos, Econômicos no Brasil," *Revista do Instituto de Ciências Sociais*, 1(2).

———, Peter Evans, Guido Mantega, and Paul Singer, 1977. *Multinacionais: Internacionalização e Crise*. (Caderno CEBRAP, no. 28), São Paulo: Editora Brasiliense/CEBRAP.

Quijano, Anibal, 1972. *Nationalism and Capitalism in Peru*. New York: Monthly Review Press.

Rezende, F., J. V. Monteiro, W. Suzigan, D. Carneiro, F. P. Castelo Branco, 1976. *Aspectos da Participação do Governo na Economia*. Monografia No. 26. Rio de Janeiro: Instituto de Planejamento Econômico e Social/Instituto de Pesquisas.

Rippy, J. Fred, 1959. *British Investments in Latin America: 1824-1949*. Minneapolis: University of Minnesota Press.

Rockefeller, Nelson, 1969. *The Rockefeller Report on the Americas*. Chicago: New York Times (Quadrangle).

Rolfe, Sidney and Walter Damm, 1970. *The Multinational Corporation in the World Economy*. New York: Praeger.

Rood, Leslie, 1975. "Foreign Investment in Manufacturing," *Journal of Modern African Studies*, 13(1):19-34.

———, 1976. "Nationalization and Indigenisation in Africa," *Journal of Modern African Studies*, 14(3):427-447.

Rowland, Robert, 1974. "Class Operária e Estado de Compromisso," *Estudos Cebrap* (April-May-June), 8:1-40.

Safarian, A. E., 1966. *Foreign Ownership of Canadian Industry.* New York: McGraw-Hill.

Santista, Grupo Industrial, 1973. "1973 Annual Report of Santista Textiles, A Division of the Santista Group, São Paulo, Brazil."

———, Grupo Industrial, 1974. "Exercício, 1/7/73-30/6/74, Relatório da Diretoria."

Scárdua, João Felício, 1974. Interview in *Opinião.* October 20:15-16.

Schmitter, Philippe, 1971. *Interest Conflict and Political Change in Brazil.* Stanford: Stanford University Press.

———, 1973. "The 'Portugalization' of Brazil," in *Authoritarian Brazil*, A. Stepan, ed. New Haven: Yale University Press.

Schmookler, Jacob, 1957. "Investors, Past and Present," *Review of Economics and Statistics* (August), 29(3):321-333.

Seikman, Phillip, 1964. "When Executives Turned Revolutionaries," *Fortune*, 70(3):147-149.

Simon, Herbert, 1965. *Administrative Behavior.* New York: The Free Press.

Singer, Hans, 1950. "The Distribution of Gains Between Investing and Borrowing Countries," *American Economic Review* (May), 60(5):473-485.

Singer, Paulo, 1971. *Força de Trabalho e Emprego no Brasil: 1920-1969.* (Caderno CEBRAP, no. 3), São Paulo: CEBRAP.

———, 1972. *O "Milagre Brasileiro" Causas e Consequencias.* (Caderno CEBRAP, no. 6), São Paulo: CEBRAP.

———, 1975. "O Brasil no Contexto do Capitalismo Mundial 1889-1930," in *História Geral da Civilização Brasileira*, tomo 3, vol. 1, *Brasil Republicano: Estrutura de Poder e Economia*, Boris Fausto, ed. São Paulo: Difusão Europeia do Livro.

Skidmore, Thomas, 1967. *Politics in Brazil, 1930-1964: An Experiment in Democracy.* New York: Oxford University Press.

Skocpol, T., 1979. *States and Social Revolutions in France, Russia and China.* Cambridge: Cambridge University Press (forthcoming).

Stein, Stanley, 1955. "The Brazilian Cotton Textile Industry 1850-1950," in *Economic Growth: Brazil, India and Japan*, Simon Kuznets et al., eds. Durham, N.C.: Duke University Press.

————, 1957. *The Brazilian Cotton Manufacture: Textile Enterprise in an Underdeveloped Area, 1850-1920.* Cambridge: Harvard University Press.

Stepan, Alfred, 1971. *The Military in Politics: Changing Patterns in Brazil.* Princeton: Princeton University Press.

Stinchecombe, Arthur, 1974. *Creating Efficient Industrial Administrations.* New York: Harcourt Brace Jovanovich.

Stopford, J. M. and L. T. Wells, Jr., 1972. *Managing the Multinational Enterprise.* New York: Basic Books.

Strassman, W. Paul, 1968. *Technological Change and Economic Development.* Ithaca: Cornell University Press.

Sunkel, Oswaldo, 1973. "Transnational Capitalism and National Disintegration in Latin America," *Social and Economic Studies,* 22:132-176.

Survey of the Brazilian Economy, 1965. Washington: Brazilian Embassy.

Survey of Current Business, 1967-1974. U.S. Foreign Investment Position and other articles.

Tanzer, Michael, 1969. *The Political Economy of Oil and the Underdeveloped Countries.* Boston: Beacon Press.

Taques Bittencourt, J. M., 1961. "Domínio do Indústria Farmacêutica pelo Capital Estrangeiro," *Revista Brasilense* (May-June), 35:13-25.

Tavares, Maria da Conceição, 1970. *Da Subsituição de Importações ao Capitalismo Financeiro.* Rio de Juneiro: Zahar Editores.

———— and José Serra, 1973. "Beyond Stagnation: A Discussion of Recent Development in Brazil," in *Latin America: From Dependence to Revolution,* J. Petras, ed. New York: Wiley.

Tendler, Judith, 1968. *Electric Power in Brazil: Entrepreneurship in the Public Sector.* Cambridge: Harvard University Press.

Torres, J. and D. Noqueira, 1959. *Joint International Business Ventures in Brazil.* New York: Columbia University Law School.

Toyobo Do. Ltd., 1974. "The Oldest and Most Versatile Textile Producer in Japan," (company report).

Trimberger, Ellen Kay, 1972. "A Theory of Elite Revolutions," *Studies in Comparative International Development,* 7:191-207.

Tugwell, Franklin, 1975. *The Politics of Oil in Venezuela.* Stanford: Stanford University Press.

Turner, Louis, 1970. *Invisible Empires*. New York: Harcourt Brace Jovanovich.

Turner, Terisa, 1977. "The Cement Racket," *African Guide*: 213-220.

Tyler, William, 1968. "A Política Norte Americana e o Impasse do Café Solúvel," *Revista Civilização Brasileira* (March-April), 3(18):87-98.

UNIDO (United Nations Industrial Development Organization), 1969a. Albert Hahn, "The Brazilian Synthetic Polymer Industry," Petrochemical Industry Series, No. 1. New York: United Nations.

———, 1969b. Alan Benton, "Selection of Projects and Production Processes for Basic and Intermediate Petrochemicals in Developing Countries," Petrochemical Industry Series, No. 2. New York: United Nations.

United Nations, 1953. *Yearbook of International Trade Statistics*. New York: United Nations.

———, 1958. *Yearbook of International Trade Statistics*. New York: United Nations.

———, 1965. *Yearbook of International Trade Statistics*. New York: United Nations.

———, 1968. *Demographic Yearbook*. New York: United Nations.

———, 1974. *Growth of World Industry*, 1972 edition, Vol. 2: Commodity Production Edition. New York: United Nations.

———, 1974. *Yearbook of International Trade Statistics*. New York: United Nations.

———, 1976. *Yearbook of Industrial Statistics*. New York: United Nations.

U.S. Bureau of Foreign and Domestic Commerce, 1898. *Special Consular Reports*, Vol. 14, *The Drug Trade in Foreign Countries*. Washington: GPO.

U.S. Department of Commerce, 1960-1973. U.S. Direct Investment Abroad, Sales of U.S. Affiliates in various years of the *Survey of Current Business*.

———, 1963. "Nationalizing Drugs," *Chemical Week* (May), 92(19):32.

———, 1967a. "The Pharmaceutical Industry of Brazil," *Chemicals*, 14(3):25-30.

———, 1967b. "Brazilian Income Tax Legislation," BBR-67-26. Washington: GPO.

————, 1968. "American Firms Subsidiaries and Affiliates," Washington: GPO.

————, 1970. *Industry Profiles, 1958-1968*. Washington: GPO.

————, 1974. "Brazil, Survey of U.S. Export Opportunities: Chemical and Petrochemical Industries." Prepared by the Office of International Commerce. Washington: GPO.

————, 1976. "Highlights of U.S. Export and Import Trade: December, 1975." Washington: GPO.

U.S. Tariff Commission, 1973. *Implication of Multinational Firms for World Trade and Investment and for U.S. Trade and Labor*. Report to Committee on Finance, U.S. Senate. Washington: GPO.

Vaitsos, Constantine, 1974. *Intercountry Income Distribution and Transnational Enterprises*. Oxford: Clarendon Press.

Vaupel, James and Joan Curhan, 1969. *The Making of Multinational Enterprise*. Boston: Harvard Graduate School of Business Administration, Harvard University.

————, 1973. *The World's Multinational Enterprises*. Boston: Division of Research, Harvard Graduate School of Business Administration, Harvard University.

Veblen, Thorstein, 1942. *Imperial Germany and the Industrial Revolution*. New York: Viking Press.

Vernon, Raymond, 1963. *The Dilemma of Mexico's Development*. Cambridge: Harvard University Press.

————, 1966. "International Investment and International Trade in the Product Cycle," *Quarterly Journal of Economics*, 80:190-207.

————, 1968. "Economic Sovereignty at Bay," *Foreign Affairs* (October), 47(1):122.

————, 1970. "Organization as a Scale Factor in the Growth of Firms," in *Industrial Organization and Economic Development*, J. W. Markham and G. F. Papenek, eds. Boston: Houghton Mifflin.

————, 1971. "Multinational Business and National Economic Goals," *International Organization*, 25(3):693-705.

Versiani, Flavio, 1972. "Industrialização e Emprego: O Problema da Reposição de Equipamentos," *Presquisa e Planejamento Econômico*, 2(1):3-54.

Villela, Anníbal and Wilson Suzigan, 1973. *Política do Governo e Crescimento da Economia Brasileira, 1889-1945. Serie Monografica No. 10. Rio de Janeiro: IPEA/INPES.

Visão, 1974. Quem é Quem na Economia Brasileira. Special Issue (August), 45(5).

———, 1975. "Brasil: Capitalismo de Estado," 46(8):43-94.

———, 1976. "A Face Oculta do Estatização," 48(13):73-86.

Walker, G. E., 1963. Industrial Management in Brazil. Washington: National War College.

Wallerstein, Immanuel, 1974a. The Modern World System: Capitalist Agriculture and the Origins of the European World-Economy in the Sixteenth Century. New York: Academic Press.

———, 1974b. "The Rise and Future Demise of the World Capitalist System: Concepts for Comparative Analysis," Comparative Studies in Society and History (September), 15(4):387-415.

———, 1974c. "Dependence in an Interdependent World: The Limited Possibilities of Transformation within the Capitalist World-economy," African Studies Review, 17(1):1-26.

———, 1976. "Semi-peripheral Countries and the Contemporary World Crisis," Theory and Society, 3(4):461-484.

Warren, Bill, 1973. "Imperialism and Capitalist Industrialization," The New Left Review, 81:3-46.

Weffort, Francisco, 1972. Participação e Conflito Industrial: Contagem e Osasco 1968. (Caderno CEBRAP, no. 5), São Paulo: CEBRAP.

Wells, Louis T., 1972. Product Life Cycle and International Trade. Boston: Harvard Graduate School of Business Administration, Harvard University.

Whyte, George, 1945. Industry in Latin America. New York: Columbia University Press.

Wirth, John, 1970. The Politics of Brazilian Development. Stanford: Stanford University Press.

Wortzel, L., 1971. "Technology Transfer to Developing Countries in the Pharmaceutical Industry," UNITAR Research Report No. 14. New York: UNITAR.

Zeitlin, Maurice, 1974. "Corporate Ownership and Control: The Large Corporation and the Capitalist Class," American Journal of Sociology, 79(5):1073-1119.

———, L. A. Ewen, and R. Ratcliff, 1974. "New Princes for Old? The

Large Corporation and the Capitalist Class in Chile," *American Journal of Sociology*, 80(1):87-123.

———— and R. Ratcliff, 1975. "Research Methods for the Analysis of the Internal Structure of Dominant Classes: The Case of Landlords and Capitalists in Chile," *Latin American Research Review*, 10(3):5-61.

————, W. L. Neuman, and R. Ratcliff, 1976. "Class Segments: Agrarian Property and Political Leadership in the Capitalist Class of Chile," *American Sociological Review*, 41(6):1006-1029.

Index

Library of Congress Cataloging in Publication Data

Evans, Peter, 1944-
    Dependent development.

    Bibliography: p.
    Includes index.
    1.   Capital—Brazil   2.   International business
enterprises.   3.   Government business enterprises—
Brazil.   I.   Title.
HC190.C3E92   332'.041'0981   78-70291
ISBN 0-691-07606-5
ISBN 0-691-02185-6 pbk.